HEBRIDEAN ISLAND
MEMORIES OF SCARP

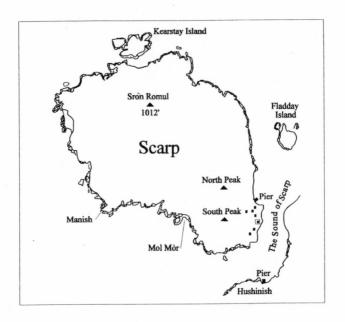

Kearstay Island

Sròn Romul
▲
1012'

Scarp

Fladday
Island

North Peak
▲

Pier

South Peak
▲

Manish

The Sound of Scarp

Mol Mòr

Pier

Hushinish

HEBRIDEAN ISLAND MEMORIES OF SCARP

Angus Duncan (1888–1971)

Edited by A. Duncan

TUCKWELL PRESS

First published in Great Britain in 1995 by

Tuckwell Press
The Mill House
Phantassie
East Linton
East Lothian EH40 3DG
Scotland

British Library Cataloguing in Publication Data
A catalogue record for this book is available on request
from the British Library.

Typeset by Hewer Text Composition Services, Edinburgh.
Printed and bound by Cromwell Press, Melksham, Wiltshire.

This volume is Dedicated to the
Memory of the People of Scarp.

The Author's original Dedication was:

To
My Wife
who was with me on
The North and South Peaks:
and
To the Memory of
My Father and Mother.

Contents

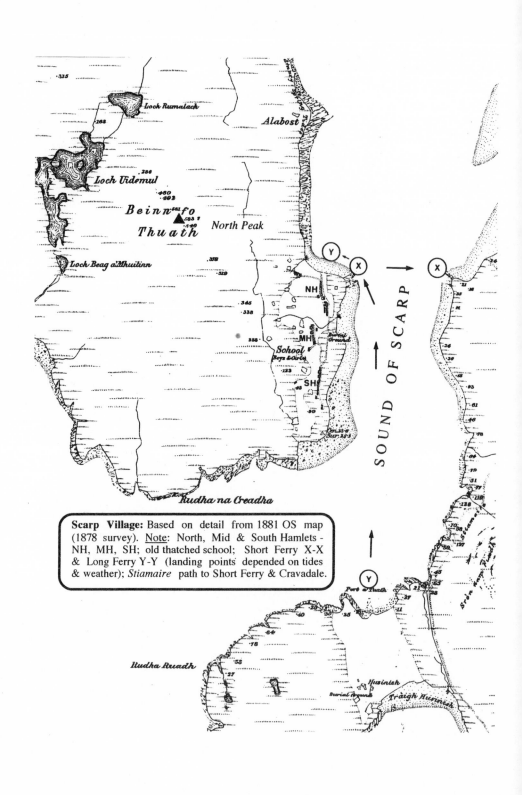

Scarp Village: Based on detail from 1881 OS map (1878 survey). Note: North, Mid & South Hamlets - NH, MH, SH; old thatched school; Short Ferry X-X & Long Ferry Y-Y (landing points depended on tides & weather); *Stiamaire* path to Short Ferry & Cravadale.

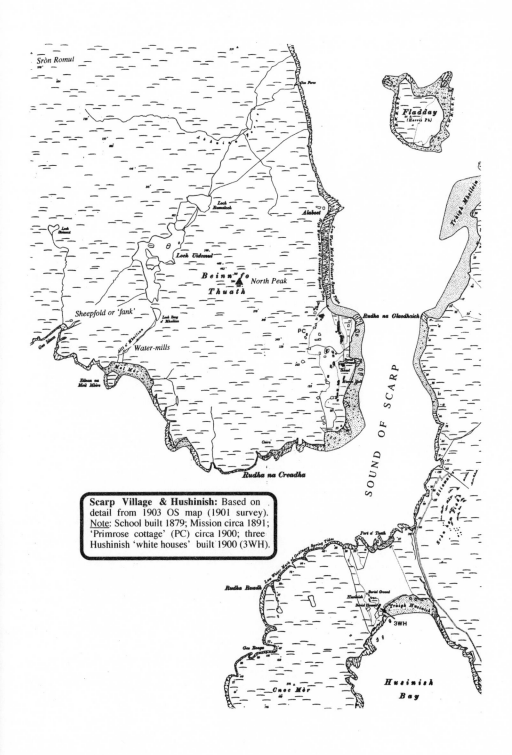

Scarp Village & Hushinish: Based on detail from 1903 OS map (1901 survey). <u>Note</u>: School built 1879; Mission circa 1891; 'Primrose cottage' (PC) circa 1900; three Hushinish 'white houses' built 1900 (3WH).

Foreword

The island of Scarp lies off the west coast of Harris, in the Western Isles of Scotland. It has seen more than four hundred years of human settlement, with just over two hundred souls being recorded there in 1881. The village lies on a sandy machair shelf at the southern end of the island's east coast. The people were crofter-fishermen and tweed weavers, making little more than a subsistence living from the land and the sea. They became a particularly outward-looking and vigorous community, with many natives of Scarp making their mark beyond the island's shores – many others, whom force of circumstance decreed should remain at home, were people of character and high intelligence. The natives of Scarp and their descendants still take great pride in the island of their forebears.

A steady drop in population occurred after 1881, with less than one hundred being recorded in 1931. By 1971 only twelve persons were noted on census night, and by the end of that year the last family had left the island.

The author, Rev Angus Duncan, was brought up on Scarp, where his father was schoolmaster. Although most of his adult life was spent on the mainland of Scotland, he retained a lifelong interest in his native island, its people – many of whom were his close relatives – its culture and its history. During the 1940s and 1950s he prepared an English manuscript describing the way of life he knew as a boy. In this he did not directly name Scarp or any of the places near to it. Place-names were given in free translations from their Gaelic or Norse origins, and Scarp itself was simply referred to as 'our island' or 'the island'. Extracts from the manuscript featured in twenty articles in the Gaelic/English magazine *An Gaidheal* between March 1951 and June 1953, under the title 'Our Island', by *Eileanach*. Other preoccupations prevented him from bringing the full text to publication. He died in 1971.

The manuscript has now been extensively revised, by introducing familiar place-names throughout, and generally updating the text. The opportunity has also been taken to introduce a few Gaelic words, phrases, or verses, where that might add colour for the bilingual reader, or spark the interest of the non-Gaelic reader. Some of this is taken from the author's own Gaelic writings or from other published sources, but the rest has been contributed by people with direct knowledge of the local culture and traditions.

In addition to the thirty chapters of the author's narrative, an Appendix contains commentaries on subjects of particular interest. In some cases these take the form of monographs by contributors having a special interest in the topic.

Among 'ground-rules' used in editing were: the place-names have been taken, as far as possible, from the Ordnance Survey 1:50,000 Landranger maps, Sheets 13, 14 and 18, and the OS 1:25,000 Pathfinder map of Scarp; 'imperial' measurements have been used throughout; people featured within the text or in the photographs have on the whole not been named, except for members of the author's own family; all 'Mac' names have been rendered with a second capital – e.g. MacDonald; and lastly, the editor's own shameful lack of Gaelic has allowed only a 'taster' of that language to be included. He is indebted to Morag MacLeod for making it possible to add that sprinkling. Where it is included Gaelic is shown in italic print and a translation is normally given.

The author sometimes pointed out that there was an extensive literature dealing with St Kilda, but that Scarp – which in early days had many cultural similarities – had been largely neglected. It is hoped that this volume will in some ways make amends.

Finally, visitors to the island should remember that Scarp has a rugged and potentially dangerous coastline; that sudden weather change could leave a visitor stranded; that the island's remaining buildings and the burial ground should be fully respected; and that – despite an example within the narrative – no attempt should be made to cross the Sound of Scarp on foot!

A.Duncan,
Edinburgh.
1995.

The Author

Angus Duncan was born in the schoolhouse at Strond, South Harris, on 25 September 1888. His father, William Smith Duncan, was schoolmaster at Obbe Public School from 1886 to 1889, when he was reappointed to Scarp Public School. The author was ten months old when the family returned to Scarp, the home of his mother. His childhood there, on an island containing many close relatives, must have been a carefree one, protected from some of the hardships experienced by less fortunate children of that time. On census night 1891 the schoolhouse held his parents, himself, and his four sisters. On the same date he had nineteen first cousins in Scarp, as well as seven more at nearby Luachair, at the head of Loch Resort.

At the age of fourteen he went as county bursar to Inverness Royal Academy, under W.J.Watson, the Rector of the day. Watson was then in the final stages of preparing his classic work *Place-names of Ross & Cromarty*. Angus Duncan was among the senior pupils who helped prepare the alphabetical place-names index for the book. This was the first volume he ever bought with his own money and he was never without a copy thereafter. This, along with his bilingual upbringing on Scarp, laid the foundations for a lifelong interest in Celtic matters.

During the First World War he served in the 4th (Ross Highland) Battalion, the Seaforth Highlanders, being invalided out with the honorary rank of lieutenant in May 1918.

After short periods working with the Supply Department of the Navy and Army Canteen Board in Edinburgh, and with Lord Leverhulme in Harris and Lewis, he matriculated at Aberdeen University in the autumn of 1920. He graduated MA in 1923, with Celtic as one of his subjects. In 1925 he was awarded an Honours Diploma with High Distinction at United Free Church College, Aberdeen. He gained a BD degree in 1926.

He was licensed by Aberdeen U.F.Church Presbytery in 1925. After serving as Assistant in Aberdeen South U.F.Church, he was ordained and inducted to his first charge, Sorbie U.F.Church, Wigtownshire, in March 1926. In 1929, just after the union of the United Free Church and the established Church of Scotland, he was called to Kilmeny Parish, Isle of Islay, where Gaelic services formed a major part of his preaching commitments, Gaelic being at that time the everyday language of most of his parishioners.

In 1936 he was inducted to Kerr Memorial Church, Ladybank, Fife, where he served until 1947. During this period he prepared the greater part of the manuscript 'Our Island'. He also gave a series of Gaelic talks on the radio, and a Gaelic play – *An t-Suiridhe Thubaisteach* or 'The Elder's Wooing' – written by him shortly after the First World War, was broadcast in 1946. His final charge was at Boston Church, Duns, Berwickshire. He was a contributor, in English and Gaelic, to a number of newspapers and magazines, usually under the initials 'A.D.' or the name *Eileanach*. Only occasionally – for a friend sometimes used that name – did he adopt the pseudonym *Scarpach* when writing on matters relating to Scarp.

On his retirement the author took part-time employment, dealing with Scots and Gaelic folklore manuscripts, in the fledgling School of Scottish Studies at Edinburgh University, at the same time extending his connections with scholars of the other Celtic cultures through membership of the Celtic Congress, which met in turn in each of the six Celtic nations. He was an active member of a number of Celtic societies, and was in his later years a Council Member of the Royal Celtic Society.

In a tribute in *The Scotsman* following his death on 19 September 1971, Hamish Henderson, a School of Scottish Studies colleague, wrote:

> The foundation of the school in 1951 enabled Angus Duncan to devote several years of his retirement to the cause dearest to his heart - namely, the recording and placing on permanent record of the folk-song and folklore of his native country. As his father's family came originally from Aberdeenshire, he was as interested in Lallan lore as in Gaelic.
> Nobody who knew him during the years he worked with us could fail to be impressed by the wide range of his knowledge of comparative ethnology, but even more impressive was the devotion (and the word is not used lightly) which he brought to his pioneer task in Scotland's first university folklore institute.
> Modest and diffident to a degree, he nevertheless had a keen and ironic eye for the comedy of the academic scene and when he needed to he could employ an infinitely gentle deflationary humour.

The full tribute appears in Hamish Henderson's book *Alias MacAlias*.

In February 1917 the author married Jane Mary MacLeod – *Sìneag* – a daughter of Murdo MacLeod, the Lewis evangelist and bard *Murchadh a' Cheisdeir*, whose best known song *Eilean an Fhraoich* tells of an exile's longing for his native Lewis. In 1962, along with his wife, he published *Bardachd Mhurchaidh A' Cheisdeir* – 'The Songs and Hymns of Murdo MacLeod'. They had five children, three of whom survive.

The Author's Father

William Smith Duncan, the author's father, a son of John Duncan and Ann Smith, was born in Aberdeen on 26 February 1834. On 13 March 1834 he was baptised in Aberdeen by Rev James Foote, a notable north-east minister of the day. Little has been handed down about his boyhood, but he was brought up, along with four brothers and two sisters, in a farming community in the parish of Tarves, Aberdeenshire. He is thought to have attended King's College, Aberdeen University, for two sessions, before training and becoming a 'certificated teacher'. His first full post was in the Free Church school at Oldmeldrum. In 1860 he married a fellow teacher, Christian Wilson. They had three children, two of whom died in infancy, and the third, George, grew up to engage in a business career in the North of England and in Glasgow. W. S. Duncan's wife Christian died in 1866 at twenty-six years of age.

In October 1869 the schoolmaster married Helen Campbell or Clark, a widow with two sons of her own. In September 1870 twin daughters, Christian Wilson and Helen Campbell, were born, and in March 1872 a son, Arthur, was born. In 1874 he was once again left a widower, for his wife Helen died that April.

He taught in Oldmeldrum, first in the Free Church school, then in the public school, until 1880. Ill-health forced his retirement soon after that. He offered private tuition until fit to take up full-time employment again.

In October 1883 W. S. Duncan was appointed to Scarp Public School, taking up residence in the schoolhouse with his twin daughters, Helen and Christian, and his son Arthur. On 8 January 1885 he married Marion MacInnes, the school sewing mistress. She was a native of Scarp.

In July 1886 he transferred to Obbe Public School, South Harris, where the first two members of his new family were born, Alexandrina in 1887 and Angus – the author – in 1888. The teacher who had replaced him in Scarp died suddenly in July 1889 and that August W. S. Duncan was reappointed in his place.

A daughter, Rachel, was born in Scarp in 1890. In 1892 his daughter Christian died in Renfrew, and that same year Alexandrina – 'Drina' – was born. Christina Ann – 'Chrissie' – was born in 1894 and William James in 1897. Helen died in Glasgow in 1896. Like her twin sister Christian, she was struck down by the then incurable disease, tuberculosis.

W. S. Duncan retired in 1901 at the age of sixty-seven. The family moved

W. S. DUNCAN'S FAMILIES

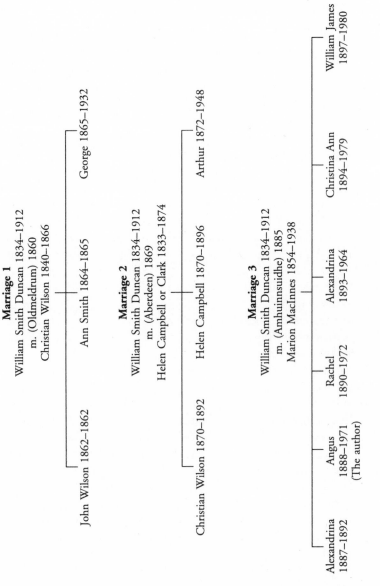

Marriage 1
William Smith Duncan 1834–1912
m. (Oldmeldrum) 1860
Christian Wilson 1840–1866

John Wilson 1862–1862   Ann Smith 1864–1865   George 1865–1932

Marriage 2
William Smith Duncan 1834–1912
m. (Aberdeen) 1869
Helen Campbell or Clark 1833–1874

Christian Wilson 1870–1892   Helen Campbell 1870–1896   Arthur 1872–1948

Marriage 3
William Smith Duncan 1834–1912
m. (Amhuinnsuidhe) 1885
Marion MacInnes 1854–1938

Alexandrina
1887–1892

Angus
1888–1971
(The author)

Rachel
1890–1972

Alexandrina
1893–1964

Christina Ann
1894–1979

William James
1897–1980

to Primrose Cottage, built for them on *Cnoc a' Ghlupa* high in the village of Scarp. From there he could watch the activities of the village, including the comings and goings of the schoolchildren of the island. Failing health marred his years of retirement and he died in Scarp on 27 May 1912, aged seventy-eight years.

Chapter 20 and the Appendix Notes on 'The School' tell a good deal about him, and the Notes on 'Flora' tell something of his skills as a botanist. A tribute published in *The Highland News* soon after his retirement gives a further taste of his qualities, as the following extracts show:

> He is a most capable and painstaking teacher – no man could be more devoted to his profession – and his going to Scarp was a veritable Godsend to the place. When Mr Duncan went to Scarp there was not a single lad from the island trying to push his fortune in a larger sphere: of his pupils there are today two in the ministry of the Presbyterian Church of Canada, and another has only a session to put in in one of the colleges of that Church, one is in the ministry of the United Free Church, and there are eleven in Glasgow . . . all well-doing and getting along nicely. These attribute any success which has attended their efforts to succeed in life very largely to the early training they received from Mr Duncan. There were many more of his pupils equally fit to face a wider world had circumstances permitted . . .
>
> Mr Duncan is a man of varied accomplishments: he is an enthusiastic botanist and petrologist, and seldom, if ever, missed a Saturday, health and weather permitting, without exploring among the hills and rocks of Scarp and the neighbourhood. When his pupils visited him of an evening, he used to delight us by showing sections of plants and bits of rock under the microscope. He is also an accomplished musician, and used to be a charming singer. His varied gifts, combined with his sterling Christian character, enabled him to exercise a unique influence over his pupils and the inhabitants of the island generally; and the Christian character of the young people who have left Scarp would be a credit to any master and any place . . .

This is part of a tribute, written on behalf of fellow pupils, by Rev Donald John MacInnes, by then United Free Church minister at Kilchoman, Isle of Islay.

Like many of the men of Scarp, the schoolmaster had a Gaelic nickname. He was known as *Am Bodach Liath* or 'the grey-haired old fellow'. Going by contemporary photographs, this seems to have been a good description of W.S.Duncan.

MARION MACINNES'S FAMILY

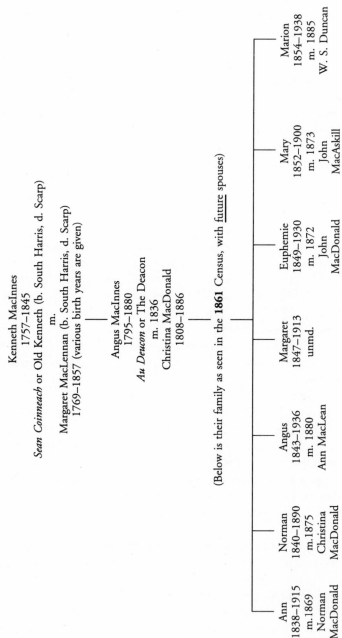

Kenneth MacInnes
1757–1845
Sean Coinneach or Old Kenneth (b. South Harris, d. Scarp)
m.
Margaret MacLennan (b. South Harris, d. Scarp)
1769–1857 (various birth years are given)

Angus MacInnes
1795–1880
An Deacon or The Deacon
m. 1836
Christina MacDonald
1808–1886

(Below is their family as seen in the **1861** Census, with <u>future</u> spouses)

Ann	Norman	Angus	Margaret	Euphemie	Mary	Marion
1838–1915	1840–1890	1843–1936	1847–1913	1849–1930	1852–1900	1854–1938
m.1869	m.1875	m. 1880	unmd.	m. 1872	m. 1873	m. 1885
Norman	Christina	Ann MacLean		John	John	W. S. Duncan
MacDonald	MacDonald			MacDonald	MacAskill	
(Scarp)	(Scarp)	(Scarp)	(Scarp)	(Scarp)	(Scarp/Luachair)	(Scarp/Obbe/Scarp)
						(The author's parents)

The Author's Mother

Marion MacInnes, the author's mother, was the youngest daughter of Angus MacInnes and Christina – sometimes rendered as Kirsty or Chirsty – MacDonald. Angus MacInnes, shown in the 1851 census as a farmer of 3 acres and in subsequent censuses as a crofter, was known on Scarp as *An Deucon*, or 'The Deacon'. In Chapter 15 the author describes how his grandfather led the men of Scarp when the tacksman called on their services to help with his sheep in the Hushinish area or in South Harris. This may have come about because his own father, Kenneth MacInnes or 'Old Kenneth', had been born in South Harris, where he, or his father before him, had possibly been a shepherd on one of the farms of the machair lands there, before circumstances – whether overcrowding or clearance – led him to settle in Scarp. But it was common at that time for tenants to have an obligation to help the tacksman in this way. The tacksman held a lease direct from the Proprietor, and in turn granted tenancies to the crofters of Scarp.

Marion – *Mòrag* or *Mòr an Deucoin* – was born on 9 September 1854, the youngest of seven children. She grew up, no doubt as busy as any other farm or croft child of the day, and by 1871, at the age of sixteen, she was listed in the census as being a general servant living at home with her parents. Her father died in 1880 and the 1881 census shows that Marion, her sister Margaret, and her widowed mother, were living together, partly dependent on the support of her brothers. The next note we have on Marion records her appointment, in 1884, as sewing mistress at Scarp Public School. It is uncertain whether she received training off the island before taking up this post, but she would by then have had ample experience of the skills which an island girl required at that time. Her marriage, less than a year later, to the schoolmaster, seems to have been an entirely successful and happy one. In 1891 she was still recorded as being sewing mistress, although by then having three young children of her own to care for. As school and schoolhouse formed parts of the one building, her sewing classes for the island's girls would have posed no domestic difficulties. On her husband's retirement in 1901 the family moved from the schoolhouse to Primrose Cottage, where Marion remained, cared for by her youngest daughter, Chrissie, until her death on 8 December 1938 at the age of eighty-four.

Acknowledgements

I am grateful to the following for their help in various ways during the preparation of this book: to *An Comunn Gaidhealach* for their agreement that I could draw from those parts of the manuscript already published in *An Gaidheal*; to the following writers whose contributions feature in the Appendix: Dugald Campbell, Peter Cunningham, Andrew Currie, James Shaw Grant, Allan MacLean, Dr Una MacLean, Rev Donald MacRae and Dr Douglas Peacock; to Hamish Henderson and *The Scotsman* for permission to quote from the tribute written on the author's death; to Morag MacLeod, of the School of Scottish Studies, for her wise advice and careful preparation of the Gaelic within the book; to all who have provided, or loaned for copying, original photographs; to the ever-helpful staffs of The Scottish Record Office, The National Library of Scotland, Edinburgh Central Library, the library of The Royal Botanic Garden, Edinburgh, and public libraries in Inverness and Stornoway; to the Curator at Dunvegan Castle for giving access to historic MacLeod manuscripts, and to the many relatives and friends in the Islands and elsewhere, who have provided information and answered endless questions as I researched the subject-matter of the book. Finally, I – and the completed book – have benefited greatly from many constructive suggestions and the stalwart support of my brother Murdo and sister Morag; not least from Murdo's painstaking assistance at the editing and proofreading stages.

Maps and Illustrations

1. Front cover: Scarp and the Sound, from the slipway at Hushinish, by the editor.
2. Outline map, showing location of Scarp, by Norman R.Harris, Culross.
3. Two maps showing Scarp village, based on 1881 and 1903 OS maps, with permission of The Ordnance Survey, Southampton.
4. Black & white photographs:
   RAF survey photograph made available by RCAHMS, Air Photographs Library, with permission of The Ordnance Survey, Southampton.
   The 1967 Scarp school closing group, and 'the briefcase mail', made available by, and the copyright of, Bill Lucas, Hebridean Press Service, Stornoway.
   'The Scarp Parliament', courtesy of Chirsty MacDonald, Tarbert.
   The R.M. Adam photographs, courtesy of The Keeper of Manuscripts, The Library, University of St Andrews.
   The *turskar*, or peat-iron, courtesy of D. W. A. MacInnes, Bedersaig.
   The 'knocking-stone' and rotary quern, courtesy of The Highland Folk Museum, Kingussie.
   The 'Rocket Mail' envelope, owned by and courtesy of Gillies Campbell, Kirkliston.
   The Angus MacInnes photograph, courtesy of Annie MacInnes, Bedersaig.
   The photograph of 'the king', courtesy of Murdo John MacInnes, Govig.
   The Luachair photograph by Alasdair Alpin MacGregor, with permission of The Scottish Ethnological Archive, National Museums of Scotland.
   The 'JMB' (J.M.Barrie) window etching photographed courtesy of Helen & John Murdo Morrison, The Harris Hotel, Tarbert.
   The 'men rowing' photograph, courtesy of Katie MacLennan, Hushinish.
5. Colour plates:
   The Hawkweed photograph by, and the copyright of, Dr R. J. Pankhurst, Royal Botanic Garden, Edinburgh. The other colour photographs are by, and the copyright of, the editor.
6. 'The nine planks of a skiff' diagram, based on a hand-sketch by Allan MacLean.
7. Back cover: The Island of Scarp from Husival Beag, by the editor.

Notes:

1. Robert Moyes Adam, 1885–1967, an illustrator at the Royal Botanic Garden, Edinburgh, was well known for his fine landscape photography. In July 1937 he visited Scarp, staying with the Postmaster's family and recording scenic views and local crofting activities. A few from each category are used in the book. These were printed from Adam's original half-plate glass negatives. His collection is now in the care of the University of St Andrews..

2. All black and white photographs dated 1979 and later are by, and the copyright of, the editor. Photographs noted as 'courtesy of . . .', were taken or copied with the cooperation of the person(s) named. The others – some of uncertain origin – are mainly from family sources.

CHAPTER ONE

The Scene

When I mention that St Kilda can be seen on a clear day from the hill above my old island home, it is obvious that I am writing of an island lying off the west coast of the Outer Hebrides. It is the Island of Scarp.

Although Scarp has its own beauty-spots, the most remarkable thing I now associate with it is the view from its north and south peaks, both of which are easily and quickly ascended. Imagine a summer's day, with the clear atmosphere which seems peculiar to the Western Highlands. Looking west, we have a broad expanse of sea, with only two rocklets or skerries breaking its surface. These are six miles away and of the same shape, but as one is larger than the other, they are called *Gasker*, or 'Goose-skerry', and *Gasker Beg*, or 'Small Goose-skerry'. I was once allowed out to these rocks in a fishing-boat, and then I saw a sight I have never forgotten. As we drew near to the smaller rock, it seemed to heave and toss before our eyes like a living thing. Then someone said, 'Seals!', and sure enough, scores of seals, every one of them as large as a bull minus the legs, were lumbering down the face of the rock into the water. It is interesting that Martin Martin, writing around 1695, said of these skerries: 'The natives kill seals here, which are very big'. On the far horizon in the same direction, the St Kildan group of islands can be seen on a clear day. As they are fifty-five miles from Scarp, we did not distinguish them as Hirta, Soay, and Boreray, as modern writers do, but regarded the whole group as Hiort. The main stacks which rise out of the sea, and have their own names, are also seen.

To the south-west of Scarp, the headlands of North Uist show up clearly thirty miles away, with the island of Haskeir lying out to sea, eight miles off the nearest of the headlands.

The views on the other sides comprise both land and water. Due north is the southern boundary of Lewis, which we never failed to remember was in a different county, namely that of Ross. A massive hill of bare grey rock, like a great defensive wall, marks the boundary here, but at the extreme western end there is room for two crofting communities, the fields and houses of which are clearly seen.

Turning round to face the east, the eye first searches the entrance to two sea lochs at the landward end of the rocky hill just mentioned, the name of the widest, Loch Tamanavay, reminding one, as so often in the Outer Hebrides, of the Norse occupation, for the Norsemen called this loch 'Harbour-bay' in their language, and by this name it is still known. Further east, Loch Resort, a fine sea loch five miles long, stretches out before us, and as it has a wide entrance and does not twist or turn, the cultivated ground at the head of the loch can be seen.

The view due east of our island village is the prettiest of all, with the water of the Sound varying from deep blue to light green above its sandy bed. Silvery strands fringe the opposite side, and then, beyond the pleasant sward above the shore, is a round freshwater loch, Loch na Cleavag, with a gamekeeper's house at the further side. As if this were not enough, a second freshwater loch, Loch a' Ghlinne, peeps out of a deep glen further away in the same direction, while the head of the wide bay of Loch Cravadale, otherwise concealed by a high sandy headland, is seen between these two freshwater lochs. This is the sweetest picture in memory's gallery. The scene, with its placid surfaces and delicate tints, is more like an exquisite painting than a piece of natural scenery.

Beyond this panorama stand several high peaks, the names of which every child knew, because they were mentioned in a humorous rhyme which represented one of them as playing a fiddle, and another as dancing a reel!

A delightful vista awaits us as we face the south. There is first the green neck of a promontory to which the Norsemen gave the name, 'House Ness', or Hushinish, the sea beyond it, then the large double island of Taransay with a thread-like strand connecting its two parts, and beyond this the golden sands of the western side of South Harris, with the peak of Chaipaval standing out prominently to sea.

During a holiday, a companion and I spent the morning of our last day on the north and south peaks, feasting our eyes on the magnificent scene presented on every side. On descending to the village, I spoke to the first man we met, describing the view we had just enjoyed. My companion on the hills then spoke for the first time: 'Do you think', she asked him, 'heaven is any prettier than this?' As he was an elder of the church, such a question was a bit risky, but he took it in good part and merely covered his face with one hand to hide the smile which he could not suppress.

The view I have tried to describe can be enjoyed by a day tripper, but it takes more than a day to explore Scarp itself. As boys, our favourite Saturday outing took us to the *Mol Mòr*, or 'the Big Shore', where we gathered small driftwood, which we carried home either in roped bundles, or in a sack. Much driftwood is washed ashore here, and it was quite common to see heavy planks, or even large logs, which the islanders found and had left above the shore until required for some purpose, such as boatbuilding, or for the erection of a house. When wind and tide were favourable, the shores and coves were systematically searched, the person who first saw a piece of wood, whether washed ashore or still adrift, having first claim to it.

As a boy, I often scoured the coastline, looking for bamboo canes, which made excellent fishing-rods, the short or broken bamboo being used for rock-fishing, and the perfect bamboo for use in a boat. The ideal in this case, and indeed generally, is to see the drifting object before it reaches the rocks, so that it may be secured undamaged. What a fascination the *Mol Mòr* has! During my last visit, I lingered on it and could scarcely leave it, keeping a sharp lookout for any interesting object deposited at high-water mark. My vigilance was rewarded, for I found what is known as a Barra Bean, but is really the fruit of a tropical plant, helped across the ocean by the Gulf Stream and the North Atlantic Drift. Heart-shaped, it is two inches deep, two inches broad and five inches in circumference either way. It is perfectly smooth and of a rich brown colour. A relative of mine possesses two of these which he brought home from Bermuda and uses as pocket containers for saccharine tablets. He has removed the kernel from the one I found, and fitted it with a metal stopper, with the result that it is now used for the same purpose.

During the last war, the shores and coves exposed to the Atlantic were strewn with driftwood and other articles, presenting an amazing spectacle. The most interesting find, however, was made on the long sandy beach across the Sound, where a wooden case full of Chinese banknotes was found. After carrying the case above high-water mark, the finder went to the nearest house to report his luck. 'I am now', he said, 'the richest man in the Long Island!' When the find was reported to the authorities, it was stated that the notes were worthless. They were in two denominations, five yuan and two yuan, the former in a brown tint, and the other in blue, each with Chiang Kai-shek's head included in the front design and the same head in profile as a watermark. The reverse side gave the name as The Central Bank of China, and bore the signatures of the general manager and the assistant general manager. There was also a picture design in the centre and the date 1941. The imprint showed that the notes were made by the well-known London firm of engravers, Thomas De La Rue & Company.

As the notes were not claimed by the public authorities, and the finder had no interest in worthless paper, they found their way in bundles into Scarp homes, where the men used them as spills with which to light their pipes, no doubt experiencing in this way something of the thrill Queen Cleopatra found in drinking to the health of Antony some liquid in which a priceless pearl had been dissolved.

In my youth a small freshwater pond, with a tiny whirlpool that captivated us, lay above the *Mol Mòr*. A stream at the nearer end is known as the Mill Stream, reminding the islander of today that his forebears brought their grain here for milling. Three large millstones – two together and one on its own – lying in the stream about two hundred yards above the *Mol Mòr*, mark the site of this old mill. If one follows the course upstream one will come to *Loch Beag a' Mhuilinn*, or 'The Little Mill Loch', and a little further on, to a larger freshwater loch,

Loch Uidemul, with two islands covered with ferns and sedge, and other wild vegetation.

Tradition has it that newly married couples used to spend their first night together on one of these islands. Whether this is true or not, it is quite certain that they were used at one time as hidingplaces, or even as strongholds, the evidence being that an underwater causeway connects them with the land round the loch. Anyone following the direction given should have no difficulty in finding the stepping-stones at the south end of the loch. If he removes his shoes and socks, and walks on these stones, he will soon come to one that rocks under his weight. Knocking-stones, or sounding-stones, are found in many parts of the country, a feature in this case being that the stone is not balanced on an iron rod, but rocks on its own base. The sound made as it strikes the stones placed on each side of it is insignificant, but it is apparently magnified by the water, and clearly heard on the islet. [*Note*: The causeway described here is now incomplete, so caution is needed when trying to use it.]

From here the general contour of Scarp can be studied and is seen to consist of two ranges of hills with a valley between them. At one time parts of the valley were cultivated. I myself remember potatoes being planted just above the *Mol Mòr*, where long green ridges now mark the type of cultivated strips known by the name 'lazybed'. Near the northern end of the valley an even better example of abandoned lazybeds can be seen, though I do not remember these being under cultivation. What I associate with them is the pleasure of running down those green strips after descending the rough heathery hill which rises to a height of over a thousand feet to westwards.

In order to get to 'the back of Scarp', as we always called the west side, it is less tiring to keep to the southern coastline, of which the *Mol Mòr* is the first conspicuous landmark. A number of precipitous coves are soon passed, the best known of which I used to descend in boyhood. The only sheepfold in use away from the village is here and the sheep are gathered there several times a year. This fank, or fold, known in Scarp as *Faing glaic Isligeo*, or 'the Islaca-hollow fank', has three drystone walls, with the ends converging on a steep rock face which serves as a natural wall on the far side of the fank. The path leading past this cove, near the edge where it is fifty feet high, is both narrow and slippery, and should not be used by the inexperienced, but a safe path is found at the northern side of the sheepfold.

One may now keep to the coastline, which becomes very precipitous before the back of the island is reached, but it is better to cross the moor from the fank, keeping well to the right, and passing through the upper part of the most extensive peat moor on the island. By taking this way there is less danger of missing the island's greatest object of curiosity, namely an 'asbestos rock' known as *Clach a' Chomharra*, or 'the marker stone'. The presence of an outcrop of asbestos among numerous other rocks, from which it can only be distinguished at a short distance, is a geological puzzle. The rock is surmounted by a granite boulder. It is not surprising that the islanders, to whom the rock is a constant source of wonder, should have a popular theory regarding its origin, the explanation given to me as a boy being that it was a woman who, returning home after gathering shellfish, and carrying a sickle, was turned into stone on the spot. The asbestos rock is of a soft and fibrous nature.

Continuing due west at the three hundred foot level now reached, one crosses a broad ridge of bare rock, and finally descends into a lovely bay, which has the distinction of having the only ford on the island. In order to see and use this ford, it is necessary to come at low tide, when the strip of sandy beach between the stony shore of the bay and the rocky islet opposite is exposed. At low tide the sea does not withdraw entirely, but leaves a channel several yards wide, across which one can wade barefooted.

Anyone who walks from the village to this bay should feel satisfied with his day's outing, and although less than three miles from the village as the crow flies, the islanders will be surprised to hear he has walked so far. I often recall a boyhood adventure which I shared with my father on one of our long walks. After spending more time than we should have on a sandy beach with delicate shells of many colours, even further from the village than the bay just described, we set out for home. A thick fog soon overtook us, but we hurried on in order to get to the lower ground. Suddenly my father came to a standstill. Pointing to a patch of sand deep below us, he asked me if I recognised it. We had come full circle, and were back at the point which we left before the fog came down!

My father fortunately had a pocket compass, and this he produced, looking for a flat stone on which to place it. Before consulting the compass, he asked me to lay down his walking-stick pointing in the direction I thought we should go. Needless to say, my sense of direction was quite wrong. The fog continued, but with frequent use of the compass, we at last reached home, where we found my mother anxiously awaiting news of us.

CHAPTER TWO

The Sound

Life on an island has many disadvantages. This is not so apparent in summer, but at other seasons of the year a Sound half a mile wide, and open to the Atlantic Ocean, can be a formidable barrier. Those living on Scarp were always conscious of it and always seemed to be thinking of some means of overcoming the many difficulties it presented.

An evangelist, Mr Murdo MacLeod, who paid the island an annual visit, once told his host that he had a dream in which he himself was engaged in building a bridge across our Sound. The islander listened attentively, and then said with great earnestness *Sin an obair as fheàrr a rinn thu na do bheatha!* – 'That was the best piece of work you ever did in your life!'

An actual incident will make such problems clear. One frosty winter's day a woman fell at her own door and broke her leg. A crew at once set off in one of the open four-oared boats used by the island fishermen, to fetch the doctor, who lived in Tarbert, seventeen miles away.

I well remember the occasion, for my mother had promised to give the doctor a meal, and she had the table set in good time. Bedtime arrived without any word of the returning boat, and we all retired except my mother, who sat up waiting.

Just before daybreak the door opened and the man whose wife had met with the accident brought the doctor in. My bed happened to be in the room where the table was spread, and I have a vivid recollection of the scene as the poor man told my mother in a highly excitable voice that they had struggled all night in a rough sea and driving sleet, and were going back with the doctor in the same boat as soon as they had had a meal. Lest it should be thought that the patient was left unattended all this time, I should perhaps add that her own brother had set and bandaged the fractured limb, using wooden splints, long before the doctor arrived.

With motor vehicles now running to the ferry and a telephone service installed on the island, the hardships of even thirty years ago are fortunately now unknown.

With the sea in their blood, and accustomed to them from boyhood, our islanders were expert in handling their boats. To watch one of those boats being launched from an exposed shore on a stormy day was a thrilling experience. 'They are just like cormorants', I once heard a visitor say of the islesmen, as she saw a boat safely launched to ferry her and a few other visitors who were anxious to get home.

Only once have I seen a boat get completely out of control while being launched, and as it happened on the far side of the Sound, those of us who watched from the island could do nothing to help. We saw the crew of two struggling with the boat as it was driven, first to the right and then to the left, until at last it was flung back on the beach from which it had been launched. For a moment or two we felt anxious for the safety of the men, but we soon saw them standing clear of the boat, and apparently unhurt.

The only boat I ever saw capsize, did so in perfectly calm weather and under most peculiar and even amusing circumstances. A student and his brother had come from Loch Resort and on a fine evening in late spring or early summer prepared to return home. Normally a number of men and lads would have been on the beach to see them off, but as it happened, the whole island had had a busy day bringing home boatloads of seaweed, and everyone seemed to be indoors at the moment except myself, then a young schoolboy.

I watched the boat leave and was still watching as the two lads prepared to hoist the sail. After the mast was stepped something went wrong with the tackle, whereupon the younger man immediately climbed the mast. To my horror the mast, which must have sprung from the mast-step, leaned to one side and slowly dropped into the water, the boat keeling over at the same time. The lad held on to the mast until he was plunged into the water, when he at once struck out and swam ashore, leaving his brother to his fate. The student, however, was equally resourceful. First he secured his wooden trunk, which was beginning to float away. From his precarious position astride the gunwale he then began to lighten the boat by throwing out the ballast stones.

A crowd soon gathered, with the lad's uncle, as I well remember, wearing thick home-knitted pants into which he had just changed, and without trousers, a circumstance which did not improve his temper. After the boat had been drawn ashore and bailed, the lads were allowed to leave on condition that they left the sail alone, but they had no sooner got out of earshot than they shipped their oars and set the sail, this time successfully and without any acrobatic display.

Only thrice, I believe, has our Sound been crossed on foot, the first and second crossings having been accomplished, strange to say, by father and son. As I recall the account, current in my youth, of the older man's achievement, the crossing was made directly opposite the village, where the Sound is narrowest, though normally deep. For his son's success, I have my own eyes as witnesses, having watched him from the end of his own home, where his brother stood calling him at intervals, while his sister sat disconsolately against the wall of the house. The tide was very low at the time, and the lad, left behind by a boatful of men who had gone to gather sheep on the far side of the Sound, made up his mind to join them. Simply tucking up his trousers, as every boy did when playing on the seashore, he set off, taking a very different course from the direct route of the boat, by this time hauled up on the opposite shore. Knowing that the northern entrance of the Sound was the shallowest part of it, he followed a diagonal course which led to the northern end of the long sandy shore on the opposite side. How long he took I cannot now remember, although I distinctly remember his figure as he plodded on without once looking back.

What his brother and sister chiefly feared was that he might fall into a pit, or sink in quicksand, but as his frequent changes in direction showed, he chose his way carefully and ultimately stepped out of the water onto the dry sandy shore almost a mile away from where we stood and watched. It will not surprise anyone to hear that this adventurous youth afterwards served on an ocean-going sailing-ship, and was for many years a ship's officer with the British India Steam Navigation Company. [See page 10 note.]

In winter the northern approach to our Sound is an awe-inspiring sight. From the account given of the young lad's successful crossing on foot, it will occur to many that the Sound at that end was silted, with the result that a broad ridge of sand, known as *Am Banca*, or 'The Bank', had formed here. As a consequence of this the sea in stormy weather reared into great crashing billows at this point.

Fortunately the islanders were good weather prophets and were seldom caught at sea during a severe storm. The story goes that two neighbours, whom I remember well, once set out on a fishing expedition, determined to reach certain rocks lying west of Scarp. Conditions grew worse as they sailed on. At last the older man, who had not spoken for a considerable time, caught the eye of his companion, who was at the helm. 'Oh, Findlay!' he said, 'it is you I am talking to without a doubt! This is not good enough!' So the boat was turned about and the risky journey abandoned.

As the principal harbour faced The Bank, a succession of waves rolled towards it, and this often held up the launching of a boat or the unloading of cargo until a lull came. On such occasions the Gaelic words for 'a wave' and 'a lull' were heard on all sides as the men, alert and vigilant, watched for an opportunity of getting on with their work.

When a boat arrived off shore in the dark, special precautions were sometimes necessary. I have often seen my uncle, who had a strong voice, proceed to an eminence overlooking the harbour, and watching the fateful bank, cry a warning when he saw white breakers appear on it. I have also seen boats arrive at the northern entrance of the Sound to be held up for hours behind The Bank, waiting to get in. When a chance occurred and those of us on shore realised that a boat was coming through, we watched, with heart in mouth, as the crew bent to the oars and competed with the elements in a real life-and-death race.

Although our women took no part in the fishing, most of them were good sailors, but in all matters connected with boats and the sea they acknowledged the superiority of the men. Here at least, the proverb I first heard repeated by my aunt as we gathered round a boat on the shore was true, *B'fheàrr dòrlach fhear na dà mhnaoi dheug* – 'A fistful of men is better than twelve women'.

Some of our women could take a turn at the oar and row like a man, not only keeping perfect time but stretching well back as the men invariably did when a long stroke was necessary. My aunt was one of these. I remember her plying the oar as we once crossed the Sound on the way home with a heavy load of some kind. A sharp breeze had blown up, with the result that the sea roughened to such an extent that there was real danger of our shipping water. My aunt told us she had often heard the men of her youth advise a crew in such circumstances to strike the waves. She herself acted on this advice and whenever the sea welled up near the boat on her side she gave it a quick slap with the blade of her oar, before dipping it in the water for the next stroke.

In my youth all the ferrying across the Sound was done from the island. No one, not even the Inspector of Schools, could take us by surprise. There were actually two ferries, a longer and a shorter one. In those far-off days, the shorter ferry was used by our own islanders, whether leaving or returning. It had one disadvantage, the traveller having to walk for more than a mile on a rough path across the face of a high hill, before gaining the road at Hushinish, near the longer ferry.

As anyone leaving the island naturally did so during the day, the shorter ferry, despite the time lost and the difficult walk, could be tolerated, but it was a real hardship for anyone returning to the island at night, in darkness or semi-darkness. When the ferry was reached, the traveller had to summon up all his lung power to make his presence known to us on the island. How often have I heard our talk and laughter round the peat fire of a neighbour's house interrupted by someone saying, 'Wheesht! I hear a shout!'

The shouting, when real and not merely imaginary, might go on for some time while the folk on the island made up their minds as to who it was that wanted over. When satisfied, those related to the benighted traveller would collect a crew to bring him across. There was no regular ferry-boat and no fare was asked for except in the case of official visitors, who used the longer ferry whenever possible.

The difficulties experienced by a stranger not familiar with the steep hill-path leading to the short ferry can well be imagined. Once at least in my boyhood a traveller arriving after dark used an unorthodox way of making his approach known. This was my brother Arthur, home from Glasgow after a slight illness. As soon as he found himself on the face of the hill, he began to set torches of heather alight and in their glow he was able to keep to the path. He at least did not need to shout. Everyone guessed who it was when they saw the fire on the hill-path, and a boat, with me crouching in the bows, was waiting for him when he reached the ferry.

As there were no piers then, the question of alighting from boats, and of boarding them, was a constant problem. When the tide was favourable, that is high enough, a rock could be used, but those alighting in this way were expected to help in hauling up the boat, after the one man left in it had rowed to the part of the beach from which it had originally been launched.

When the tide was low, or the sea too rough for landing on a rock, passengers were carried to and from the boats by those members of the crew who wore seaboots. Men were carried on the back, with their legs tucked well up, clear of the water. A woman was carried in a different way. The carrier, facing her, took her over his shoulder and clasped her legs behind the knees with one hand.

A woman not accustomed to this practice felt rather nervous and either gripped her carrier's shoulders, with her head held high, or else hung down his back in an alarming manner. The isleswoman however knew exactly what to do. She leaned well over the carrier's shoulder and took a firm grip of his jersey or jacket, half-way down his back. In this position the body was horizontal, or almost so, and so well-balanced that the carrier had no difficulty with his charge. On reaching the boat, men were placed sitting on the gunwale, from which they clambered into the boat, but the women were deposited inside the boat in a standing position.

The custom of carrying passengers on the back in this way provides an amusing story from the Isle of Barra. After the Church of Scotland set up the Assembly Schools in 1825, Principal Baird of Edinburgh University, wearing a velvet suit, visited Barra in the company of Dr Norman MacLeod, who is affectionately remembered as *Caraid nan Gaidheal*, or 'Friend of the Gael'. Seeing the carrier in difficulty as Principal Baird was being taken ashore, another member of the crew asked, in Gaelic, 'Is he heavy?' – *A bheil e trom?* 'No!' said the carrier, 'but he is as slippery as a seal!' – *Chan'eil, ach tha e cho sleamhainn ri ròn!*

---

* Note: In nineteen sixty-nine a twenty year old London student was swept to his death while attempting to cross the Sound of Scarp at the sandy shallows described here. Currents there can be very strong and quicksand pockets may be present. Such a crossing is hazardous and is not recommended.

CHAPTER THREE

Cultivation

The men of Scarp are known as crofter-fishermen and this, it may be said, describes them perfectly. Generally speaking, their activities are equally divided between the land and the sea, the crofts claiming their attention in spring and autumn, and the winter being devoted to lobster fishing.

In my youth all able-bodied men were absent during the East Coast herring season, leaving home when the planting was done and returning in time for the harvest.

The spring work was a long and laborious process, the first and most difficult part of which was the securing of seaweed for manure. This had to be done during the spring tides, when the rocks were more fully exposed at low water and a boatload could be gathered, if possible at one outing, the seaweed being cut with hooks or sickles. As the children of the island had their first experience of being in a boat at such a time, no one is likely to forget the arrival of the boats, laden with seaweed and lying dangerously low in the water, while two men rowed side by side on the middle bench.

The boats used different parts of the beach for unloading, and lucky children were carried into the boats, where they could perch on the towering heap of seaweed in the prow and watch the women loading the creels for the men to carry ashore. The older boys could be of some use at such a time, being given the task of keeping the boat straight with an oar at each side, thus setting all the men free for the heavier work. To save time two creels were used for each carrier, the spare creel awaiting him refilled, each time he returned to the boat with an empty creel.

In contrast to the women who carried their creels, whether loaded with peat for fuel or fodder for cattle, with a strap round their shoulders, the men merely drew the strap over one shoulder and had no difficulty in balancing the creel on their back in this way. As we had no horses or carts on the island, the seaweed was afterwards carried from the shore, where it had been left above high-water mark, to the fields.

The 'ebb', as we called the process of securing seaweed, had another interest for children, for we expected the women taking part to bring us some of the edible seaweed of which we were so fond, as well as dulse, which was also in great demand by grownup folk. Whether carrageen grew on our rocks or not I cannot say. If it did, its value was not generally known, for I cannot remember seeing it prepared or cooked. With milk added it makes a delicious pudding and is sold in shops under the name 'Irish Moss'.

Anyone who is familiar with island life will readily believe that the weather dictated the progress of the 'ebb'. *'Thugainn!' ars an righ, 'Fuirich!' ars a'ghaoth* – '"Come" said the King "Stay!" said the wind' – was an oft-quoted proverb in Scarp. A whole month might be lost before a season's seaweed was cut, and further delay might occur in waiting for calm weather to bring it home. In good settled weather on the other hand, a crew might sail to one of the sheltered sea lochs several miles away, where seaweed was plentiful, and cut and bring home a full boatload the same day. I was once taken as a boy on such a trip and greatly enjoyed the experience.

In rough weather a quantity of sea-wrack was often washed ashore on the seafront below the village, and although considered inferior to the bladder seaweed cut off the rocks, was gathered for manure.

In the heyday of the kelp industry, from approximately 1748 to 1822, the green island facing the northern end of our Sound, Fladday or 'Flat Island', where much seaweed was secured year by year, was used as a base for cutting, drying, and burning seaweed to produce kelp ash, the tradition still lingering that a schooner with a cargo of kelp was once lost in the sea to the north of us.

In those days the landlord claimed the shore, as well as every reef and rocklet, and no seaweed could either be cut or gathered to manure the land. It all went into the kelp trench.

While seaweed was used for all crops, farmyard manure, carried direct from the byres in creels, was used for potatoes and barley, as far as it went. No artificial manure was used, but I remember bags of guano being received and used as an additional manure for oats.

When a potato field was slow in its growth, it was not unusual to see part of the thatch of a dwellinghouse being removed, and the soot-laden thatch next to the rafters being taken and spread over the backward potato crop. Some of our men had great faith in the value of soot, while others were sceptical, but even a boy could see that the crop treated with soot was a richer green than the other crops. The crops grown on Scarp were potatoes, oats, and barley, an occasional field being sown with rye-grass. It is hard to imagine what Highlanders would do without potatoes, just as it is difficult to understand what took their place in a Hebridean's diet before they were introduced in 1743. It is said that silverweed, the root of which the children of the island dug up and ate, was plentiful at one time, and formed part of the regular diet before potatoes came into general use. One thinks of the wild carrot, which we also dug up and ate raw, but the silverweed had one thing in its favour: when held before a fire, or placed for a moment or two on red-hot cinders, it was both softer and sweeter than when raw, and it also swelled a little. The truth probably is that there was no equivalent, not even remotely, to the potato, the staple food being bread, at first barley-bread, which Pliny says was the most primitive food of man, and later, oatmeal bread.

I do not know when potatoes were first grown on Scarp, but they must have been fully established long before 1846, for that year was still remembered and spoken of in my youth as the year of the potato blight. Events such as births, marriages and deaths were said to have taken place, *A' bhliadhna thainig gaiseadh a' bhuntàta* – 'in the year the potato blight came', or, *Na h-uimhir seo a bhliadhnaichean as dèidh gaiseadh a' bhuntàta* – 'so many years after the potato blight'. This habit of speech showed our dependence on the potato crop, and the tragedy of its failure, especially when the potato blight first appeared with such dire consequences for the Highlands and for Ireland. As Hugh Miller says of it: 'The potatoes had become the staple food of the Highlander; and when, in 1846 the potato blight came on, the people, most of them previously stripped of their little capital, and divested of their employment, were deprived of their food, and ruined at a blow. The same stroke which did little more than slightly impinge on the comforts of the people of the Lowlands utterly prostrated the Highlanders'.

The reference to loss of capital and employment is a reminder of what came to be known as the 'Clearances', when whole townships were broken up to make room for sheep farms and deer-forests.

Although the potato was the most important crop, it would be a mistake to think the cultivation of other crops was neglected. Such a mistake can easily be made even by an observant visitor. Some years ago a well-known writer on the Highlands set foot on the island, and afterwards reported that the only sign of cultivation seen by him was a few lazybeds at some distance from the village. As it happened, I myself had spent a holiday on the island a few months earlier, before the harvest work began. One afternoon I saw another visitor standing well above the village, surveying the scene before him. As I knew his opinion would be worth having, I crossed over to him. He told me he was amazed at the extent of the cultivated fields, and pointed out how the whole ground, from the seashore to where we stood at the foothills, was cultivated. He also drew my attention to the barley which waved in the breeze between fields of potatoes in full flower, and told me that more barley was grown for animal feeding on Scarp than anywhere else in the Long Island. As this man was an agriculturist who visited various markets in the Outer Hebrides, his remarks greatly impressed me, just as the naturalist's account, a few months later, depressed me. This was in 1930.

After the crops are gathered the fields certainly look bare, but the mere presence of boundary stones should have been sufficient evidence of cultivation. The lazybeds seen by the naturalist, having heavier soil than the sandy soil of the village, were used for oats, although an occasional rig might be planted with potatoes.

As no plough had been used on the island within living memory, the whole of the ground was dug by spade. Fortunately the men, used to hard muscular exercise such as rowing, were strong, and dug much faster than our townsmen do in their gardens or plots. I remember one man who was sometimes obliged to work single-handed, without anyone to lay the manure in the drill for him, or put in the seed potatoes. He could work at an astonishing pace, without taking a rest, and at the end of the day he would have a large field fully delved.

Mention of spade-digging leads inevitably to an account of the ancient implement used generally in the West Highlands a hundred years ago, and known to Gaels as a *cas-chrom*. Dr Johnson, who gave the name as 'crooked spade', saw one used in the Isle of Skye during his famous Tour in 1773. I myself would translate it as 'bent shaft', the Gaelic name being suggested by the long handle, or shaft, slightly curved, which gave, as Dr Johnson actually says, good leverage in digging hard ground. The shaft of a *cas-chrom* was usually five and a half feet long, the iron blade, or shoe, which was driven into the ground being twelve inches in length. This blade was only four inches broad. Eighteen inches above the iron blade was a wooden pin upon which the foot was placed. Unlike the handle of a spade, the shaft was fixed to the head at an angle of 145 degrees.

I am old enough to have seen this implement used by two, or even three different men. In one case I believe the explanation was that there were not enough spades to go round and the old man in question produced this ancient implement, used, it is said, in classical and Old Testament times. He tried by its means to help the other workers. Being much heavier than a spade, and having a step two and a half feet high, it could only be used slowly and its use on sandy soil by this particular man can only be accounted for in the way I have suggested.

In another case, of which I have a vivid recollection, the reason probably is that the old man was loth to give it up in favour of the more modern spade. An amusing incident of my boyhood has fixed this second man's use of the *cas-chrom* in my memory. A man called Disher arrived on the island selling earthenware and china dishes, when all the men and most of the women and children were away at a sheep-gathering. From the rock at which Disher landed and where a few of us met him, we could see an old man slowly delving with a *cas-chrom*. Poor Disher was disappointed to find an empty village, with no one to show an interest in his wares. At last he picked up a certain bedroom utensil and waving it aloft cried in Gaelic, 'Cas-chrom! Come down and buy a chamber pot!'

I do not remember the *cas-dhìreach*, or 'straight shaft', which was also used in the Outer Hebrides. This implement, used for the cultivation of lazybeds, resembled the *cas-chrom* in length and weight, but had a straight handle, and although it has long gone out of use, it must have been much better for its purpose than the modern spade. It still makes my teeth chatter to recall how a light spade rattled on the stony bottom of a lazybed's drain while the crofter picked up every scrap of soil with it.

Every second year the narrow strip of ground known as a lazybed was trimmed, and all the soil that had been washed off by the winter's rain was recovered from the ditch surrounding it, the latter being cleared at the same time; hence the Gaelic word *taomadh* used of this process and, significantly, for bailing a boat.

The soil recovered in this way was broken with a heavy rake with thick wooden teeth, after which it was sown with corn. Seaweed, used as manure, was spread before any spade work was done. Potatoes were planted in the same patch of ground in alternate years, when the lazybed was delved like an ordinary field and not trimmed as described.

Other implements used a hundred years ago, but now unknown or largely forgotten, were the *caibe-lair*, or turfing-spade, and the *crann-nan-gad* – delightful name! – a light plough used to turn the soil of either a lazybed or an ordinary field for sowing or planting. I am sure I have also heard of a special hoe, heavier than the ordinary potato hoe, for breaking up the clods of a newly formed lazybed.

In my youth and no doubt still, the harvest work, like the spring work, was shared by men and women, the barley being pulled, and oats cut by sickle. As soon as enough for a sheaf was cut or pulled, it was tied with a twist of its own straw, the sheaves afterwards being set up in small stooks to dry before being carried in huge loads to the cornyards, where stacks were made. Those cornyards were drystone enclosures built as a protection against cattle and sheep during the winter. Although most of the cornfields were reasonably near the enclosed cornyards, the oats grown at the north end of Scarp, where all the crofters had some ground cultivated, had to be carried a considerable distance. I can remember both men and women engaged in this heavy work.

As all the arable land was used for potatoes and corn, only the borders of fields and the rough hilly ground were under grass. The hay crop was therefore small. It was generally used to feed the hoggs or lambs that had to be wintered at home. I still remember my astonishment at the quantity of hay secured by the crofting families at the head of Loch Resort, where I used to spend my school holidays. It was built up in large ricks, shaped like a house, roof and all, which they called *dais*, either after the Scots word 'dass', or the Old Norse word *des*, both of which signify a hay rick.

Of vegetables apart from potatoes, only cabbage was generally grown, most families planting cabbage in one end of the cornyard, or in a separate kailyard, enclosed, like the cornyard, by a drystone wall. We shall hear more about these kailyards when the Hallowe'en and Hogmanay celebrations are described.

CHAPTER FOUR

Fishing, Part 1

The development of a boy in Scarp from childhood to full manhood could fairly be described in terms of his interest in fishing and his active participation in it.

At an early age, children of both sexes were sent to the shore in the autumn and winter to gather limpets for use as bait for rock-fishing. As limpets cling to the smooth surface of rocks, a sharp stone was used to dislodge them, and many a knuckle was skinned before a small pailful was obtained. These limpets were cooked and thoroughly drained, after which they were put in a jamjar or syrup tin, the empty shells being thrown away.

The boy who was lucky enough to possess a short rod, with ordinary string as line, and a small-line hook, could use some of the limpets for baiting his rod, only a small piece of the limpet being required for a single bait; but the jar or tin of bait was really intended for one of the three men on the island who owned a spoon-net, and upon whom the children depended for a catch of the small 'cuddies' which approached the rocks in the autumn and winter. The spoon-net had a long wooden handle, and it required considerable skill to raise the circular net, supported by wooden hoops, clear of the water, and slowly empty the live fish into a wooden or zinc pail held ready on the rock.

A small pocket-shaped opening on the left side of the net, close to the large hoop from which the net was suspended, helped to guide the fish into the bucket, but only a moderate catch could pass through this aperture, the rest falling either into the pail, as we used our arms to guide them, or onto the rocks where we recovered or lost them according to the nature of the surface from which we fished.

The limpet bait, which had been cooked, was chewed in mouthfuls by the man operating the spoon-net, and then ejected into the sea to attract the fish. When a good haul was likely, the net, already submerged or half-submerged near the rock, was quickly raised to a horizontal position, trapping the fish so that they could not escape before it was raised above the water.

When fish were scarce, darkness often set in before every family got enough for one 'diet', as we used to say, but when they were plentiful, it was grand to go home with a full bucket, and give a satisfactory answer to the invariable question with which our appearance was greeted, 'Did you get any?' The recollection of the spoon-net at work still thrills me and I fancy I can feel the lively 'cuddies' hammering my chest as I lay over my bucket, to keep the fish from jumping out, until they settled down.

When he possessed a long rod and could give a hand in rowing, a Scarp lad might join others in a boat, and go fishing for saithe and lythe. This was more interesting and more exciting than rock-fishing, three or four hooks with flies from seagull feathers being used on each rod. Three men could fish comfortably from an ordinary fishing-boat, with another two rowing, making five persons in all. If each brought a rod, two lads seated in the stern of the boat would attend to two rods. This was not difficult, as the rods were merely held in the water, with the rowers giving the necessary movement.

Although the appearance of mackerel was unwelcome, partly because they were not eaten in every house, but chiefly because they frightened other fish away, they provided good sport, being strong and playful. To attend to a couple of rods with mackerel taking freely was not an easy matter, but in the case of saithe it was only necessary to secure one rod between one's knees or under a bench while attending to the other.

When the boat returned and was hauled up, the catch was sorted out in shares corresponding to the number of men in the boat, and lots were cast. The system of lots was widely used in my youth. As I recall it, there was more than one way of casting lots. One way was to ask someone to turn his back, whereupon another member of the crew, pointing to a share, asked, 'Whose is this?' Someone was at once named as the owner of the share indicated, and this was repeated until all the shares were disposed of.

The other method was more elaborate. Someone was asked to collect tokens, which consisted of small articles such as a tiny pebble, or shell, or button, or match, or a particle of seaweed, and these were held by him in his closed hands. Each member of the crew then chose one of these tokens, after which one of them called the lots by saying, for example, 'This share will go to the token in the fore-part of the right hand'. The man holding the tokens would then say what it was. This was repeated for the token in the middle-part of the right hand, the hind-part of the right hand, and so on for the tokens of the left hand.

The fishing activities in which the men of the island engaged, centred mainly on lobster fishing, the reason being that lobsters were marketable. They were indeed the only 'fish' sent regularly to the market. In order to get bait for the lobster pots, it was necessary to cast small-lines, for which bait had also to be found. Various baits were used for the small-lines. There was first, the lobworm, or lugworm, as we called it, which was dug up with a spade on a sandy seashore or beach at low tide, the worm's castings in spiral coils, like an earthworm's castings, indicating where a lugworm was located. These were larger than an earthworm, with a stronger skin, and the segments more clearly marked. The variety of colours was noticeable, some being red, some yellow and some black.

The lugworm could be used as bait without any preparation and it was comparatively easy to get it on the hook, and to nip off any part not required. A large lugworm provided bait for more than one hook. As a lad I tried my hand at baiting the small-lines with lugworm, the only objection being that handling this bait left the fingers a yellow colour.

Mussels made good bait, but to gather them involved a journey to one of the sheltered sea lochs near us, where they were found in large numbers in the narrow parts of the loch. In preparing them for bait, the fishermen deftly opened the tightly-closed valves of the mussel with a pocket-knife, released the soft mussel with a flick of the knife, and dropped it into a bowl.

It was not easy to bait a hook with this soft substance, all of which was used for one hook, but by putting the hook through the small white membrane by which the mussel is fixed to the inside of the shell and by a judicious use of the tough ligaments, the lines could be successfully baited.

Children were never sent for lugworms, nor did they take part in mussel gathering, but a rare treat awaited them when sand-eels were sought for bait. For this, a bright moonlight night was necessary, as well as a very low tide. An ordinary hook, or sickle, was used to stir up the sand, whereupon the small, silvery sand-eels popped up, leaping and somersaulting. I remember gathering them in this way on two beaches, one on the island, and the other on the smaller beach at the long ferry.

In winter, when it was impossible to get fresh bait, the fishermen drew upon their stock of pickled herring, boning them first, then cutting them into small neat cubes. They were not cooked – all that was necessary was to fix the hook once in the thickest and strongest part of the bait. When I mention that one of these small-lines, as we called them, normally carried as many as six score hooks, it will be seen that much time was taken in attending to them. After use, they had to be sorted out or unravelled, as well as 'cleaned' or cleared of anything still adhering to them. An intelligent boy could do this, and he might find in the process a starfish or two that had been hooked and left on the cleared line.

In baiting the line, the fisherman sat on a low chair, with the line in an orderly heap on his left and the special board used for small-lines on his right, the bait being on a stool in front of him. The baited hooks were laid in rows from left to right on the board, each row being further forward than the last, while the line was laid down in large coils behind them. When fully baited, a length of the strong brown line was passed through the slits in the sides of the board and fastened down to keep the coil of line in position. When the tide was suitable for fishing, the lines were taken on the boards to sea, and carefully paid out by two members of the crew, after which a small leather buoy was attached to each line to mark its position.

The actual work of lobster fishing was a hazardous business, especially in winter when it was in full swing. Open boats, only eighteen feet in length, with a crew of four, were used, the few larger boats on the island being employed in ferrying seaweed, or bringing home a load of peat in the spring, or going for the island's requirements of oatmeal, flour, and general groceries, to the shopping centre at Tarbert.

As in other parts of the country, the precious lobster was fished in a net-covered pot, or cage, which we simply called a lobster creel, the base being made of several pieces of strong wood, and the top and sides of three slim wooden hoops covered with a net of ordinary twine. When ready for use, a heavy flat stone was securely tied to the bottom, inside the creel, to act as a sinker.

These creels were made by the fishermen themselves. It was fascinating to watch one of them making a creel-net, with the net hitched to his outstretched foot to keep it taut, and using a wooden needle similar to the needle used in mending herring nets, but smaller. A smooth piece of wood was used as a gauge to decide the size of the mesh and to keep the meshes a uniform width. Two sleeves were added, and a wire hoop, five inches in diameter, fastened to the end of each. When the net was fitted to the lobster creel, these sleeves, one on each side, were drawn tight, and fastened in such a way that the ends hung halfway between the roof and floor of the creel, and clear of each other, having been constructed in a position diagonally opposite, and not directly opposite, each other.

Through these sleeves, the unwary lobster entered the cage to get at the bait, which was fixed in a vertical string catch fastened at both ends of the creel. Having entered a creel in this way a lobster could not find its way out, and was therefore trapped. A simple contrivance enabled the fisherman to remove his catch from the creel without difficulty, several of the meshes on one side of the creel being made without fixed knots, so all that the fisherman had to do to make an opening was to pull a running knot.

The bait used was the fresh fish caught on the small-lines, such as haddock, flounder, gurnet, and young skate. When these were scarce, pickled herring was used, several being put in the creel to attract the lobster.

In my youth all catches of lobsters were sent direct to Billingsgate market, packed in straw in wooden boxes, and with the printed labels supplied by the London salesmen nailed to them. As I write this, the strange names of the great metropolitan fish market come to mind. They were household names in Scarp.

It was a risky business to send live lobsters all the way to London. It entailed much loss and sometimes, in warm weather, even the loss of a total consignment, but there was no alternative in those days. Until the catches were large enough to make up a consignment, lobsters were kept in a large box made of stout wood, with perforated sides, anchored with a large canvas-covered rope in a shallow sandy bay near the village, each boat having its own box. After a whole day at sea, the last, and I am sure the most satisfactory, duty was to transfer the catch to the big box through a trapdoor in the top. In order to prevent lobsters from attacking one another, it was customary to cut the tendon of the smaller movable claw, before putting them into the box.

To watch the boats come home on such occasions was a thrilling experience. How often I have watched them as they crossed and re-crossed the Sound in long and short tacks, leaning over in an alarming manner under the weight of wind striking the sail! At the end of a tack, they might shorten sail, and come home with the sail looking ridiculously small. When they made for the big boxes, we concluded they had a catch. We could judge from the time spent at the box whether the catch was large or small.

Modern methods of marketing lobsters, without any risk to the fishing community, have made this industry much more profitable than it was at the time of which I write. I do not know if a close season is now observed, but in those days there was a strong feeling that a close season should be enforced in lobster fishing, and petitions craving this were frequently sent to the Secretary of State for Scotland, or to the constituency's Member of Parliament. This attitude was no doubt strengthened by the presence off our coasts every spring, when our own fishermen were not employed in lobster fishing, of a number of large boats from a distant island, assiduously hunting the coveted lobster. These boats could stay away from home for six days at a time, from Monday to Saturday, and although they sometimes fished quite near the rocks round Scarp, the crews kept away from the village as if realising how unwelcome they were.

Only once can I remember our islanders interfering with them. On the way to dig for lugworms, one of our crews came upon the lobster creels set by the 'intruders' and cut away the corked ropes used to mark and to haul in the creels. This had a sequel which I myself witnessed. Shortly after the islanders' action, the nearest police sergeant arrived on the island and made straight for the boats hauled up on the shore. I remember watching him with mingled curiosity and fear as he entered each boat and examined it carefully.

It turned out that the 'pirates' were too subtle for our straightforward islanders. Discovering their loss, and seeing a boat left unattended on the sandy shore not far from where their lobster creels had been set, a member of the crew had landed, and making his way to the islanders' boat unobserved, he cut a few notches with a knife on the underside of one of the benches, or thwarts. The police sergeant was looking for these marks! My recollection is that the inside of the wanted boat had been tarred in the short interval, making the sergeant's task rather difficult.

Until then, none of the Scarp boats had been registered, but now a demand was made by the authorities to have all the fishing-boats registered at the port of Stornoway. The few larger boats on the island were exempt, only the ordinary eighteen-foot boats regularly used in lobster fishing being registered.

As the numbering of boats was something entirely new on Scarp, great interest was shown in the actual work of painting the numbers on each side of the bows, several men having been found on the island who proved good draughtsmen for this purpose. Names, though not compulsory, were also added in most cases.

CHAPTER FIVE

Fishing, Part 2

At one time, long-line fishing was carried on from the island, but it is now unknown and all but forgotten. For this type of fishing, a large boat was necessary, and as they went far out to sea and might be away for a day or two, it was necessary for the crew to take food with them. I have often heard the older islanders speak of the long-line fishing, their accounts showing that it was once a lucrative business, large quantities of dried fish being sent to Stornoway for sale. During my mother's girlhood, boats from the East Coast engaged in long-line fishing near us, using as base the island of Fladday, for my mother remembered being taken into one of the huts used by the East Coast fishermen, and being given tea by a woman there. As I myself can dimly recall the preparations for a fishing expedition of this kind, and also remember the boat's return with a catch of cod, hake, ling and skate, I conclude that the long-line fishing had not been entirely given up in my boyhood, although I have no recollection of the special boats, too heavy to be hauled ashore, that were once used. One of the island's regular big boats was used, I feel sure, on the occasion I remember.

On Scarp we divided fish into four kinds: white fish, grey fish, red fish and herring; grey fish standing for the class of fish that is not perfectly white, such as cod, hake and ling, and red fish comprising salmon and trout. In the native language, these descriptive words are compounds, and not separate words, a fact that shows this way of classifying fish to be of long standing.

Fishermen have many enemies. The fishermen of Scarp singled out one fish as a deadly enemy. This was the dogfish, which could play havoc with both nets and lines, and disperse shoals of herring, or scatter smaller numbers of other fish. It was nevertheless sometimes fished for its own sake, as I well remember. On one occasion I crouched for several hours in the bow of a boat fishing near a promontory exposed to the open sea. Single lines, with one large hook and a sinker of lead, were used, and these, baited with small portions of herring, were cast from the boat while two men rowed slowly. It was soon apparent that dogfish were present, and a good catch was taken.

It is a most difficult fish to handle. Wearing oilskin jackets and trousers, the fishermen were protected from the spines of the dorsal fins, but had to take care of their hands when unhooking the fish, which lashed out at them with its tail. Another objectionable feature was that some of the catch deposited in the boat embryo dogfish, with yolk-sacs, but without the protective 'mermaid's purse' common to dogfish and skate when the embryo is normally released. As fresh dogfish was not too appetising, it was usually salted and dried, and was eaten when nothing better could be got.

In recalling our islanders' occupation as fishermen, only one kind of fishing remains, namely, herring fishing, the mention of which awakens pleasant memories. For this there was no fixed season. The sea lochs already described were our fishing ground, the men of the island waiting for signs of the presence of herring in one of these lochs, or for news that catches had been taken by other boats. To see flocks of excited seagulls in a loch was regarded as a sure sign of a shoal being present. Men could then be seen making for the shore, with heavy herring nets in bundles on their shoulders, and carrying ropes as well as large home-made buoys of skin, black with tar. As the boats left in the afternoon or the evening, according to the time of year, young children could watch their departure. This was an occasion on which everyone took food with him, the nets being left in the water all night, and only being drawn at daybreak.

As I often spent my school holidays up Loch Resort, I was able to see how our men spent their time. After setting the nets, they rowed up the loch, and landed near the small hamlet of Luachair, where they spent the night. This hamlet consisted of two crofters' houses by the lochside and a gamekeeper's house a few hundred yards further away. On the opposite side of the loch – on the Lewis side – was one occupied house, while another gamekeeper's house stood above the head of the loch, with two salmon rivers between it and the first houses. The respective gamekeepers served two estates which marched with the loch and the river at the end of the sea loch. Our island crews divided themselves between these houses – apart from of the gamekeeper's house on the Lewis side, which was too far away – and sat up all night. In my early boyhood, three families lived in the hamlet of Dirascal, two miles further down the loch, and this hamlet was used in the same way if it happened to be nearer the fishing ground. After all, the crofters of both hamlets originally came from Scarp and had many relatives there. The removal of the three crofting families from Dirascal to a new site at Hushinish is described later.

Until bedtime the visitors, divested of their oilskin jackets and trousers, but still wearing their long seaboots, exchanged news with those on whom they had billeted themselves for the night. Sooner or later the question of whether the nets should be tried was sure to be raised, the younger members of the crew being impatient to know if there were any signs of success. If a blank was drawn when the nets were examined the whole set of nets in that part of the loch might be drawn at once and shot elsewhere, an operation which took some time.

As the nets were drawn very early, before the catch could attract marauders such as dogfish or seals, all the boats returned home in the early forenoon. This was a great occasion. As the boats approached, we could tell from the depth of water drawn whether they came well-laden or empty. What a joy it was to stand on the shore watching the nets being shaken, and to see the shapely silvery fish still held in the narrow meshes. When they came inshore, and the cry, 'Bring a creel!' was heard, our excitement was great. The creel, with its larger interstices stuffed with seaweed or straw, was used for unloading, the whole catch being dumped in a single heap on the clean pebbly shore and afterwards divided into shares, for which lots were cast in the usual way. Even when only one boat happened to be engaged in a night's fishing, it is true to say that no family on the island was left without 'a fry'. Herring, with my fingers stuck through the gills, was the first fish I ever brought home. Sometimes the boys and girls brought light metal basins to the shore, and went home with as much fish as they could carry in them.

The presence of the herring in the coastal lochs depends largely on the weather. When a storm overtakes the great shoals in their migration from one feeding ground to another, they are often driven inshore, and find their way into sheltered sea lochs, where they may stay for several weeks. Only once have I known of herring being caught close to the sandy shore of our village. It happened in the springtime when tillage was in full swing. Our men had had a good herring season and had stored their nets. Then one afternoon a dark shape was seen moving slowly up the Sound under the water, and as it contracted and expanded, and also changed direction, the watchers concluded that it was a shoal of herring taking this unusual course on its way from one of the lochs to the open sea. A few nets were hastily brought out, and the largest boat launched. The shoal was quickly intercepted and there, within a hundred yards of the shore, we saw some unorthodox fishing, the young men in the boat standing on the benches and driving the fish into the nets by plunging the oars obliquely through the water. Whether the nets were ruined by the heavy catch taken in this way I do not now remember. The quality was poor, and while some may have been used for feeding cattle, most of it was put into pits and afterwards used as manure.

When herring fishing began, every family laid in a supply of coarse salt, a bag of which was usually shared between two families. The family's share of a catch was cleaned by the women and then laid neatly and tightly in a large wooden barrel by one of the men, who covered each layer with salt. When the salt dissolved and a good pickle had formed, it was usual to re-lay the whole barrelful, using less salt, in a fresh barrel, where the fish could be left all winter if necessary.

The sale of any of this pickled herring was the exception, not the rule. It was the family supply, and only after a particularly successful season, when the quality of the cured herring was very good, do I remember a few barrels being sold outwith the island. Although not confined to a 'tattie and herring' diet, the islanders believed that a good supply of both potatoes and herring was the best security against the rigours of winter, when the island was often stormbound. Salted herring was also taken without potatoes, and tasted well with either oatcake or scones, both of which were, of course, home-baked. A cup of tea taken with such food tasted doubly sweet.

CHAPTER SIX

Sheep Gathering

In such a small compact community, common planning was often necessary. This accounted for the informal meetings at the end of one of the village houses, which the islanders, especially the women, usually referred to as 'the parliament'.

Of a morning, two or three men might be seen arriving in a slow leisurely way at the regular rendezvous. An hour later this number might have increased to twelve or twenty, with some of the men sitting down, or leaning against the low wall of a thatched house. Others stood in front, or walked a few steps backward and forward, as the discussion proceeded. If too much time was allowed to pass before the adjournment, it was obvious that nothing unusual was to be done that day, and the women waiting at home could adjust their domestic work accordingly. However, if something involving the whole community was agreed upon, the meeting could be seen breaking up hurriedly, the men going off at a quick pace in all directions to tell those at home and to get ready for the day's work. A sheep-gathering, of which every islander has pleasant recollections, was one of the events always decided upon in this way.

Although Scarp had a 'king' he seldom attended the parliament. How or when he got the nickname *an righ*, or 'the king', I do not know, but as he was neither crofter nor fisherman but a merchant, his life was different from the common life of the village in much the same way as was that of the schoolmaster and the missionary. He nevertheless had the largest stock of sheep on the island, and might intervene in order to persuade his fellow islanders to undertake a sheep-gathering if he thought a 'gathering' – as we always called it, whatever its purpose – was due. On such an occasion he might have been seen walking down from his house and approaching the parliament with an expression of impatience in his eyes. He was a strong, heavily-built man, who had a habit of keeping his hands in his jacket pockets with the thumbs sticking out. This habit gave another islander occasion to indulge in a witticism which I still remember. Seeing 'the king' coming towards them, he remarked to the other men: 'You may be sure he is after something when you see the big guns mounted in that way!'

But a sheep-gathering: the event of events in a boy's life! There was of course common grazing for sheep, and as they wandered all over the island and could be found on the highest peaks as well as on the low ground, the task of gathering them was a long and difficult one. The young and more active men set off first with a few dogs, keeping to the northern half of the island. A few hours later the rest of us, including women and children, set off by the shortest route for the fank, or sheepfold, described in the first chapter. Once there we selected a site near the fank, where we deposited the creels, bags, and binders we had brought, as well as our lunch, which we carefully concealed from inquisitive dogs, under an upturned creel or in a bundle of bags. Although we were away from home most of the day, no fire was kindled and no tea was made. Oatcake and scones, with milk carried in bottles, served our purpose until we came home ravenously hungry in the evening.

The hill-pasture of the island was divided into two parts by an iron fence running north and south, the southern end resting on the top of the precipitous cove beside the fank. Except in winter, all sheep were kept outside this fence as a protection for the village crops, and a day's sheep-gathering was therefore usually done in the western half of the island, which is much higher and rougher than the other half. When the sheep arrived, they were rested for a while on the even green ground of the steep gully and afterwards driven into the fank. While two men kept the door of the fank, the other men moved among the sheep and picked out their own, which they led out, holding them by the neck or horns.

The fascination of this scene for children watching from a high perch at one end of the drystone wall of the fank, where the ground almost reached the top of the wall outside, can be imagined. How keenly we watched our own men wading through the dense flock. At last they saw one of their own and kept their eye on it until, having segregated it from the swirling woolly mass, they trapped it in a corner of the fank and laid hands upon it.

The excitement on such an occasion was intensified by the fact that most of the children could claim a personal interest in some animal, or in more than one animal, every family owning sheep that nominally belonged to individual members of the family. The word 'nominally' is used here in its literal sense, the regular expression being that such a sheep was named after such a person, in the same way as it was said that such a person was named after his father or grandfather. As a lamb was sometimes given to a young child as a present by a relative richer in stock than the child's father, the custom of giving children a nominal share of the flock may have sprung from that.

There could be disappointment too on a fank day. Some sheep were as difficult to round up as a roe or a hind, and defied man and dog, while a few of those gathered sometimes broke out and escaped. In the case of the latter, they might form part of a second drove which was brought from the south-westerly quarter of the island after the first fank was disposed of.

Sometimes the whole flock was dealt with and set free again at this fank. This was the case at shearing time, an interval of two or three weeks separating the shearing of the ewes with lambs following them, and shearing of the hoggs and wedders. For shearing, the light, sharp-pointed, double-bladed shears were used. After the fleece was taken from the sheep in one piece, the animal's feet were untied and the children given the opportunity of sending it away by smacking it with the hand and saying, *Falbh gu lom 's thig gu molach* – 'Go away bare, and come back fluffy!' In the case of ewe-sheep, they added a line asking it to 'bring a speckled ewe lamb'.

My earliest memories of a sheep-gathering on Scarp go back to an earlier period of childhood. Twice a year the flock, or part of it, gathered as described, was driven along the coast to the village. This happened in the late autumn when the lambs were removed from the flock and in winter when the whole flock was brought home for smearing. Those were memorable days for children of all ages.

There was no permanent fank in the village in my young days. The roofless walls of an old house, with a heavy lobster box for door, served the purpose. With this type of fank, even the tiniest children could watch the lambs which had to spend a night in it, the grass-covered top of the thick wall providing a perfect balcony. The first I remember was needed as a home for an islesman on whose croft it stood. It was duly roofed and dressed inside, but in spite of such a change and the passing of many years, I still think of it as the sheepfold of my early years, waiting empty, and even isolated, throughout the year, and assuming great importance as soon as the bleating flock came in sight.

A similar fank was used for many years, the only difference being that this fank had dwellinghouses on three sides of it. This also was required to provide a home for a newly married islesman, after which a fank with a high stone wall was built in the same locality, but at a distance of a hundred yards from the dwellinghouses. The choice of this site for a permanent sheepfold was no doubt dictated by its proximity to the shore, from where the lambs were taken to Fladday, where they were left untended long enough to forget their dams and to look after themselves. This period of isolation usually lasted six weeks.

The practice of bringing the island's flock to the village for smearing in winter has undergone a revolutionary change. The whole flock was gathered at the fank beyond the boundary fence. The first lot gathered was sometimes put into the fank for security, but they were sometimes watched outside the fank on the bare green slope overlooking the creek, until the second lot were brought in, when both lots were driven home together.

Once secured in the home fold, the men got in among them and picked out their own sheep, to lead them one by one to the barns, or where there was no barn, to the owner's house, for smearing. The boys loved to help at this stage, for it was almost as good as a ride on horseback to go astride a full-grown sheep, especially if it was a wedder, and let it go as fast as possible without escaping. This sometimes led to spills, a broken arm resulting in one case.

The actual work of smearing had a great fascination for children, and no islander took his place on the smearing stool, as we called it, without eager helpers waiting for the order to fetch one of the animals loose in the barn or in the unoccupied end of the house, as the case might be. Younger children were allowed to sit up late to watch the smearing.

The smearer, clad in oilskin jacket and trousers and wearing, as an additional means of protection, oilskin sleeves drawn tight at the wrists, sat astride the narrow end of the stool. A smearing stool was made of two strong wooden sidepieces, supported by four round wooden legs, and connected by tapering wooden battens. A tub of smearing tar stood on the smearer's right.

The animal to be smeared was placed on the stool, but not tied, its feet being left free. If it kicked too much, its feet might be held, but as far as I can recollect, the smearer held it in position by tucking its head well under his left arm. In smearing, a shed was made in the wool, from neck to tail. The wool was pressed down on both sides to make a wide shed, and the smearer then applied as much of the tar as he could conveniently lift with cupped fingers to the animal's skin, beginning at the end furthest away from him. When the whole shed was treated with tar, a new one was formed in the same way on the right side of it, and close to it, the tar-filled shed being covered in the process. Even for the owner of a comparatively small flock the whole evening was spent on the smearing stool, and those with large flocks stayed up all night. As each sheep was smeared, it was marked with the red or blue keel used for identification at a distance and then released outside the door, which was otherwise kept shut all the time. As it was winter, with no crops exposed, it was not necessary to drive the sheep away. They soon found their own way to their old haunts. Smearing has long since given way to chemical dipping, so this laborious task is now but a memory.

CHAPTER SEVEN

Games

In Scarp, as in rural society generally, the children were encouraged to give a helping hand in any activities in which adults were engaged, but they nevertheless had their full share of children's games and other forms of fun.

So far as my own experience goes, no adult, not even any of the teachers, led us in our play or taught us new games. Our games were apparently handed down from generation to generation with little or no change, and if some of them were introduced by incomers, as may have been the case, they were perpetuated in a local version of our own. They were, in other words, assimilated and naturalised by the islanders before attaining popularity or general acceptance.

It is strange to recall that we had only two ball games. One of these was the national game of shinty which quite young children of both sexes played, using a round piece of cork for ball. A discarded walking-stick with a short shaft was good enough as a caman, or shinty stick, for the younger children. The bigger boys acquired strong and better shaped home-made clubs which they tried to keep from the younger children. I have reason to remember this. As a small boy I was once sent into the middle playground to throw back the ball, when it came over the wall, to the senior boys playing in the larger playground. All of a sudden the schoolmaster's whistle blew and before I could get out of the way a shower of shinty sticks descended upon me. I suffered to some extent, but I had discovered where the best clubs could be found for a game after school hours or on a Saturday.

The other ball game was a cross between baseball and the common game of rounders, and may be identical to the game of baseball mentioned by English writers of a century ago. As in baseball, a stick was used for hitting, and the ball could be hit any distance without being considered out of bounds. The ball was made of woollen thread wound tightly round a centre of cork, and stitched all round to prevent ripping. A bat with a blade three or four inches broad and a round handle was used, and there were two corners or halting places, besides the den. A catch, or a hit on one's clothes, got a player out, but no one was allowed to run with the ball. Only one step could be taken by the person who had the ball and if it was necessary to chase anyone the ball had to be thrown from player to player. Anyone who ran a whole round successfully without stopping at either corner got an 'out' member of his side back in; and the last survivor, to whom corners gave no protection, by completing a successful round could get his whole side in again.

This game was so popular that it was often played in winter in an open field behind a row of dwellinghouses, ordinary boundary stones marking the 'corners'. On such occasions lads who had left school took part, while many adults, sitting or standing at the end of a barn behind the den, watched the game.

As played by us this game required great skill. Ability to hit well, run fast, and avoid the ball by jumping, drawing up suddenly, or bending low, was necessary on the one hand, and alertness and a good aim on the other hand.

When the bat used had an 'X' and an 'O' carved on its front and back respectively, the side to go in first was decided by throwing up the bat and spinning it like a coin, while the boy throwing it asked, 'X or O?' If the bat came to rest on the ground with the figure called by the opposing leader uppermost, his side went in first. A wrong guess gave the other side first chance. If the bat was not marked, the cry was, 'Wet or Dry?' the wet side being produced by the simple expedient of spitting on it.

Jumping games were very popular on Scarp. I have taken part in a game of leapfrog on the long sandy beach below the school, but leapfrog was not a popular game, games requiring more skill being preferred. In one of these, a boy stood, with head and shoulders bent, near the edge of a firm grassy bank, with his back to the bank. All the other boys taking part lined up some distance up the bank, each boy holding his cap in his hand. The game consisted of jumping over the waiting boy and leaving one's cap securely on his back while in flight. When all the caps were disposed of in this way the reverse process began, each boy as he jumped over picking up his own cap. If he failed in this, or knocked any of the caps down, he was 'out', and had to take the crouching boy's place at the face of the bank.

Much more exciting was the jumping game known as 'King Jock'. After sides were picked, the side to have the first jump was chosen by tossing a button, with the cry, 'Head or Tail?' and letting it fall on the ground, the front of the button being regarded as the 'head' and the reverse side, on the analogy of a coin, as the 'tail'. The side losing the toss then crouched in a row at right angles to a wall, against which the foremost member of the row supported himself, the others crouching behind, and holding onto one another by the hips, or upper part of each leg, with the head kept well down as in a good rugby scrum.

When ready, the first member of the other team came running up, and after the warning cry 'Coming!' leapt as far forward as he could, using his hands to give leverage, and then held on. If any part of him touched the ground the whole side was out. If he succeeded, the others repeated the jump, getting as far forward as possible in order to leave room for those coming behind, especially the last jumper, who was regarded as the key to a successful round. This boy had to find a perch somewhere when he jumped, and was obliged to repeat the formula, 'King Jock a-ro high, Jock a-ro high, Jock a-ro high', before either he or any of his side touched the ground.

Having often played this game, I have a vivid recollection of every feature. When as many as a dozen boys took part, making six a side, it was a test of endurance as well as agility. In a game in which one of the sides played such a burdensome role, it was inevitable that various devices should be used to get the other side out. The row of crouching boys might begin, for instance, by extending as much as possible in order to prevent early jumpers from getting well forward. As the number of boys on their backs increased, the row might contract so as to leave less room for late jumpers.

Another device was to place a tall boy at each end of the row. In this case the jumper had to decide whether to drop into the sagging centre of the row, and risk touching the ground with his feet before he could recover, or spring forward to the first boy's back and risk breaking his head against the wall. When the last jumper's turn came, he might find his comrades occupying the saddle to the last inch. With such a possibility in view, the smallest boy was often given last place in jumping because, being light, he had a better chance of clinging to the end of the row for the few seconds it took to repeat the formula. If necessary, the little fellow might be supported by one of his team-mates.

Some boys were so clever at this game that they could leap right over members of their side who had failed to get far enough forward. I have seen jumpers come to rest in all sorts of positions, sometimes hanging over the bearers' sides, and sometimes slipping right underneath, but holding on with hands and feet in an inverted position. Once a leap was completed, no one was allowed to creep forward, or improve his position by a hair's breadth.

This game is remembered on the mainland of Scotland, where it was known as 'Hunch Cuddy Hunch'. A lad always stood against the wall, facing outward, providing his own side with a good grip and preventing those on the other side from colliding with the wall.

High and broad jumps were also popular, but only in an island version of our own. The high jump consisted of a leap from the top of a shore rock known as *Sgeir an Teampaill*, or 'Temple Rock', to the sandy beach below, and the broad jump was from the high grassy bank of a sandy trench near the school, to the lower bank on the opposite side. As the dry ditch or trench was of considerable length, and varied in width, it provided a test of skill for boys of all ages.

The Temple Rock was graded naturally, so that three different heights were available. To encourage a timid jumper, a large sandcastle was sometimes built by his companions, affording him a soft landing, as well as a point at which to direct his leap.

The returning exile who laments the passing out of use of his favourite jump, may also find that the elements, in this case heavy winter seas, have also changed the aspect of the Temple Rock, washing much of the sand away and leaving huge boulders where he used to land safely after a jump from the topmost peak. He, however, knows that the damage here is not irreparable and that those ugly and menacing boulders may again be buried out of sight when the sea, in a more gracious mood, returns the sand it has roughly wrested from the shore.

I can recall two hopping games. In one, opposing sides faced each other, standing on one leg with their arms akimbo. At the signal 'Go!' they hopped forward and pelted each other in a manner reminiscent of rams fighting, their tightly folded arms being used both to give a blow and to receive the force of a blow on impact. The boy who forced the other to set down his raised foot won. This game was known to us as 'Creeping Charlie' and could be played even by two boys. When enough boys were present to form sides, and they played as two opposing teams, a collective attack might be made on the survivors of the losing team, unless the sides happened to be well matched and the casualties were even.

In the other hopping game our caps were again brought into use. In this game, the caps were set down in a row on the ground, about eighteen inches apart. The owner of the first cap then hopped over every cap, turned at the far end, and hopped back. He then got down on one knee in front of his own cap, caught it with his teeth, and without raising his hands off the ground, tossed it backwards over his shoulder, clear of his body. If he touched a cap in hopping over them, or set his raised foot down at any time, or touched the ground with knee or foot when kneeling, or raised a hand off the ground in the effort to throw the cap over his shoulder, he was disqualified. This was repeated until all the caps had been retrieved, the last boy having very little hopping to do.

Throwing the cap was the most difficult part of this game. It could sometimes be tossed more than the length of one's body. There was no rule restricting the method of gripping the cap, as long as this was done with one's teeth. Some boys held it by the hard peak and some by the back, or the top, while others liked to hold the cap the other way round. As we were not allowed to use our hands, it was amusing to see a boy pick up his cap with his teeth, turn it over, grip it anew, and then balance it several times well off the ground before attempting to throw. If I have succeeded in describing this game as I knew it, the resemblance of its last stages to a kitten playing with a mouse will occur to some.

The common game of 'tig' was popular in several elaborate forms. In one, known to us as 'Hen with Chickens', all the children available formed up in a row behind a leader, holding onto each other's waists, while one boy or girl, facing the leader or 'hen', tried to 'tig' one of the 'chickens', the 'hen' meantime holding the assailant off in an effort to protect the brood. Those 'tigged' were transferred to the enemy and thus the game proceeded until the enemy had caught the lot. When this happened, the 'hen' itself was chased over the school playground until caught, unless the enemy's unwieldy following broke up and the game was abandoned.

My most amusing recollection of this game reminds me that a large smooth rock protruded in the main playground. As we once swirled round to evade capture, the living chain of one side was drawn across the slippery rock surface and thrown in all directions.

In another fine game of 'tig' the players stood in a circle with hands joined. One boy or girl then walked round the outside of the circle, and at length 'tipped' someone softly and ran. As soon as he realised what had happened, the person touched gave chase, while the pursued player ran in and out through the gaps in the circle. The pursuer, who might lose time in a slow start – the object of an almost imperceptible touch – had to keep his head up and follow the movements of the pursued. Failure to follow the precise course taken by the pursued disqualified him and he had to take his place once more in the ring.

The girls, who had their own playground, sometimes played 'Drop the Hankie' in the larger common playground. For this imported game, the girls sat in a wide circle on the ground. One took a handkerchief, and walked round the circle behind the girls, chanting, in English, the words:

> I sent a letter to my love;
> And by the way I dropped it;
> Adee, adee, I dropped it;
> I dropped it, I dropped it.

ultimately dropping the handkerchief behind someone and running. The player with whom the handkerchief was left got up and chased the other, who ran round the ring until she reached the place where her pursuer had been sitting, where she sat down, if not caught. Very young boys sometimes joined the girls at this game. That is why I remember it.

CHAPTER EIGHT

More Games

'Smuggle the Keg' was a favourite game both in the school playground and elsewhere. It was played by boys and girls together. Sides were chosen, and the side 'in' first went off to hide while the others turned their faces to the wall at the den, whether the playground wall or the wall of a dwellinghouse. One of those in hiding took possession of the 'keg' which was represented by a button or a small piece of slate pencil. Any article easily concealed in one hand served the purpose.

When the game was in the school playground, the whole side which had gone off to hide reappeared in a row and tried by swift and evasive running to reach the front wall, any part of which served as the den. Their opposite numbers ran out to intercept and catch them. When one was caught, his or her captor slapped the head several times with the open hand, saying, 'Keg or no keg, one, two, three!' If the person caught did not carry the keg, he would say, 'No keg!' When the keg was found, the holder simply showed it, whereupon the captor cried, 'Keg caught!' If the boy or girl entrusted with the precious keg got safely through, this player cried, 'Keg in!' as he or she touched the wall.

This may appear too simple. Some variation was however possible even in the school playground. A few players might go outside the wall at the far end, and work their way back unnoticed, outside the northern boundary wall, then leap into the playground a few yards from the den, or enter by the main gate and touch the end of the front wall next to the gate. Some might even go round the school and schoolhouse and force their way to the den if it was lightly guarded.

There was more scope for a boy's ingenuity when the game was played, as often happened after school hours, at the end of one of the dwellinghouses. On the more restricted approach to the den fleetness of foot was less important than clever scheming. A boy, for example, might move unseen among the cluster of thatched roofs, or even hide in the dockens growing between them, until he saw the den clear, whereupon he would dart forward and leap down into the den.

In 'Smuggle the Keg' the key player was of course the one who had charge of the keg. When this player was caught, the whole side was 'out' and those still at large might as well come in. If the smuggler reached the den safely, the whole side was 'in' for another round.

I now come to a game entirely different from any of those described. This was 'The Soldiers' Battle' played by the boys on the shore. Two rows of large stones were set up about twenty yards apart, either on the sandy beach or on the pebbly shore above the beach. Apart from the labour involved in carrying them, it was easier to set up the stones on the beach, with the sharper ends driven into the sand. If set up where they lay, it was necessary to choose stones with an even base, so that they could stand securely on top of other stones. The space between individual stones in the same row might vary from a few inches to as much as a foot, or even more when set up on an uneven rocky shore. A tiny stone known as the 'king' was set up at the higher end of each row, a few feet away but in line with his 'soldiers'.

As soon as sides were drawn the battle began, the choice of sides being determined by telling a boy to turn his back, after which he was asked, 'Whose side is that?' His answer would be, 'It will be our own', or 'It will be your own'.

The side to draw first blood was decided in an interesting way, each of the two leaders throwing a stone in an effort to knock down one of the 'soldiers' in the rank opposite where he stood. This went on with single alternate throws until a soldier fell, the side represented by the successful thrower taking the first round.

In this stone-throwing game only one boy at a time threw the four stones he was allowed, all the other boys meantime standing behind the row of stones from which he was aiming at the opposite row. When each member of the side had thrown his quota of stones, all the boys walked over to the other row, after which the second team tried, in the same way, to knock down as many of the enemy's soldiers as possible.

Although not a rule of the game, the king was usually left to the last. The most likely reason is that it was by far the most difficult unit to hit and early attention to it was uneconomical. It was necessary, however, to dispose of the king before either side could claim a victory. When the stones were erected on a flat sandy beach, the king occupied a humble position, but when set up on the rocks, or large stones, above the beach, the highest site was chosen for him. He then occupied a commanding position from which to survey the scene of battle and direct his men. In this position I have seen a king survive all his men for several rounds before finally being knocked out. On the other hand a ricochet, or some other unintentional hit, might get rid of him at an early stage.

'The Soldiers' Battle' was fought with great keenness. As any size of stone could be used for throwing, the older boys had an advantage over the rest, especially when the game was played on a shore of loose stones and a large missile churned up the ground, inflicting several casualties. If the shore was steep as well as stony, a falling soldier might roll down the file for a few yards, involving others in its own fall. Advantage was sometimes taken of sloping ground to enfilade the opposing file, a thrower being at liberty to discharge his missiles from any angle as long as he kept behind his own line of soldiers. The ideal way of getting the single file all out was to begin at one end and knock the stones down one by one without leaving gaps, a solitary stone proving a much more difficult target than a group of stones.

'The Soldiers' Battle' was a most popular game, which often left the boys with sore fingers as a result of the large number of stones thrown. When possible, smooth stones were chosen for throwing, but we were sometimes obliged to use sharp-edged stones which hacked the thumb and forefinger. While the other games described were good for the development of brain and muscle, this game made good marksmen, at least with a stone. Even yet I cannot resist the temptation of picking up any loose pebble I may come upon on a country road or in a field, and throwing it at a distant object.

When we could not muster enough boys for a game of 'The Soldiers' Battle' we used to set up a few small stones on the rocks near the water's edge, and sitting or standing on the bank of loose stones higher up the shore, try to knock them off.

I can remember only one other outdoor game that could be said to be popular on the same scale as those already described. This was our island's version of 'Pitch and Toss', confined to the boys and always played with buttons. So anxious were we to get a good supply of buttons that we often played until it was too dark to see where one's button landed when pitched up to the pin, which usually consisted of an empty mussel shell fixed to the ground, with the front facing us. A wooden pin, or an open pocket-knife with the blade stuck in the ground, was sometimes used, but we preferred the mussel shell, into which the button could be pitched to gain the best and safest possible position.

As I have no personal knowledge of the game of 'Pitch and Toss' as played in the south, I shall describe it as it was played in Scarp. The lads, with an underhand movement, pitched a button towards the pin from a mark ten feet away. If satisfied with his throw, he called, 'I'll lie!' but if not satisfied, he picked his button up, and awaited his turn for a second try. Players were allowed three tries in each round.

I fancy I can still hear the lads who had pitched and 'laid' and therefore stood behind the pin, call to a lad who had newly pitched, 'Will you lie?' The lad addressed might carefully study the position of his button before coming to a decision. If he thought he could not improve his position, he would 'lie'. When the pitching was over, the owner of the button nearest the pin gathered all the buttons and after giving them a good shaking between his hands, threw them up in the air. Those that alighted with the front of the button uppermost were picked up by him as his own. The owner of the button that lay in the second position repeated this process and so it went on until no button was left. The pitching was at once resumed, those who had lost their button ruefully produced another, while those whose stock of buttons was done, or who could not afford to risk further loss, fell out of the game. So far as I remember, this was the only game in which the age-long measurements of finger-breadths and hand-breadths were used on the island. Both measurements were often resorted to during this game.

There was a fine discrimination in the matter of buttons. Only men's buttons were accepted, the favourite size being that of a trouser button, whether made of bone or metal. Waistcoat buttons were too light for accurate pitching. Coat buttons on the other hand were too big, and frowned upon, even if sometimes tolerated. No women's buttons were ever used, nor were cloth buttons, or those of the neck type without holes. Buttons having two holes instead of four were suspect, even if otherwise suggesting masculine use.

The buttons won by a lad in this game had a great fascination for him. Although he had them loose in his pocket when playing, at home he had them strung on a piece of twine like a girl's row of beads. He was constantly counting them, knowing them individually, and frequently changing their order on the string. Some were new, or in new condition; there were strong bone buttons of different colours, brown being the favourite colour, and light metal buttons, some of which were white, while others had a glossy surface with a trade motto such as 'Ne Plus Ultra' or 'Best Ring Edge' stamped on them.

The best buttons were kept at the inner end of the string and old or damaged ones at the free end ready to be used in a game. A lad's ambition was to get rid of the poor specimens and acquire more and more of the newer ones, hence the need for restringing, as well as the delight it gave when things were going well.

I cannot remember now what our maximum gains were, or what might be regarded as a record collection of buttons, but I remember being told that a young lad who lived sixteen miles away, and had relatives on Scarp, had won two hundred buttons.

In spite of the temptation to cut buttons off garments in use, I cannot recall any trouble on that account. Discarded clothes, however, were stripped of their buttons without compunction. As cast-off clothing was sometimes thrown out into the fields and left there to decay, we often searched the fields, and picked up a button or two in the loose sandy soil. Worn-out garments were also left among the dockens and nettles on the wide wall tops. I distinctly remember finding a ragged pair of trousers in this way, with a complete set of good white buttons clinging to them.

When the weather was too wet for Pitch and Toss, an interesting substitute was found in a house game for which a square top was used, the letters 'D', 'N', 'T' and 'A' being carved on its four sides respectively. The top was spun by each player in turn on a small wooden table or stool. When the top stopped with 'D' uppermost, a button was set down; when 'N' was uppermost, nothing happened; when the figure 'T' was uppermost, the lad who spun the top took one button; and when 'A' appeared, the lucky lad who had spun the top took all the buttons on the stool. What the four letters stood for was remembered by the formula : 'D' for 'down', 'N' for 'nothing', 'T' for 'take up one'; and 'A' for 'all'.

CHAPTER NINE

Children's Pastimes

Other pastimes, in which quite young children could take part, may now be mentioned.

The simplest game I can recall was played by two children sitting or kneeling on the green sward below the school, among the buttercups and daisies which literally covered this meadow in summer. It is the game known in some places as 'Carl-doddie'.

A couple of ribwort stalks, known to us as 'giants', were plucked for this game. As one giant was held in a horizontal position, the other giant was used to slash at it in an effort to knock off the exposed head. This went on until one of the giants lost its head, each competitor being allowed only one try at a time. As the flower-stalk of this plant is hard, though slender, it might hold out for a considerable time, especially when both contending giants had suffered damage and cautious attack was necessary. The larger stalks were not always the strongest and many a stalwart giant lost his head speedily to a small but tough opponent who scarcely merited the name of giant. The secret of success, as I remember the game, lay in a sharp stroke near the top of the stalk, but not directly on the head.

Girls found the giants useful for making daisy chains. Their method was to pluck the daisy tops and string them on the tallest giants they could find.

Bird's-foot trefoil, which children plucked and ate, also grew there, the flower being thrown away and only the small calyx supporting the blossom being eaten. In our native language, the trefoil was known as *bàrr-a-mhìlsein*, or 'honey', but that name would have been more appropriate for the basil, light purple in colour, which contained a sweet liquid obtained by sucking the tube-shaped flower after plucking it.

The tufted vetch was also found here, and we often stripped it of its bunches of bluish purple blossom and ate them in handfuls. No trimming was necessary, as in the case of trefoil, for the blossoms were eaten whole.

This meadow produced the popular wild carrot – white and not red like the cultivated variety – which we carefully dug out of the ground with a sharp wooden stick specially made for the purpose. Once the wild carrot had flowered it was left severely alone. Like a garden carrot that has sprouted, the wild carrot in flower was as hard as the small mattock used for digging it up, and no longer edible.

The early purple orchid, which also grew on the machair, as this meadow was appropriately called, was of absorbing interest. It was known to us as the 'dappled cow', and was easily recognised by the conspicuous purple or dark brown spots on the leaves of the plant. When found before the flower had formed, children dug round the plant until its white tuber was uncovered, and when a larger and smaller tuber were found together – the new tuber which takes over from the previous year's tuber grows alongside the old – the excitement was great. A dappled cow with its calf had been found! The children could carry the implications of the Gaelic name further and milk the dappled cow by compressing the udder-like tuber, but I have no recollection of any desire to taste the sap squeezed from it in this way. As a rule no damage was done to the plant, and the dappled cow was covered up again and left to chew the cud, or rear its calf, in its own way.

Playing in the fine dry sand so plentiful in the village was a favourite pastime for small groups of children. Here they could play at boats on dry land, even if their boat was only a mussel shell, with a smaller shell of the same kind set up as a sail in a cargo of sand. A boatload of lambs was the favourite type of cargo. With our love of lambs, we were fond of carrying small periwinkles of different colours, and pretending they were lambs. Other shells, a variety of which I have on my desk in front of me as I write, served as hoggs, ewes, and rams.

It goes without saying that as children much of our time in summer was spent on the seashore. A shallow pond among the smooth rocks at the east end of the harbour was used for sailing home-made toy boats, while sticklebacks could occasionally be seen darting through the water. The rocks at the western end of the harbour were more irregular. It was possible to catch partans there in the pools left by the receding tide. To attract the partan it was only necessary to string a few shelled limpets, and lower the string, with a small stone attached to the end, into the pool. The unwary partan left its hidingplace and embraced the row of limpets, whereupon the string was gently drawn up, with the partan clinging to it.

Although barefoot, except in winter, it was exciting to practise jumping to and from an isolated rock without wetting one's feet. As a wave receded far enough to leave the sand behind the rock exposed, a lad would run up and leap to the rock dry shod, or at least dry footed. As the next wave was about to encircle the rock, the lad would spring off, racing the incoming water until it reached the point at which it began to recede again. When the tide happened to be flowing, and not ebbing, the sport became more and more difficult and therefore more thrilling, until it had to be abandoned unless another suitable rock could be found.

The only bogeyman game I remember is associated with the long beach which faces the Sound. While one boy or girl went off to hide, the others knelt on the beach, playing with the sand and chanting the words, 'There will be no bogey tonight!' until the bogeyman appeared and chased them. The boy or girl caught was obliged to play the bogeyman for the next round.

When compelled by rain or darkness to remain indoors, the younger children found ample means of entertaining themselves. An hour or two could be spent with a home-made spinning-top carved out of an ordinary cotton reel, one reel making two tops. For a handle, it only required a short round piece of wood wedged tightly in the hole, with the lower end protruding only a little and sharpened to form a point. I was fortunate in having a cousin who could make good tops like this.

Boats, large and small, were found in most homes, but as I write I recall some of the more unusual toys my much-loved cousin made. One was a small handsaw, all of wood, but a perfect copy of a real saw. As I still remember every detail, this tiny saw must have been a prime favourite for quite a long time, but it lost its interest when the wooden teeth began to break off. I also remember another toy of the saw type made by him. It consisted of a solid wooden man, with a long saw attached to his arms, and a weight fixed to the lower end of the saw. When this *Bodach-sàbhaidh*, or 'Sawing Mannie', as we called the toy, was set up on the edge of a table or stool and set going, it gave an excellent imitation of the top man at work when a log or large plank of wood was sawn with the 'great saw', which was always operated by two men, one of whom stood in a deep sandpit below the level of the ground.

The most popular of a number of string tricks also gave the impression of a saw at work. When the string was ready to be slipped off one's fingers, the person holding it caught the strand nearest him in his teeth, while some other person caught, with one hand, the corresponding strand on the other side. The string was then slipped off, leaving a loop in each of the performer's hands, as well as in his mouth. By pulling and slackening the four ends, the strands of string rubbed against each other in a way and with a sound reminiscent of wood being sawn.

Even toy animals were not unknown to us. An old boot sole made of gutta-percha was occasionally found in the fields. When held in front of a fire it became soft and pliable. I still remember the well-formed animals – rams and bulls with enormous horns – made in this manner by my clever cousin.

A 'hummer' consisting of a circular piece of leather fastened to the middle of a double string was also popular. When the string, rotated several times to tighten it, was drawn and slackened with both hands, the leather spun round quickly making a loud humming sound.

A sling made out of the tongue of a boot or shoe was favoured for short periods by some boys, and home-made bows and arrows by others. More difficult to construct was a 'squirting gun' as we called it, which made an occasional appearance to the detriment of the unwary. It was of wood and

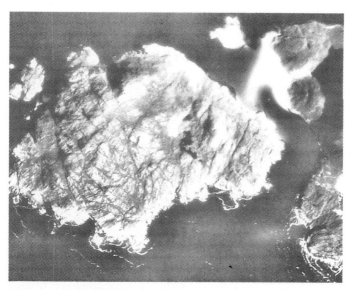

Scarp from the air. RAF survey photograph taken in 1946 from 16,600 feet. Note Hushinish peninsula at bottom right and the sandy shallows crossing the Sound of Scarp, with Fladday Island catching the sun towards the top. (Copyright: The Ordnance Survey.)

The author's parents, William Smith Duncan, Scarp schoolmaster from 1883 to 1886 and 1889 to 1901, and Marion MacInnes, a native of the island, were married in 1885. This was probably a wedding portrait.

The author's favourite photograph
of his wife, Jane Mary MacLeod—
Sìneag—taken in 1917, the year of
their marriage.

The author with his children, Murdo (left), Anna, Morag, and Angus, on holiday
at Dunoon in 1931—taken by *Sìneag* with a Box Brownie camera. A third boy, 'Innes'—
Angus MacInnes—had died in infancy in 1927.

The author, Rev Angus Duncan, in the early 1940s.

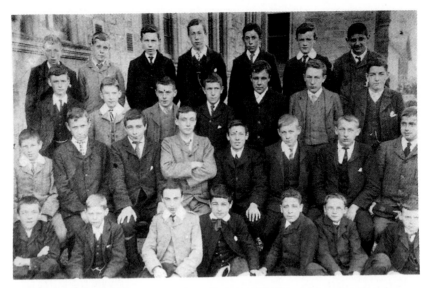

An Inverness Royal Academy class of 1903-1905. The author, who went there from Scarp at fourteen years old, is third from the right in the top row.

The closing of Scarp School in June 1967. The author is fifth from the right. The last teacher, Joan MacLennan, is eighth from the right, and the last two pupils are immediately in front of her. (Copyright: Bill Lucas, Hebridean Press Service, Stornoway.)

The author's mother, Marion MacInnes, aged seventy-five and by then severely arthritic, with his children Morag and Murdo and his sister Chrissie, outside Primrose Cottage, Scarp. (Summer 1930.)

Scarp and Hushinish people prepare to go to Amhuinnsuidhe in an early post-bus. Chrissie—fifth from the left—was taking chickens to the castle. The Hushinish postman stands in the foreground. (Mid-1930s photograph.)

The schoolhouse, on the right, was the author's home from 1889 till 1901. School and schoolhouse, with playgrounds and kitchen garden, are surrounded by a fine stone wall. The ground was feued to the Harris School Board in 1879. (July 1994.)

Primrose Cottage, high in the village, was built for the schoolmaster's retirement. He lived there until his death in 1912, and his widow, Marion, remained there until she died in 1938. Both are buried in Scarp. (May 1994.)

A charming group of young *Scarpachs* among the summer flowers at the end of the mission-hall. A creel lies on the large stone, and the Missionary, John MacDonald, stands on the right. (Marjory Duncan, 1930.)

A familiar view for generations of visitors—the mission and school buildings seen from the Sound, with the burial ground near the shore to the right. *Sgeir an Teampaill*, or 'Temple Rock', is in the foreground. (May 1994.)

The mission-hall (left) and mission-house, with the gable-end of the schoolhouse beyond it. The machair flowers, absent here, had been heavily grazed by sheep during lambing time. The flowers quickly recovered once the sheep were driven beyond the village. (May 1994.)

Tilley lamps still hang in the fine mission-hall, but there was no sign of the long-handled wooden ladles once used for taking up the collection. (July 1994.)

A funeral in Scarp. The author's sister Chrissie is brought back to her native island after being ferried from her home in Hushinish. (April 1979.)

Led by Rev William MacDonald and Rev Donald MacRae, the men take turns carrying the coffin to the burial ground. By tradition only male mourners attend Scarp interments. (April 1979.)

The burial ground, Scarp. Most graves are marked by two sea-smoothed boulders carried from the adjacent shore at the time of an interment. There is no formal record of the boulder-marked lairs. (July 1994.)

'The Scarp Parliament', described in Chapter 6, gathers to discuss the day's activities. Two cousins of the author are in the foreground, while the dog 'Prince' lies at his master's feet. (Photo circa 1939-1940.)

Scarp boats being prepared for the day's work. Some of the island's notable men of the time are in the photograph. It illustrates the joint effort needed when launching or hauling up boats. (Mid-1930s photo.)

Boats pulled up in the harbour area at the north end of the village. Thatched houses and one of the first 'tin houses' can be seen. Glen Cravadale and the rugged hills of North Harris lie across the Sound. (R.M. Adam, July 1937.)

A 'blackhouse' in Scarp with thick stone walls sandwiching a fill of small stones, soil or sand. Ropes holding down the thatch at the roof ends are looped round the projecting 'crow-sticks' on the ridge. Primrose Cottage can be seen on the left. (Mid-1930s photo.)

A 'blackhouse' interior in Scarp, taken 'by available light'. A kettle hangs over the peat fire and a spinningwheel stands ready for use. (R.M. Adam, July 1937.)

was built on the principle of a bicycle pump, with a cloth pad fastened to the end of the plunger.

Several good indoor games were played during the long winter evenings. The 'Peat crumb game' was one of these. For this game a boy or girl took a peat crumb, while all the others taking part sat in a circle with their hands on their laps. The first player went round them all, pretending to leave the peat crumb in each lap. He then put his hand in his own inside jacket pocket, saying, 'If I myself am found with it, it will be in my oxter pocket'. It was understood that someone in the circle or the first player himself now had the peat crumb. Someone was then asked, 'Who has it?' The player addressed at once named someone. If his guess was right he was given the peat crumb and the first player took the vacant place in the circle. If wrong, the boy or girl named was asked, 'How many strokes would you like him to get?' When the number was stated, the boy or girl who had guessed wrongly held out a hand and received from the first player, either with the hand or with a strap, the number of strokes determined by the person he had suspected of having the peat crumb.

I say 'suspected' because every effort was made to deceive the others. Everyone pretended he had received the little black token, closing his hands tightly, or hiding them under his jacket or behind his back, and trying to convey to the others by word and look that he knew the secret. After one wrong guess the game was resumed as already described.

When quite young, children were taught to take part in the game, 'Bite him partan'. In this game the children brought their hands together, palms downwards, each player gripping the back of another player's hand with the forefinger and thumb. The pile of hands was then moved up and down, while the children chanted the lines:

> Bite him, bite him, partan!
> Whoso finds it smarting,
> Let him drop it!

This was repeated until one of the players lost his grip, or felt compelled to let go in order to escape from the grip that pinched him so sorely. When only two persons took part, a round might last for some minutes, but when more than two pairs of hands were involved, the weight often caused a quick collapse. In this game the mere effort to get under way, pinching and being pinched in the process, was part of the fun.

Games in which the performer played another child a trick were indulged in, the one I remember best taking the form of question and answer, as follows:

> Where were you last night?
> > In the brown hound's house.
> What did you get there?
> > Bread and ale.
> What did you leave for me?
> > A cuff on top of the head!

Action was suited to the words of the last line, the performer giving the other player a blow on the crown of the head with his clenched fist.

No account of our fireside games would be complete without mention of the most interesting of all, namely 'Knuckle-knocks'. For this game one lad, known as *am boc adhairc*, or 'the horned he-goat', sat on a stool while another lad, standing over him, drummed on the sitter's head with his knuckles as he repeated the rhyme:

> *Aon, a bhuicein!*
> *A dhà, a bhuicein!*
> *Maide-sùirn, cùl an dùirn;*
> *A' chearc bhìodach, bhadach, bhàn*
> *Anns an t-sabhal, anns an àth;*
> *Beiridh i ' n t-ubh air an spàrr;*
> *Brisidh e mun ruig e ' n làr:*
> *'S tomhais romhad 's as do dhèidh*
> *Cia meud adharc th'air a' bhoc!*

The English lines are:

> One! you goatie! Two! you goatie!
> Furnace stick and back of wrist:
> > The tiny, tufted, white hen,
> > In the cornkiln, in the barn;
> > It lays its egg upon the spar,
> 'Twill break before it reach the floor:
> Guess before you and behind you,
> How many horns the he-goat has!

When the rhyme came to an end, the drumming stopped and some fingers were held up to represent horns. A wrong guess brought the knuckles into action again, the victim being released only when he correctly guessed the number of fingers held up by the other player.

Before the actual game began, an intricate method of counting was used to determine who would take the goat's place, one of the players hiding a hand behind his head, and then bringing it down in front of him for a moment, with some fingers cocked. The other player at once held out his own hand with the 'same' number of fingers stuck up. If he made a mistake, the count went against him, and thus they continued what is regarded in some Highland districts as a game in its own right, until one player had amassed fifteen points, the lad who lost being obliged to take the horned goat's place in the game.

The finger-counting was not as simple as it seems. A boy with supple finger joints manipulated his digits in a way that confused his opponent, who would not always find it easy to display the correct number on his own hand.

Grown-up lads, and even mature men, sometimes imitated the knuckle-knocks when a boy's bare head was within their reach. An island wag, with big sharp knuckles, was fond of such a trick. Scarp folk still remember how this man and a man from the east side of Harris indulged in a game of Knuckle-knocks while at the summer herring fishing at Lybster or Wick. A Caithness man, seeing them, and not realising that they were merely playing a game, came up to them excitedly and said in his own dialect of Gaelic, 'Lord preserve me, men! Be at peace!'

A traditional story suggests that this game was known in Norway and may either have been introduced to the Hebrides by the Norsemen, or copied by them from the Hebrides. The story is that a Hebridean boat's crew, after landing on the coast of Norway, went to look for shelter. Seeing a house, they went up to it, but were afraid to enter on account of the noise inside. When they at last ventured in, they were astonished to find a houseful of men engaged in a game of Knuckle-knocks!

Although only one pair at a time played this game on our island, while any others present watched the fun, there is no reason why several pairs should not play it simultaneously. If this was done in Norway, it would account for the shouting that surprised and frightened the Hebridean crew.

EDITOR'S NOTE

The author had provided a Gaelic version of the 'Knuckle-knocks' rhyme. Morag MacLeod has provided the following versions of 'Bite him partan' – a *partan* is a common crab – and 'Where were you last night?' She has made slight adjustments to the traditional rhymes to suit the author's English ones:

> *Bididh, bididh partan*
> *Ga b'e leis as goirt e*
> *Leigidh tu fhèin, fhèin, fhèin*
> *Leigidh tu fhèin as e.*

Cà 'n robh thu an-raoir?
'N taigh a' mhadaidh dhuinn
Dè fhuair thu ann?
Aran agus lionn
Dè dh' fhàg thu agamsa?
Sgailc air bhàrr a' chinn.

CHAPTER TEN

The Ceilidh, Part 1

Most people are familiar nowadays with the Gaelic word *cèilidh*, used for an informal gathering where Gaelic songs are sung and stories are told in that language. It is a misnomer when applied to an entertainment, whether Highland or Lowland, at which only English songs and recitations are heard.

In the Isles the word is primarily used in the same way as the English word 'visit' and like its English equivalent it is employed both as noun and verb. The Gaelic word, however, suggests a visit of some length and not a mere call. It is used in a derogatory sense when a house-to-house gossip is said to be *math air cèilidh*, or 'good at the visiting', but it is generally heard in such phrases as, *Cuin a tha thu/sibh a' tighinn a chèilidh?* – 'When are you coming to visit?', that is to say, going to pay us a visit; *Cha robh an cèilidh fada* – 'The visit was not long!', on the visitor's leaving; and *Nach dean thu/sibh cèilidh?* – 'Will you not make a visit?', that is, make a stay long enough to merit the name.

The word embraces a wider connotation when used of the common practice among islesmen of gathering in some favourite house for the evening. Sedate householders make their way alone to such a house, but the boys and younger men prefer to go in groups. As dusk falls, a boy may be heard asking another, *Bheil thu dol a chèilidh?* – 'Are you going visiting?' or calling to a chum, *Thig a chèilidh* – 'Come and visit!'

For some reason the children of Scarp learned at a very early age the habit of spending the evening in a neighbour's house instead of at home. At first this might be at the home of a relative, such as an uncle or aunt, where less restraint was imposed and where other children lived. As I write these words I am thinking of the house which was my own second home as a little boy, and of the hundreds of times I was taken home on someone's back when bedtime came. On a stormy night I was muffled up and covered in such a way that I saw and felt nothing until I was safely lowered into my mother's arms and unpacked. Later, three of us regularly spent the evening in a house where we helped to fill the bobbins for the weaver, a woman who was not related to any of us.

It is not surprising that a habit formed so early should continue throughout life and that married men, as well as groups of younger men, should be drawn of an evening towards some favourite hearth. The very furniture of these thatched houses seemed to invite visitors. Each house had a long wooden bench against the front wall, on one side of the fire, which was in the middle of the room. Members of the family sat on low chairs or stools, but rarely on the bench, which was usually higher. The result was that when the nightly callers began to arrive, they crossed over to the bench as a matter of course and almost as a matter of right. When the bench became crowded, the cry, 'Move up!' could be heard from latecomers.

There was always a low chair for the guidwife, or mistress, at one end of the hearth, 'the upper side of the fire' as we called it, and another for the guidman, or master, at the end next the door, 'the lower side of the fire'. Any other chairs remained in the next room where the family slept.

Most houses had a stool or two on the far side of the fire opposite the bench. I remember one stool on which three children could sit together, but it was not very safe. The seat consisted of a block of wood, roughly crescent-shaped, mounted on three round legs. It was obviously a piece of driftwood in its raw undressed state and as the seat was uneven young children kept slipping forward, threatening all on the stool with a spill. More than one house had a more solid and secure seat than this, in the form of an old whale vertebra, or segment of backbone. As the one I remember had turned a dark colour and was smoothed and polished with use, it must have been quite old. It was too heavy for a child to pull in to the fire or away from it, even by a few inches, but it made a comfortable seat. The way the owners removed this piece of furniture when sweeping the floor was to raise one side from the earthen floor and roll it along on edge in the same way as a heavy tub or barrel is rolled. As it had no protuberances showing where the ribs had been attached to it, the first owner must have taken more pains to convert it into a seat than the owner of the three-legged stool just described. If the bench was too full for the children to use and all other seats were occupied, they brought three or four peats from the peat corner and laying them flat on top of each other sat comfortably enough on these for the rest of the evening.

A good peat fire burned on the hearthstone, which was raised only a very little, if at all. If the guidwife needed the fire for baking or for cooking the milch-cow's supper, a broad girdle or three-legged iron pot hung over the fire, but she knew the company felt happier when the full glow of the fire could be seen and she did her best to please them in this. If she had a silent-running spinningwheel, she might sit at it all evening and hear every word spoken, only stopping the wheel when some novel or serious matter was mentioned and she wanted to give her full attention, along with the rest of the company, to the narrator.

The guidman, or host, was usually free to entertain his visitors and to hear what they had to say. When the first visitors arrived they might find him engaged in some work, but this would soon be set aside, especially when his wife kept advising him, as often happened, to put it away. Quite obviously such preoccupation on the part of the host was considered out of place.

The older men usually spent the whole evening in the same house, but the young men moved on after a while and sought new entertainment further afield. In this way several houses might be visited on the same evening,

Although the women of the village stayed in their own homes after dark and did not wander about in the same way, they were always curious to know where their menfolk had been. The answer to their question might surprise them for two different reasons. It might show that the men had merely been next door, in which case the women were almost sure to say that it had not been worthwhile leaving their own fireside to spend a whole evening next door. If the men had reached one of the houses furthest away from their own, the women were as ready to say, 'Well done!' in mock admiration. However, this critical mood soon passed and the women were all attention as they listened to the answer given to the second question, 'Who were there?'

With the passing of the years, changes occurred by which one house might lose its regular visitors while another house gained in popularity. On this account, an islander home on holiday from the south was almost sure to ask, as he recalled his own life on the island, *Dè 'n taigh-ceilidh a th'agaibh a-nis?* – 'What visiting-house have you now?' using the compound word *taigh-ceilidh*, or 'ceilidh-house', a fact which in itself conveys, as far as this practice is concerned, a sense of popularity and general recognition.

The conversation at these informal gatherings usually began in a conventional, matter-of-fact way. The first question from host or hostess might well be, 'Where were you today?' If the answer referred to some sort of work connected with the croft, it might remind both host and hostess that it was time for them to bestir themselves. How often have I heard the host remark on such an occasion, 'Well, I myself have also that to do!' or 'I myself have that to do yet!' and saying it in a serious tone that suggested he was resolved to get on with it as soon as some more pressing work was done. If the visitor had spent the day among the peat 'lifting' or stacking it, he was sure to be asked, 'How did you find it?' the form of the question referring to the condition of the peat. When the visitor could announce that he had spent the day on the hills the conversation at once turned to the sheep on the common grazing. Was he north or south? How far had he gone? Did he happen to see in such a place a sheep of such a description? In a small community which had so much in common, there was no limit to the topics which might be discussed. When one of the visitors was just back from a visit to the mainland, as we called the rest of the parish, his news was eagerly sought.

The ceilidh's chief interest lay in the opportunity it gave the younger members of learning something of the island's past history. A casual remark might lead to an account of some forgotten custom, the older men present supplementing each other's contributions with their recollection of what their parents or grandparents had told them. When appendicitis became 'fashionable' after King Edward VII's successful operation in June 1902, some of our islanders remembered hearing of an illness known as *an greim mòr*, or 'the great pain'. As nothing could be done to relieve the pain, and the patient lived only a few days, it had been regarded on the island as some mysterious disease, although it could have been nothing more or less than appendicitis. So at least we all concluded, especially when told of two islanders who had to leave their work hurriedly when planting potatoes in spring, and whose spades, on the day of their funerals, were still standing where they had stuck them in the ground.

Discussing old customs one night, someone once told of a way of relieving flatulence. A certain liquid was prepared and swallowed by the sufferer, the effect being that it brought on a bout of vomiting that gave immediate relief. 'That is what they called the emetic', said another man, the Gaelic name quoted showing, or at least suggesting, that it had once been widely used.

Those assembled in this way liked to hear of the men and women who formerly lived on Scarp. Genealogical details were always interesting. In the common way of referring to islanders by their father's first name and often with their grandfather's first name added, we were curious to know more about the bearers of those names. Our seniors were able to satisfy our curiosity and sometimes prove at the same time a blood relationship among ourselves, of which we had been quite unaware.

Certain men had almost legendary feats ascribed to them, and we listened with interest and delight to the tales of their prowess, whether on land or at sea. Stories of the sea were numerous. When I hear of the Loch Ness Monster I recall the story heard at such a ceilidh, of how a whale once gave a Scarp crew a real fright. After losing sight of it and when they thought it had gone away, a member of the crew saw it submerged under the boat and quite close to the keel, as if on the point of overturning them. He at once picked up one of the ballast stones and heaved it overboard. The whale dived after the stone, and was not seen again. This story was told with the comment that the whale had lost its young and mistook the stone for it.

When it was time to go home, we would leave the ceilidh-house with as little ceremony as we used on entering it. In winter any latecomers were asked on arrival if it was dark. If there was a moon, rising late, we were sometimes persuaded to wait until it was up. If we could not wait, we were given a hook or sickle, which we thrust into a glowing peat and carried as a torch to enable us to keep to the path home.

CHAPTER ELEVEN

The Ceilidh, Part 2

I have described a conventional ceilidh as it may be found any evening in summer or winter, and have left for a new chapter my recollections of such gatherings when few adults were present and the host and hostess were free to entertain the children visiting them.

Riddles provided good entertainment on such occasions. A typical riddle was rhythmical in form and therefore pleasant to hear and to repeat, whether it consisted of a four-line stanza, or only a couplet. As examples I will give in translation a few popular riddles.

>   i.   Glintie, Glintie, a little black man,
>   Three legs underneath, and a bonnet of wood.

If the children looked round the room, they could probably see the 'little black man'. He might even be so near that he could be touched, for he is none other than a three-legged pot, with a home-made wooden lid. As these pots varied in size, we were in the habit of giving 'a little pot', as the answer to the riddle; that is, the very small three-legged pot found in most houses and used, for example, for cooking an infant's food.

>   ii.   What neither is, nor was, nor will be,
>   Stretch your hand out and you'll see.

The answer to this riddle is that no two fingers are of the same length.

>   iii.   The little child can lift it in his fist,
>   But twelve men cannot lift it with a rope.

The answer is, 'an egg'.

The first four-line riddle refers, like the first two-line riddle, to an article of domestic use, but is cleverer and more difficult:

>   iv.   The guidwife clinking,
>   And the guidwife clattering:
>   The guidwife taking her food,
>   And she never asked a blessing on it.

The answer is, 'a spinningwheel', the food being the rolls of wool it greedily 'swallows', a word which is used metaphorically in ordinary conversation for the action alluded to in the third line. In some versions of this riddle, the verb in the third line is 'swallowing' instead of 'taking' or 'eating'.

The second four-line riddle concerns an object not found in any house. It runs thus:

> v.   A big black whale,
> Lying at the burn-mouth;
> And no one in Ireland or England
> Can leap on its back.

This riddle, repeated slowly, and with emphasis on the first line, used to scare us, and yet the answer is comparatively easy – it is 'a millwheel'.

As an example of the more tricky class of riddles that do not refer to a common object, I give the following three as the most popular:

> vi.   A man without eyes,
> Saw a tree with apples on it,
> He took not apples off it,
> Nor left he apples on it.

The clue in this case is to be found in the plural forms 'eyes' and 'apples'. The man was one-eyed and the tree had two apples growing on it, one apple being taken and the other left.

> vii.   I pose you a riddle:
> 'Tis not your clothes, nor your hair,
> Nor any part of your flesh:
> Yet you bear it, and guess what it is.

The answer is, 'my name'.

The last specimen is only slightly rhythmical, at least in the form which has survived on Scarp, but as I consider it very clever I give it here:

> viii.   I went to the wood, and sought it not,
> I sat on a knoll, and found it not;
> As I did not find it, I brought it home:
> I still have it, and guess what it is.

The answer is, 'a thorn in the foot!'

Tongue-twisters were a form of entertainment that caused much amusement. The difficulty encountered was due, as in the English tongue-twister, 'The scenery was truly rural', to the proximity of groups of consonants in a rhyme we were asked to repeat quickly. There was however more to it than that. The mere difficulty of repeating the rhyme did not amuse us, although the attempt to *Abair 'Mac an Aba' gun do chab a dhùnadh* – 'Say MacNab without closing your gab' – was an exception. What really amused us was that a misplaced consonant or a vowel-change often resulted in a new conception of a grotesque kind.

Puzzles were also popular with the older children, whose ingenuity was tested in showing how a fox, a goose and a sheaf of corn were ferried across a river in a boat that could take only one at a time. The solution was that the goose was taken over first; then the sheaf of corn, and the goose taken back; then the fox was ferried over; and finally the goose. More complex puzzles were also popular, including a variety generally called, 'The Tinkers' Ferrying'. These involved people wishing to cross a river without breaching certain defined limitations, such as the maximum weight the only boat could carry, or who might cross with whom – for example a wife might only cross with her husband. In one puzzle a husband and wife and their two boys reached a river which they wished to cross. The only ferry-boat could carry only one adult or the two boys. How did they cross? First the two boys crossed together, and boy 'A' returned alone. Then the wife crossed, and boy 'B' returned with the boat. The two boys again crossed together, and boy 'A' returned alone. Then the man crossed, and boy 'B' brought the boat back. Finally boys 'A' and 'B' crossed together, completing the ferrying!

There were stories suitable for the younger children, one of the most popular relating the disappointments met by a woman who could not carry her boy and a load of firewood home at the same time. This is our island version of a folktale of various titles, which J. F. Campbell says is the best known of all Gaelic tales. It is the story of 'Big Birken and Her Son' which, with much repetition in it, took a long time to tell.

BIG BIRKEN AND HER SON

Big Birken went to the forest to gather firewood and took little Birken with her. As big Birken gathered wood, little Birken gathered nuts and ate them. When they were ready to go home, little Birken had eaten so many nuts that he could not walk. Big Birken told him he must go home on his own feet as she could not carry both him and the load of wood, but little Birken refused to walk. 'Well,' said big Birken, 'I will go for a switch to beat you with.'

When she found the switch, she said she wanted a switch to beat little Birken so that he could go home on his own feet, as she could not carry both him and the load of wood. 'I am not obliged to do that,' said the switch, 'unless you get an axe to cut me.' So she went for an axe.

When she found it, she said she wanted an axe to cut a switch, and a switch to beat little Birken so that he might go home on his own feet, as she could not carry both him and the load of wood. 'I am not obliged to do that,' said the axe, 'unless you get a grindstone to sharpen me.' So she went for a grindstone.

When she found it, she said she wanted a grindstone to sharpen an axe, an axe to cut a switch, a switch to beat little Birken so that he might go home on his own feet, as she could not carry both him and the load of wood. 'I am not obliged to do that,' said the grindstone, 'unless you get water to moisten me.' So she went for water.

When she found it, she said she wanted water to moisten a grindstone, a grindstone to sharpen an axe, an axe to cut a switch, a switch to beat little Birken so that he might go home on his own feet, as she could not carry both him and the load of wood. 'I am not obliged to do that,' said the water, 'unless you get a deer to swim me.' So she went for a deer.

When she found it, she said she wanted a deer to swim water, water to moisten a grindstone, a grindstone to sharpen an axe, an axe to cut a switch, a switch to beat little Birken so that he might go home on his own feet, as she could not carry both him and the load of wood. 'I am not obliged to do that,' said the deer, 'unless you get a hound to chase me.' So she went for a hound.

When she found it, she said she wanted a hound to chase a deer, a deer to swim water, water to moisten a grindstone, a grindstone to sharpen an axe, an axe to cut a switch, a switch to beat little Birken so that he might go home on his own feet as she could not carry both him and the load of wood. 'I am not obliged to do that,' said the hound, 'unless you get butter with which to rub my feet.' So she went for butter.

When she found it , she said she wanted butter for a hound, a hound to chase a deer, a deer to swim water, water to moisten a grindstone, a grindstone to sharpen an axe, an axe to cut a switch, a switch to beat little Birken so that he might go home on his own feet, as she could not carry both him and the load of wood. 'I am not obliged to do that,' said the butter, 'unless you get a mouse to scrape me.' So she went for a mouse.

When she found it, she said she wanted a mouse to scrape butter, butter for a hound, a hound to chase a deer, a deer to swim water, water to moisten a grindstone, a grindstone to sharpen an axe, an axe to cut a switch, a switch to beat little Birken so that he might go home on his own feet, as she could not carry both him and the load of wood. 'I am not obliged to do that,' said the mouse, 'unless you get a cat to hunt me.' So she went for a cat.

When she found it, she said she wanted a cat to hunt a mouse, a mouse to scrape butter, butter for a hound, a hound to chase a deer, a deer to swim water, water to moisten a grindstone, a grindstone to sharpen an axe, an axe to cut a switch, a switch to beat little Birken so that he might go home on his own feet, as she could not carry both him and the load of wood. 'I am not obliged to do that,' said the cat, 'unless you get milk for me to drink.' So she went to the dun cow for milk.

When she reached the dun cow, she said she wanted milk for a cat, a cat to hunt a mouse, a mouse to scrape butter, butter for a hound, a hound to chase a deer, a deer to swim water, water to moisten a grindstone, a grindstone to sharpen an axe, an axe to cut a switch, a switch to beat little Birken so that he might go home on his own feet, as she could not carry both him and the load of wood. 'I am not obliged to do that,' said the cow, 'unless you get a wisp of hay for me.' So she went to the barn-boy for a wisp of hay.

When she found him, she said she wanted a wisp of hay for the dun cow, a cow to give milk for a cat, a cat to hunt a mouse, a mouse to scrape butter, butter for a hound, a hound to chase a deer, a deer to swim water, water to moisten a grindstone, a grindstone to sharpen an axe, an axe to cut a switch, a switch to beat little Birken so that he might go home on his own feet, as she could not carry both him and the load of wood. 'I am not obliged to do that,' said the barn-boy, 'unless you get a bannock for me from the baking-woman.'

So she went to the baking-woman, and asked for a bannock for the barn-boy. 'I am not obliged to do that,' said the baking-woman, 'unless you bring me water from the well in a sieve.' Big Birken took the sieve, but every time she filled it, all the water ran out before she reached the house. She at last sat down and began to cry. A hooded crow flew over her and said, 'Push red clay and moss in it! Push red clay and moss in it!' Big Birken put red clay and moss in the holes in the sieve, and brought the baking-woman water to mix the bannock. So she got a bannock for the barn-boy, a wisp for the cow, and milk for the cat, a cat to hunt a mouse, a mouse to scrape butter, butter for a hound, a hound to chase a deer, a deer to swim water, water to moisten a grindstone, a grindstone to sharpen an axe, an axe to cut a switch, a switch to beat little Birken so that he might go home on his own feet, as she could not carry both him and the load of wood. But when she returned to the forest, little Birken had burst!

When we grew older we were told stories of a more exciting nature, many of which did much to encourage superstitious fears. Two tales in which a graveyard figured were typical. In one, a tailor laid a bet that he would sit in the graveyard at midnight and do his work there. He was not there long when a phantom appeared and said, 'Do you see my big fist, without flesh or blood, threatening you, tailor?' This happened three times, and each time the bold tailor answered, *Chì mi sin,'s fuaighidh mi seo!* – 'I see that, and I sew this!' In another tale, a crippled tailor laid a bet that no one would undertake to carry him through the graveyard at dead of night. A volunteer was found, and off he set with the tailor on his back. It so happened that two men had chosen that night for sheep-stealing, one of them going for the animal, while his companion lay concealed in the graveyard. When the man in hiding saw the tailor being carried into the graveyard in the dark, he thought it was his companion returning with the wedder for which he had gone. In his excitement he cried, 'Is he fat?' – the masculine pronoun being used in Gaelic of a ram or a wedder. The man carrying the tailor got such a fright that he at once dropped his burden and took to his heels. 'Fat or lean,' said he, 'there he is and do what you please with him!'

For the sake of those who would like to know these tailor yarns in full, I may say that an English version of the first tale is given in Nicolson's edition of MacIntosh's *Gaelic Proverbs and Familiar Phrases*, while a good Gaelic version of the second tale is included in Neil MacLeod's *Clarsach an Doire*.

EDITOR'S NOTE

Morag MacLeod has provided Gaelic versions of the riddles shown in this chapter. She has made slight adjustments to fit the author's English versions:

i. *Diotaman, dòtaman, duine beag dubh*
   Trì chasan fodha is bonaid fhiodh. – (Poit)

ii. *Rud nacheil 's nach robh 's nach bi*
    Sìn do làmh is chì thu e. – (Na meuran)

iii. *Togaidh an leanabh beag 'na dhòrn e*
     'S cha tog dà dhuine dheug le ròp e. – (Ugh)

iv.   *Tha bean an taigh' a' gliogadaich*
      'S tha bean an taigh' a' glagadaich
      Tha bean an taigh' ag ith' a biadh
      'S cha do ghabh i riamh an t-altachadh.
      - (Beairt fhighe no cuibheall shnìomh)

v.   *Muc-mhara mhòr dhubh*
      'Na laighe am beul an t-sruth
      'S chaneil an Eirinn no 'n Sasainn
      A leumas air a muin.
      - (Roth a' mhuilinn)

vi.   *Chunnaic fear gun shùilean*
      Ubhlan air craoibh,
      Cha tug e ubhlan dhith
      'S ch a do dh' fhàg e ubhlan oirre.
      - (Fear air leth-shuil a chunnaic dà ubhal
      air craoibh agus a bhuain a h-aon diubh.)

vii. *Cuiridh mi tòimhseachan ort*
      Chan e d' eìdeadh 's chan e d' fhalt
      'S chan e ball sam bith dhe d' chorp
      Ach tha e ort 's tomhais dè a th' ann.
      - (M' ainm)

viii. *Chaidh mi don choill 's cha do dh' iarr mi e*
      Shuidh mi air cnoc 's cha d' fhuair mi e
      O nach d' fhuair mi e, thug mi leam dhachaigh e
      Tha e agam fhathast – tomhais dè tha ann.
      – (Bior nam chois)

CHAPTER TWELVE

The Ceilidh, Part 3

Many quaint and picturesque expressions used in Scarp can be traced to traditional tales told round the peat fire.

For example, a common way of excusing ourselves when told to do something was to say, 'I am not obliged to do that, said the cat!', a clear allusion to the story told in the last chapter. In the same way, we had several people on the island, both men and women, who never saw my brother William, when a boy, without exclaiming, 'William be seated!' This was said in a spirit of banter or fun, one particular woman usually adding the words, 'and by Mulruba, you will fare no better!' It was obvious that a story lay somewhere in the background. It is in fact the story of 'Niggardly Mary'.

NIGGARDLY MARY

Once upon a time there lived a woman who was known as Niggardly Mary because she never gave anyone food. A certain man was determined he would get food in her house, and off he went one day as darkness fell. The man's name was William.

When he reached Niggardly Mary's house he said, 'May God bless this dark smoky house!'

'Oh!' answered Niggardly Mary, 'As you have blessed the house, get out of it!'

'The birds have roosted', said William, 'it is fitting that I should stay.'

'Oh!' said she, 'These are but spring birds, full of disease. But what is your name?'

'William-be-seated', he replied.

'William-be-seated!' exclaimed Niggardly Mary in surprise.

'Indeed I will', said William, 'when the guidwife invites me.'

'If you do', said she, 'by Saint Mulruba you will fare no better! You will have a bare floor and broken ground, and fleas to bite and torture you.'

'Tuts woman', said William, 'give me some food, and may God protect me!'

'I have no food for myself', said she.

'What does for you and your kindred will do well enough for me for one night', said William, 'whether sorrel from the hill, or limpets from the shore, or hot water and nettles.'

A small quernstone lay on the floor by the fireside. Niggardly Mary laid her head on the quernstone, thinking he would go away, and said, 'This is the sleep of inhospitality.'

William went and fetched a stout piece of wood.

'And this', he said, 'is the awakening of trouble!'

'Stop, stop, you wicked man', said she, 'and get some food.'

A sheep's head was ready for singeing, and Niggardly Mary asked William if he would singe it for her. He said he would if he got the head-singer's reward. This she promised him. She then brought a bowl, put a little meal in it, and laid it down beside the fire.

'Leave that there', said she, 'until I return from the well.'

When she left, William filled the bowl with meal, and when she came back she said, 'I rather think this has grown big since I left'.

'Oh!' said William, 'Were you a kind, generous woman, you would always have plenty of food at hand like this.'

When the head was singed and cooked, William asked Niggardly Mary what her own share of it was. 'As much as I can claim in a single verse', said she.

'So be it!' said William.

She then said:

> Two ends, two bends,
> Two crooked jaw-bones,
> Eight cloven hooves,
> And four shank-bones.

And William, claiming the head-singer's reward, said:

> Mouth, cheek, and brain,
> Two ears to the bone,
> The head's preservers,
>   (the eyes)
> The skull's loud clapper,
>   (the tongue)
> And the marrow of the four trotters.

William thus had all the meat, and Niggardly Mary the bones.

When morning came William left and went to a neighbour's house.

'Come in William', said his friend, 'where have you been?'

'In Niggardly Mary's house', said William.

'Sit in man, sit in and have some food', said the other, 'for no one has ever had food in that house.'

'I, at least, got food there', said William.

'No! No!' said the other, as he brought William a plate of mashed potatoes and milk.

As he ate, William glanced at the door, and saw a pair of eyes over the half-partition, watching him.

'Lonely do you eat!' said Niggardly Mary, for it was she.

'Alone have I bought it', said he.

'Many a man bought, but did not pay!' said she.

'Cast that up to the man who ate your share', said he.

'Heavy is the load on the thin handle!' (the handle of the spoon), said she.

'It is easier to descend than to ascend', said he, 'but the journey is not long.'

'But it is upwards!' said she.

'No sooner up than down', said he.

'Oh!' said she, 'I rather think your father was a bard!'

Saoilidh mi gur e bàrd a b' athair dhut!

'He was neither tall nor small, but of medium height', said William.

Cha b' àrd 's cha b'ìseal, ach anns a' mheud chumanta.

Niggardly Mary, who had met her match, then withdrew, and William-be-seated saw her no more.

(Note : The word-play on 'bard' – *bàrd*, and 'was tall' – *b' àrd* – is only effective in the Gaelic lines.)

This tale is known as *A' Chailleach Bheur* in some published versions. Including two unpublished versions in J.F. Campbell's manuscript collection of *West Highland Tales* in the National Library of Scotland, twelve versions of this short folktale are known to me. In each tale, the visitor uses the same ruse, with the same name, to gain entrance to Niggardly Mary's house. An interesting variation is found in the version published in *The Celtic Monthly* for March 1909, in which William-be-seated turns out to be her own son, who had left home as a young man, to seek his fortune, and had now returned, a very wealthy man. When he has claimed his share of the sheep's head, his mother says that only one man could have done it, but that he had died long ago, whereupon her visitor reveals his identity in a good four-line verse in which he tells her that she is a strange woman who scarcely recognises her own first-born child.

In his book, *The History of the Celtic Place-names of Scotland*, Professor W.J. Watson rightly points out that the asseveration, *Ma-Ruibhe!* or '(By) Mulruba!' is often heard in Harris. The professor got this information from his friend and former student, the late Rev Malcolm MacLean, a very fine Celtic scholar, who was a native of Scarp.

As islanders condemn niggardliness in any form, a number of short stories with the same *motif* were current among us, the common factor being a bowl of brose that was shared, and the artifices used to get the lion's share of it, for example by turning the bowl round to illustrate something said.

The theme was brought up to date with the story of how a Communion visitor unexpectedly got hospitality from a family of the Niggardly Mary type. At a certain Communion season one of the visitors announced to his fellow travellers that he would spend every night with a family that was never known to invite or welcome visitors to their home. He went uninvited to the house, where he got some supper, a bed, and breakfast in the morning. When he left in the morning, he suddenly stopped at the door, as if he had heard someone call to him, and said, 'Yes, yes! I'll come, I'll come!' He returned the same night, bringing another guest with him. The story adds that the whole household was converted at family worship that night, and the house was always full at Communion seasons thereafter.

A child's delight in the mysterious and uncanny was satisfied by listening to the prophesies attributed to the Brahan Seer, or *Coinneach Odhar* – Swarthy Kenneth – as he was usually called. His real name was Kenneth MacKenzie. Although born in the Outer Isles early in the seventeenth century, *Coinneach Odhar* went to live on the Brahan Estate, in Easter Ross, hence the name 'Brahan Seer'. His gift of predicting future events was attributed to the possession of a divining stone found by his mother in the old graveyard of Kirkton, in Uig, Lewis. He was the Highland counterpart of Thomas the Rhymer.

An interesting forecast attributed to *Coinneach Odhar*, was of the erection of three white houses, that is, modern stone and lime houses, at Hushinish, a prediction that was fulfilled in the year 1900. Another local prophesy attributed to him alarmed us not a little. It was the prediction that an enemy force would overrun the Outer Isles, until turned back at a pass just to the south of East Loch Tarbert, by 'Donald of the three Donalds', using as his only weapon a caber taken off a thatched house. As we were assured that a certain Donald whose father, grandfather, and great-grandfather bore the same name, actually lived in the vicinity of the pass in our day, we regarded the fulfilment of this prediction as imminent.

We even heard tales of hidden treasure, such as were common to all countries in ancient times. Our treasure, which consisted of an ordinary three-legged cooking-pot full of gold, was buried within sight of three isthmuses, or narrow necks of land. This was the only clue as to its location. Some maintained that the pot of gold had been found and that a woman in Taransay, to the south of Scarp, had the actual pot and used it in her home.

From such traditional tales and local lore, to an actual occurrence within living memory, was an easy transition, and we listened with thumping hearts to the story of a dangerous character who roamed over the Western Isles a hundred years ago.

The man, *Mac an t-Srònaich*, or 'Stronach' by name, who spent seven years in hiding among the high hills and deep dales of our end of the parish, fled from his home near Inverness after killing his sister in mistake for a Skyewoman who spent the night in his house, and whose name was given as Marion, daughter of Magnus. Feeling suspicious, the traveller had strung her beads to the neck of Stronach's sister, a ruse that saved her life when he sought her in the dark. When she was missed, the wild man set out after her, but she was able to persuade a passing carter to hide her under the hay in his cart and so she escaped.

The information that she was the grandmother of a certain Magnus, who lived near our island, and of whom we shall hear in a later chapter, greatly impressed us.

This wild cateran somehow crossed the Minch, and wandered about the Long Isle, keeping out of sight as a rule, but sometimes waylaying travellers, whom he attacked and robbed. Our island tradition had it that he was hanged in Inverness after confessing that he had committed seven murders, one of which was in our parish. This victim's name, as still remembered in my youth, was given as Hector MacAskill, or *Eachann Mac Chaluim 'Ic Iain 'Ic Choinnich* – 'Hector, son of Calum, son of John, son of Kenneth'. Other details remembered were that the fugitive fell in with Hector as the latter was returning from Stornoway with the refreshments for his own betrothal reception; that is, the reception that precedes by two weeks a wedding in the islands. He confessed that Hector was his most formidable opponent and this crime the one he regretted most. The islander, he said, had him down twice, but released him each time at his own request. He found only half-a-crown on MacAskill. Pieces of the earthenware jar carried by Hector are said to have lain for many years at the Scaladale River, near Ardvourlie, although Hector's body was found in a field some distance from the ordinary footpath.

On another occasion, this fierce man met an island stalwart, known as *Dòmhnall Bàn Mac Aonghais*, or 'Fair Donald MacInnes', who had lived in eight different parts of the parish, including Scarp. 'He made seven flittings', I was told. The story was that the freebooter came up with MacInnes while the latter was on his way to Stornoway, and followed him for a long time, but did not challenge him. To illustrate MacInnes's strength, it was said that he once carried home from Stornoway, a distance of forty-one miles, a boll of meal, enough nails to make a boat, a pair of boots weighing fourteen pounds, and a new spade. This was when he lived in a village just east of the pass mentioned in connection with 'Donald of the three Donalds'. I have only heard Fair Donald MacInnes's name in this connection, but that of his brother *Iain Donn*, or 'Brown John', is well-known throughout the parish. Our island 'king' was indeed the son of Brown John, of whom feats of strength are also related.

It was said that the wild man lived for some time in a cave near the head of Loch Resort. The cave was situated high among the rocks above Glen Ulladale and was known as *Uamh Ulladail*, or 'Ulladale Cave'. It had a narrow opening, admitting one person at a time, and was reached by a steep and winding path. Inside the cave there was a well or spring. As evidence that the cave was used in the way indicated, we were told that ashes had been found in it. This cave, by the way, is described by Martin Martin in his book, *A Description of the Western Islands of Scotland*. When we asked how Stronach lived, we were told his method was to steal food at night. It was known, for example, that he stole potatoes from the small settlement of Luachair at the head of Loch Resort, and took them away in a shoulder-plaid belonging to a woman whose name was given as *Mòr Nigh'n Dhòmhnaill Oig*, or 'Marion, Young Donald's daughter'.

Only one good deed is told of Stronach, namely that he helped a woman at Loch Tamanavay, the sea loch north-east of Scarp, to raise the mill-lock on a stream, so that she might get her corn ground.

The hills of our deer-forest, as well as those seen in the heart of the parish north of us, provided excellent cover for fugitives, whether singly or in bands. The tradition that some of the MacLeod Chieftains took refuge in the caves of the deer-forest was probably true. One thinks of Donald MacLeod of Berneray, popularly known as 'The Old Trojan', who was 'out' in both the '15 and the '45, and who was hunted by Redcoats and Government independent companies. His own son, commanding one of these companies, was his most ruthless pursuer.

Thus old and new blended in the talk to which we listened round the peat fire. Short stories and anecdotes about some historical or even mythological figures were better appreciated by children than a long folktale. A love for the old folktales, told in the traditional way, came later.

CHAPTER THIRTEEN

The Ceilidh, Part 4

It was my good fortune to know a man who was a genuine storyteller and who could narrate a long folktale in the grand manner. He was well educated and had such a good memory that he claimed to remember any Gaelic song or story ever heard by him. Once when I mentioned the eighteenth-century Gaelic poet William Ross, he repeated from memory, and without a pause, one of his long poems.

It is strange to think that I first heard the English nursery rhyme, 'The House that Jack Built', from him. He could repeat it at incredible speed, as though this should be one's aim in repeating the well-known rhyme. He once surprised me in another way. I had been reading one of Scott's novels, and complained to my friend that we had no great writers in our day. He at once reached for a volume that lay on a small shelf against a wall, and there and then read to me one of Conan Doyle's stories. When he had finished, he looked at me with a smile playing on his face, as much as to say, 'Are you satisfied now?'

A long folktale was related slowly and leisurely, the narrator telling his listeners when and where he first heard it. My old friend used to introduce his longest folktale by saying that he had heard it from a tinker woman who sometimes visited Scarp and lived with her children in the island's cornkiln, the foundation of which still remains. Placing her hand on a small fellow's head, she would say, *Is e leth-fhear de dhithis eile tha'n seo!* – 'This is one of triplets!' Once she amused the village lads who had come to visit her in the kiln, by saying, 'I brought fourteen children into the world and had they not killed my tinker, I would have won the prize!'

With such an introduction, my friend the storyteller would embark on the story of, 'Big John, The King's Son', which he had heard from her. It was a typical Gaelic folktale, with well-balanced phrases and passages to hold the tale together and make it easier to remember. It also contained one long 'rune', or rhythmical passage, which is a feature of many folktales. Some of the incidents in the tale – for example, the small bannock with a blessing or the big bannock with a curse – are found in popular folktales that are otherwise unrelated; but the tale as a whole is obviously related to one noted by the famous folklore collector J. F. Campbell and published under the title: 'The Brown Bear of the Green Glen', in the first volume of his *West Highland Tales*. They are really two versions of the same folktale, though differing widely. The 'rune' is not given in Campbell's version, but is found, with slight differences, in several of the other tales in Campbell's collection.

I give the Scarp version here in translation, as I partly memorised it, and partly wrote it down, while the storyteller was still living.

BIG JOHN, THE KING'S SON

There once was a king who had four sons, the youngest of whom was a fool. One day, as the king's sons were out hunting, they saw the most beautiful feather ever seen anywhere from the beginning of creation to the end of time. Away they went after it, but the nearer they thought they were, the further away the feather really was.

They went home and told the king what they saw and what had happened. Said the king: 'That was a feather from the golden bird owned by the Brownie of the Distant Island of the Green Earth, who is placing the world under spells. Many a king's son and knight's son, poor man's son and rich man's son, has gone to seek it, but never returned home'.

A day or two later the oldest son asked leave to go and seek the golden feather. The best horse was made ready and a new saddle was laid on it, and before he left his mother asked him whether he preferred a small bannock with a blessing or a large bannock with a curse. He said he preferred the large bannock and plenty with it.

He had not gone far when he came to a green hillock, where he dismounted and began to eat the bannock. Presently he heard a voice crying, 'Piece! piece! A piece for me, as I am faint!' 'You goggle-eyed, squint-eyed, swarthy, grizzled beast', said the king's son, 'it is little enough for myself.' 'So will things turn out for you', said the voice.

The second son and the third son left in the same way, and as their brother fared, so they fared.

Then the youngest son said: 'Words and vows I give that I shall not pause nor rest until I find out where the feather came from'. There were cries of, 'Bad luck to you!' here and cries of 'Bad luck to you!' there, as Big John prepared for his journey. By that time there was no beast or harness left but the white gelding and a saddle that had lain in the window unused for seven years. Before he left, his mother asked him which he preferred, the small bannock with a blessing or the large bannock with a curse. Big John replied that a mother's blessing was worth having in any case. 'So will things turn out for you', said his mother.

Big John set off, and before long the pretty pillared clouds of day began to desert him, and the dark dismal clouds of night to appear. At last the white gelding fell into a pit. Said Big John: 'As I have no other place to rest tonight, I will disembowel the white gelding and sleep in its trunk'.

As soon as he was settled he began to eat the bannock. He then heard a voice say: 'Piece! piece! A piece for me, Big John the king's son, as I am faint!' 'Yes beloved one', and, 'yes adorable one', said Big John, 'come in here for you may need it more than I myself do.' The owner of the voice came in and who should it be but the splay-footed Beast of the Wood.

As soon as morning came the splay-footed Beast said to Big John: 'Mount on my back, and keep good hold between my wings'. Big John did so and with the splay-footed Beast's first leap Big John's head hit the clouds. 'My ruin and bane! I am dead at this rate!' said Big John. 'Have no fear', said the splay-footed Beast, 'but keep a firm grip between my wings and tonight we shall be with the Knight of the Black Shield.'

'Now', said the splay-footed Beast when they reached the Knight's house, 'you will go in and ask if you can have a night's lodging. They will tell you "No!" but that you will be killed and a piece of you hung on every spit. You will then ask if you can get lodging for the sake of the splay-footed Beast of the Wood. They will answer "Yes beloved one", and, "yes adorable one, with soft water to wash the hands and warm water to wash the feet, as we lift it in our palms".'

It all turned out as the splay-footed Beast said and they got both food and shelter from the Knight of the Black Shield. Big John noticed that they had no loaf-bread and said that it was strange that there was none. 'Well', said the Knight, 'we have none.'

Next morning they set off again and after the splay-footed Beast's first jump only one hill remained between them and the clouds. They came to the house of the Knight of the White Shield and were received and entertained as on the previous night. Big John saw that they had no flesh, and said that it was strange that there was none. 'Well', said the Knight, 'we have none.'

On they went the next morning and on this third day two hills stood between them and the clouds. They ultimately reached the house of the Knight of the Red Shield and spent the night comfortably there. Big John saw they had no wine and said it was strange there was none. 'Well', said the Knight, 'we have none.'

Early next day they went to the shore and there found a large block of wood. 'Put your hand in my ear', said the splay-footed Beast, 'and you will find a club there.' Big John did so and found the club. 'Strike the block with it', said the splay-footed Beast. This was done, and there before their eyes was the finest galley ever seen from the beginning of creation to the end of time.

The splay-footed Beast went to the stern and Big John to the bow, and they launched it at the first attempt.

> Then they hoist the red and speckled sails,
>   towering high,
> 'Gainst the tall and tough masts of timber;
> Not a mast was unbent,
>   Not a sail unrent,
> As they sped through the lashing and
>   splashing sea.
> Blue Book, and Red Book, and Green Book
>   of Northmen!
> Their music and song were
> The roaring of whales and the wailing of boars,
> While the black, curved periwinkles of the seafloor
>   rattled on the hull,
> As Big John, the king's son, deftly steered it.

In this way, they at length came to the Distant Island of the Green Earth. They hauled the galley ashore, struck it with the club, and it became a block of wood again.

'Now', said the splay-footed Beast, 'you must be quick, for the castle is guarded by a hundred lions, a hundred giants, and a hundred archers, but I shall bring upon them an hour's sleep.'

In the first room Big John entered, there was the golden bird, perched on a chair of gold. 'I will put this at least in the scarlet plaid', said Big John. Looking at the other side of the room, he saw there a bottle of wine, with writing on it to the effect that even if a hundred men drank from it, it would never go dry. This too went into the plaid.

He went into the next room and there saw a leg of mutton. This went into the scarlet plaid. He went into another room and there saw a loaf of bread, and this he put into the scarlet plaid.

As he glanced around the room before leaving he saw the fairest creature ever seen from the beginning of creation to the end of time, asleep on a high bed, and he thought it a pity not to kiss her. This he did and hastened out.

At that moment the lions and giants and archers began to awaken, but the splay-footed Beast carried him away in the twinkling of an eye.

To make a long story short, it need only be said that when they reached the Knight of the Red Shield, Big John gave him the bottle of wine. When they reached the Knight of the White Shield, Big John gave him the leg of mutton. And when they reached the Knight of the Black Shield, Big John gave him the loaf.

A year and a day passed, and then the Brownie of the Distant Island of the Green Earth and the fair creature, with the giants and archers, came to the king's palace, and the Brownie cried: 'Come out whoever took my golden bird, else the highest stone of the palace will be the lowest and the lowest stone the highest'.

The king's eldest son came out. The Brownie asked him how he found the golden bird, and he said he found it among the bens and glens and rough places, but not without much wandering. 'Off with his head!' said the Brownie, 'And quarter him and toss him behind me in the chariot!' This happened to the king's three sons, one after another, for they all claimed to have found the golden bird. The Brownie then asked the king if he had not yet another son. The king said: 'No, except one fool, and if he went to seek the golden bird, he certainly had not found it'.

Upon this, Big John came out and told his story from beginning to end. The fair creature, who was none other than the Brownie's daughter, recognised him, and there and then gave him her hand in marriage.

She struck the king's sons with the magic wand and the healing water, and they were all as hale and hearty as they had ever been. And a wedding feast was held, lasting a year and a day.

I now give, by way of contrast, in an English dress, the folktale traditionally known by the title: 'The Parish of Saint Kellog'. It is surely one of the most amusing stories in any language.

THE PARISH OF SAINT KELLOG

Once upon a time, a certain young man went to the parish of St. Kellog to look for a wife, and having married a farmer's only daughter, settled down with her parents.

When peat-cutting time came round, all four went to the peat moss and when it was time for dinner the younger woman was sent home for food. When she entered the house, she saw the grey mare's pack-saddle on a rafter above her head and began to weep, saying: 'What would I do if the pack-saddle fell and killed me and my brood?'

When the others got tired of waiting, her mother was sent to see what kept her, and when the old woman reached home she found her daughter weeping within. 'Woe is me!' she said, 'What has come over you?' 'Oh!' said the daughter, 'When I came in I saw the grey mare's pack-saddle on the rafter above my head; and what would I do if it fell and killed both me and my brood?' The old woman wrung her hands. 'Me the day!' said she, 'If that should happen, what would you and I do?'

As the men in the peat moss wondered why neither of the women returned, the old man went home to see what kept them, and when he entered the house he found them wringing their hands and weeping. 'Woe is me!' said he, 'What has come over you?' 'Oh!' said his wife, 'When your daughter came home she saw the grey mare's pack-saddle on the rafter above her head, and what would she do if it fell and killed both her and her brood?' 'Me the day!' said the old man, wringing his hands, 'What if that should happen!'

As night fell, the young man came home tired and hungry and found all three weeping together. 'Dear, dear!' he said, 'What has come over you?' His father-in-law told him. 'But', he said, 'the pack-saddle has not fallen!'

Next morning the young man left the house saying that he would neither pause nor rest until he had found three other people as foolish as his wife and her parents.

As he walked through the parish he saw three women sitting at their doors, spinning on distaffs. 'I rather think you do not belong to this place', he told them. 'Indeed no,' they said, 'and we do not believe you belong to it either.' 'No!' he said. They then declared: 'The men of this parish are so simple that we can make them believe anything we like.' 'Well', said the young man, 'I have a golden ring here which I will give to the one that makes her husband believe the most impossible thing.'

When the first husband came home, his wife said to him: 'You are ill!' 'Am I ill?' said he. 'Oh yes', she replied, 'take your clothes off and go to bed.' When he got into bed she said: 'You are now dead'. 'Am I dead?' he asked. 'Yes', she said, 'you are dead. Close your eyes and do not move a hand or foot.'

When the second husband came home his wife said to him: 'It is not you!' 'Is it not?' said he. 'Oh no!' replied his wife. So he left the house and took to the wood.

When the third husband came home, nothing unusual happened. But next morning, when invitations to the 'dead man's' funeral were sent round, his wife would not allow him up. When the funeral procession had passed by, however, she told him to get up at once and go to the funeral. He jumped out of bed and began looking for his clothes, which his wife had concealed. 'Where are my clothes?' he said. 'You are wearing them!' said his wife. 'Am I wearing them?' said he. 'Yes', declared his wife, 'hurry up and you will overtake the others.' So off he went as fast as he could run, and when the funeral party saw the naked man bearing down on them, they thought he was mad, and scattered, leaving the coffin on the road.

As the naked man stood at one end of the coffin he was joined by the man from the wood. 'Do you know me?' said the newcomer. 'No!' said the other. 'Oh no!' said the man from the wood, 'I cannot be Thomas when my own wife does not know me. But why are you naked?' 'Am I naked?' said the other, 'My wife told me I was wearing my clothes.' 'My wife told me it was not I!' said Thomas. 'And my wife told me I was dead!' said the man in the coffin.

When the men on the road heard the dead man speak, they took to their heels; but their wives came and took the three men home, and the woman whose husband had been 'dead' got the golden ring. So the young man had found three people as foolish as those he had left behind, and he returned home.

When he went out the next day he saw a boat with twelve men going to sea, but when it returned only eleven men could be found, and no one knew which of the twelve men was missing. As he watched, he saw that the man who counted the crew always forgot to include himself. 'What reward will you give me', asked the young man, 'if I find the missing man for you?' They said they would give him anything he asked if he found the missing man. After making them sit down in a row on the ground, he took a club, and giving the first man a clout on the head, said: 'You will remember that you were on the boat'. He did the same for the next man, and the next, and so on until he had counted twelve. In spite of the bruised and broken heads, they were so pleased that the missing man had been found that in addition to the reward, they set about preparing a feast for the young man.

It so happened that the parishioners had a loch that was being stocked with fish. The young man suggested to the twelve men that they should drain this loch and get fish for the feast. So they drained the loch and found only a large eel in it. 'This', they said, 'is the beast that ate up all the fish!' So they caught the eel, took it down to the shore, and went off to sea to drown it.

As the young man turned to go home he saw four men trying to lift a cow onto the wall of a thatched house, so that it might eat the grass growing on top of the wall. 'What reward will you give me', he said, 'if I bring down the grass for you?' They looked at him, astonished. He then climbed the low wall, cut the grass, and threw it down to the animal.

He finally saw a man coming along with an ox in a cart. The men of the hamlet knew that the ox had been stolen, and said that a Court should be set up and the thief tried. This was done, the decision of the Court being that the horse should be put to death for drawing a stolen ox!

There is an allusion to this last folktale in a poem by the seventeenth-century

Gaelic poet John MacDonald, who complains that his banishment from his native Lochaber, because he had sought redress for the murder of the heir of Keppoch, resembled 'the ancient law of the Parish of St. Kellog, by which the gelding was sentenced in Court'. We have an allusion to the same incident in the expression used by Highlanders to indicate a miscarriage of justice. 'A more unreasonable judgment', they would say, 'was not given even in the Parish of St. Kellog.'

CHAPTER FOURTEEN

The Land

Until the year 1779, Scarp was included in the territory of the MacLeods of Dunvegan. In that year our parish, along with Berneray and St Kilda, was sold by the trustees of General MacLeod of MacLeod, the 20th Chief, to Captain Alexander MacLeod of the East Indiaman *Mansfield*, second son of the famous Donald MacLeod of Berneray, for the sum of £15,000. In 1834 the parish was bought by the 5th Earl of Dunmore, whose grandson, the 7th Earl, sold the northern half to Sir Edward Henry Scott in 1871. In my youth, therefore, the Scotts, the last of whom was Sir Samuel Edward Scott, who died without issue in 1943, were our proprietors.

It would be interesting to know the early history of Scarp, small though it is. Dean Monro, writing in 1549 says it was: 'fertile and fruitful, good for corn, store (i.e. store cattle) and fishing', but as the Dean uses practically the same words for many places mentioned in his *Description of the Western Isles of Scotland*, his witness is of limited value.

Martin Martin's account, about a hundred and fifty years later, is disappointing in a different way. Unlike the Dean of the Isles, he gives a very full account of all the places visited, but he seems to have bypassed the island, although he paid a lengthy visit to St Kilda. Reading Martin's account, I feel quite certain that he only saw Scarp from a distance, probably when he visited the Flannan Isles twenty-five miles north-west of us. My reasons are that his description of it as, 'a high land covered with heath and grass', is too general, and that he shows Hushinish on his map as being situated north of Scarp, instead of south of it.

MacCulloch's account, published in 1819, is equally meagre. He states that it was a conspicuous island on the west coast of Harris, consisting of a single mountain about one thousand feet high. Had the island been all hill, as he seems to suggest, this would have been a good guess, for the highest point is one thousand and twelve feet above sea level.

The extent of the village, as well as its configuration, may throw light on its past history. It really consists of three hamlets, known to this day as, *Am Bail' a Tuath, Am Bail' a Deas,* and *Am Baile Meadhonach* – 'The North Hamlet', 'The South Hamlet', and 'The Mid Hamlet' – a circumstance which points to the old land system by which one superior held the land from the Clan Chief, while cottar families, living in small compact groups, carried out the work.

The change from the feudal system, which created such hamlets, to the modern crofting community, must have been gradual. Long ago an islander may have acquired the land to the south of South Hamlet, for cultivation as a croft, for this part of the village still goes by the name *A' Bhuaile*, or 'The Croft'. The rest of the land would follow suit, being divided, at some time or other, among the islanders, who continued to live as tenants in the thatched houses, built end to end and back to back, in the three compact clusters that had formed the earliest farm communities.

In my own lifetime a great change has taken place in this respect. In all three hamlets, former neighbours have moved away from each other, the tendency in every case being to spread out. There is not a single pair of back to back or end to end dwellings now. In my early youth, no crofter or cottar lived in a stone and lime house, only the missionary, merchant and schoolmaster living in houses of modern type, whereas as I write, more than half of the island's families live in modern houses.

If local tradition is trustworthy, the sandy soil of the village was very much deeper at one time, when the ploughshare, to repeat the picturesque description still remembered, only struck against one stone in the whole of the ground cultivated. This seems incredible, although it is not difficult to believe that the contour of the village has undergone change. Such a change can be seen on a smaller scale in a lifetime. Not only does the soil thin, it also fills up in places, changing the conformation of the surface and turning sandy hollows into green fields, with the ubiquitous daisy plant providing a protective covering.

If the islanders' conjecture is right, that *A' Chlach Ruadh*, or 'The Red Stone', below North Hamlet, is the solitary stone once feared by the ploughman, the additional information is elicited that the sea has encroached upon the land to a considerable extent, for The Red Stone now stands clear of the soil, on the upper part of the shore. There is some support for the theory regarding the encroachment of the sea. Tradition, with some exaggeration, says that at one time a woman, washing blankets in the loch on which we sailed our toy boats, could throw her wooden beater right across the Sound at that point!

The mention of a plough is interesting. An islander of over ninety years, who died in the year 1935, remembered the last pony kept on the island and could describe its colour, but I never heard him speak of a plough being used in his time.

As a result of the greater freedom enjoyed by our islanders, and the value of the potato crop in raising a family, an expansion of population took place in the nineteenth century, giving rise to agitation to have some families resettled elsewhere. Intensive cultivation must have been the rule then. Anyone looking across to our island from the long ferry at Hushinish cannot fail to see an indication of this in the long green ridges among the hills, facing south, which mark the position of fields which were once cultivated. The difficulty of carrying manure to those fields must have been very great and would not be attempted nowadays for any consideration.

A hundred years ago Scarp accommodated eight farming families. By 1870 the island was divided into sixteen 'lots', as these small crofts are called, one person being responsible for the rent of each lot. In addition, there was, as is usual in a crofting community, common hill-grazing, with the number of sheep and cattle kept by each crofter being limited by the system known as 'summing', or 'souming'. It shared with every other part of the Long Isle the evil results of the subdivision of single crofts among the crofter's married sons or brothers, and the provision of at least a few potato fields for cottars, that is, people who had no hereditary claim to any of the land and paid no rent. The distinction between 'crofter' and 'cottar' is no longer recognised however. The runrig system, by which families shared the various plots, changing over every third year, was not known on the island.

Scarp had in addition its own peculiar difficulties. Being exposed to the wild Atlantic, the fishing often proved a failure. As there was no sheltered harbour and no piers, the large boats used for long-line fishing could only operate in the summer, when they rode at anchor, after which they had to be sold. There was no road nearer than Amhuinnsuidhe, five miles beyond the long ferry. A cargo of oatmeal, unloaded there in stormy weather, was sometimes carried to the ferry on one's back. The doctor lived seventeen miles away. The absence of a road and the distance from a doctor were genuine grievances, especially when one recalls that our islanders paid their full share of taxes, as well as school and poor rates.

The greatest grievance, however, was the loss of the grazing once enjoyed by the islanders across the Sound. At one time much of the island's livestock spent the summer there, but this privilege was withdrawn without any compensation in land or reduction in rent, when the extensive deer-forest of 40,000 acres was cleared in the first quarter of the nineteenth century. This seems to have been our island's main share of the infamous 'Clearances', which caused so much suffering throughout the Highlands in the first half of the nineteenth century. Although Scarp escaped, several hamlets on the parish mainland to the north and south of us were cleared to make room for the tacksman's sheep and the proprietor's deer.

Our islanders asked for two things, namely the resettlement of those areas by some of the island's forty families, and the restoration, to those left on the island, of the grazing privileges once enjoyed across the Sound. Appeals to the estate factor only brought the retort, 'Go to America!' But in the year 1885 the trustees of Sir Edward Scott, who had died two years earlier while his son and heir was still a minor, granted our islanders land in seven localities near to the island.

All this happened a few years before I was born, but the boys and girls then on the island must have found the flitting of households in different directions an exciting event. The date is still remembered as, *A' bhliadhna a dh'fhalbh na daoine as a'bhaile* – 'The year the people left the village'. By the time I was old enough to visit those small communities, my contemporaries and I did not regard the people as islanders, even though we knew the heads of families in each of them had brothers and sisters living in Scarp.

It is significant that Hushinish, the nearest vacant land, as well as the best, was not at that time granted as a new settlement. Who lived there in the eighteenth century, where they went and what their numbers were, was forgotten, but some information can be gleaned from the fact that certain families in the parish still use the burial ground there, just as the small communities set up to relieve the congestion on Scarp still use our island graveyard.

A certain concession was however made in regard to Hushinish, four island families, including the missionary and the merchant, being given permission to cultivate fields on the north side of Hushinish, facing Scarp. As Lady Scott's brother, Mr Edward Packe, was one of the trustees, his name has always been associated with this particular favour.

Fifteen years later, Hushinish was actually reoccupied, when the families of Dirascal, the nearer of the two small hamlets set up in 1885 near the head of Loch Resort, were transferred to it. Had I not been in the habit of spending my school holidays at an early age with my aunt in Luachair, I would not have known the present Hushinish community in its old home. I distinctly remember seeing the children come to the small village at the head of the loch, where my aunt lived, to attend the Ladies' School there. As it was less than three miles away, with a tolerable path for the schoolchildren, I visited the hamlet of Dirascal more than once and still remember the position of the three houses, near the water, in a quiet bay of the loch. But it was claimed on behalf of the proprietor that the presence of the houses frightened the deer away, and prevented them seeking winter shelter on the lower levels by the shore.

As Hushinish was offered in exchange, a second flitting was willingly undertaken, and so in April 1900, in time for the spring work on their new land, the three families were transferred. I remember seeing the boats pass down the Sound with the furniture and other household articles, and have a vivid recollection of the cattle appearing across the Sound, opposite the South Hamlet, and being driven by the women of the community along the precipitous path towards their new home. At first the people lived in small thatched houses, where I remember visiting them, but before winter set in three modern houses were ready, the proprietor having given each family a grant towards the cost of a house. Thus in the year 1900 the Brahan Seer's vision of, 'three white houses in Hushinish', was realised!

By the time this transplantation took place, the island missionary had left, but the other islanders mentioned earlier were permitted by the proprietor to continue cultivating their fields there. From the new Hushinish tenants' point of view this was a real snag. In addition to good crops of potatoes, much hay was taken off those fields and carried across to Scarp, the merchant having a large flock of sheep and a cow. Complaints were made that the islanders trampled good grass which lay between the fields and the harbour. But no change was made until the merchant gave up cultivation, whereupon the only surviving cottar, who had no cow and only a few sheep, was requested to take no more grass. As the last of those fields was given up many years ago, they are now part of the resident Hushinish crofters' land, to use as they please, but Mr Packe's name is remembered in Scarp and a few are still left who recall his interest in them.

Only once have whole families left the island in my time. That was in 1919, after the First World War, when four Scarp families were transferred to unoccupied land used as a deer-park at Cliasmol, seven miles beyond Hushinish. Like the vacant places resettled in 1885, this place had also been cultivated at one time. The tradition was that it had been occupied by a leaseholder whose farm servant was fed on seal flesh. This servant, not surprisingly, ultimately rebelled and ran away.

CHAPTER FIFTEEN

The Sheep Farmer

As nobody lived at Hushinish in my early youth, I had the queerest conception of *Fear Hùisinis*, or 'the Hushinish Man', whose name was so often heard in Scarp. That he was a person of some importance and in a class by himself was obvious; nevertheless I pictured him as a recluse, living a lonely life on the green, grassy isthmus at our long ferry, and when we found coins dating from the early Georges, as we sometimes did, on the ground cultivated by our island cottars, we believed they had once belonged to *Fear Hùisinis*.

The name really pertains to the sheep farmer to whom the western side of our parish was let early in the nineteenth century, and for whom the villages mentioned in the last chapter were 'cleared'. Hushinish itself was the first place to attract the factor's attention. Although local tradition regarded *Fear Hùisinis* as having lived at the other end of the western seaboard of the parish, over twenty miles away, it is likely that he lived in Hushinish first, and only moved when he leased a second large tack, or sheep-run, situated at the other end of the parish. A later factor was, indeed, responsible for clearing the southern half of the parish, and creating sheep-runs there. The name Hushinish, or 'House Ness', is no guide in this connection, being from the Norse language, and therefore belonging to a much earlier date.

Hushinish was an ideal gathering place for the large flock of Blackface sheep scattered over the hills and glens of the vast deer-forest. A high strongly built wall across the base of this neck of land enclosed it in such a way that it formed a huge fold or fank, while the long sandy beach on the south side, with stones only found at the inner or eastern end of it, would help to receive the flocks that entered by the only gate, which was placed at the southern end of the wall. It would also provide safe and suitable grazing ground for weaned lambs.

As Hushinish has a highly lime-rich machair its value for grazing, indeed for cultivation, is apparent. The first Statistical Account of Scotland, of 1794, describes Hushinish as being arable, and adds the information that horse-drawn ploughs were used there. Part of the hill outside the wall at the southern end was quite obviously cultivated at some time, but it is now vain to ask when this was done. Was Hushinish itself once overcrowded, or do those green strips represent the portion allotted to some cottars or servants for their own use?

As our islanders paid their rent to *Fear Hùisinis*, Scarp must have formed part of the extensive tack held by him, even if he did not stock it for his own use. He had, however, a claim on the islanders' services. They helped with the sheep-gathering, not only in Hushinish but also on the isthmus further south, where he finally lived.

My grandfather – usually known as 'The Deacon' – led our islanders on such occasions, taking with him his collie, 'Lassie', which my mother remembered well. A number of stories were told of this faithful and intelligent dog. Once when she was away working at Amhuinnsuidhe with the Scarp men, she returned home alone to feed her pup, swimming the Sound to do so. By morning she had rejoined her master at the fank! In my youth I heard so much about my grandfather's work among the sheep that I thought he had been a shepherd. Instead, he was described in the 1851 Census as being 'a farmer of 3 acres, employing two labourers'. Later censuses, and his death certificate, described him simply as being 'a crofter'.

At the time of which I am now writing, *Fear Hùisinis* had a Highland shepherd living across the Sound at Cravadale, on the far side of Loch na Cleavag. Before the small communities were formed in 1885, this was the only place within six miles of our short ferry in which a stormstayed islander could pass the night. It is, therefore, not surprising that at a certain Communion season, no less than forty of our islanders spent a night in the shepherd's house beside the loch. That was the age of the 'shakedown', when in an emergency all the spare blankets in a house were laid on loose straw on the floor to form beds. So well-known was this custom that the saying, 'A straw out of each shakedown', was applied to anyone who possessed only what he or she could borrow from others.

Gaelic editors too, have borrowed the short and simple phrase, *sop as gach seid*, as a title for miscellaneous matter, in the same way as an English editor might use the words, 'here and there'.

The tacksmen's shepherds led an arduous life. They not only tended large flocks, gathering them, with assistance, several times a year, and even ferrying them to and from islets to which they were sent to pasture, but they were also obliged to drive those for sale – both sheep and black cattle – to the Falkirk Tryst, after seeing them conveyed by boat to the Scottish mainland. No provision was made for the shepherds during their long absences from home. They either took food with them or provided for their own needs as they went along.

There is an interesting sequel to such trips in the case of the Highland shepherd to whom I have just referred. Realising the value of a knowledge of English and a good general education, he resolved to have his family educated, no matter what the cost in personal sacrifice. The result was that two of his sons became schoolmasters, one being an Arts graduate of Glasgow University, while the other members of his family were all well-read and spoke fluent English.

By the time I was old enough to pay my first visit to Cravadale, a modern house had been built near the old thatched house by the side of the loch, with one of the sons serving our proprietor as a shepherd. I may add here that when Hushinish was resettled in 1900, the proprietor's sheep were withdrawn from it. A few years later the whole flock was sold, the shepherd turning gamekeeper and remaining where he was. Stone fanks, as well as a roofed house used at smearing time, remained as witnesses to the supremacy of the sheep in Hushinish – both the tacksman's Blackface sheep and the proprietor's Cheviots – for upwards of a hundred years.

Fear Hùisinis is only a memory in Scarp. Nevertheless, I have personally known several tacksmen of the better sort in the Outer Islands, and would describe them as prosperous gentlemen-farmers. Once when spending a holiday with my aunt at Luachair, one of those, a man of gigantic stature, appeared on the north side of the loch, near the shepherd's house there. He had come to arrange a sheep-gathering, and as usual wanted the assistance of the men on the south side of the loch. When I crossed over with my cousins the next day, and climbed up to the sheepfolds above the shepherd's house, I was astonished at their size, there being several drystone fanks grouped together. The men sheared the sheep, while the shepherd's sisters packed the fleeces in bags which were afterwards taken in a large boat, kept by the shepherd, to the nearest port, twenty miles away. Incidentally, the tall man whom I saw waving across the placid Hebridean loch on that far-off day was the grandfather of Duncan J. MacRae, that fine Scottish rugby internationalist of the late nineteen-thirties.

It may be appropriate at this point to indicate some of the circumstances which brought about such a radical change in the Highlands during the early part of the nineteenth century, when so much of the land was occupied by large leaseholders:

1. With the abrogation of the clan system after Culloden, in 1746, the close tie between landlord and tenant was severed and much of the land was either sold to distant relatives of the chief, or let out on lease by absentee landlords.

2. The social and political changes which ensued, created a demand for money, for the lairds and other large landowners no longer lived off the land or spent the greater part of their lives on their own estates.

3. The collapse of the kelp industry, which had proved so remunerative for landowners, who raised the rent as the price of kelp soared, aggravated the situation thus created. Dr Johnson, for example, wrote in 1773 that the rental of a farm in North Uist rose in ten years from thirty pounds to one hundred and eighty pounds – a six-fold increase. The repeal of the duty on barilla and salt after

the Napoleonic Wars reduced the price of kelp from a maximum
of twenty-two pounds per ton to two pounds per ton in 1831.

4. There was a ready market for wool, the woollen industry being
the greatest industry in England, encouraged and protected by
Parliament.

5. Finally, those living in the Highlands and tilling the soil there,
whether as tenants or sub-tenants, had no security of tenure, and
their occupancy of the land could be terminated at will.

As is well known, the outcry raised in the Highlands ultimately led to
the appointment of a Royal Commission in 1883, and three years later
the Crofters Holdings (Scotland) Act was passed, giving crofters security
of tenure, with the power to bequeath their right in a holding, so long as
the beneficiary was a member of the same family.

A permanent Crofters Commission was also appointed, one of the most
important matters referred to it at the outset being the fixing of fair rent for
every district that applied to it for revaluation of the holdings. In this way a
survey was carried out in our parish in 1890, when the extent of arable land
and outrun of each croft was recorded, as well as the extent of the common
hill-pasture, the rent paid, and what the surveyors regarded as a fair rent for
each township. I think I am right in saying that, in spite of several changes
in the ownership of the estate, the 'Fair Rent' then fixed for our island is
the rent still paid.

It is sometimes claimed that sheep were unknown in the Highlands before
the eighteenth century. The truth is that sheep were comparatively few. Cattle,
horses, goats and pigs were reared in large numbers, but the occurrence in
the Outer Isles of such place-names as Sheep Island, Sheep Hill, and Sheep
Ridge, as well as Meadow Isle, and Pasture Isle, all in the old Norse tongue,
is proof that sheep were well known in the islands as far back as the Norse
occupation, which lasted from the middle of the ninth century to the middle
of the thirteenth century. That many of the islands off the west coast of
Scotland, including the Outer Hebrides, were good for grazing sheep may
be assumed from the fact that many of these were 'cleared' in the early
nineteenth century, and added one by one to existing tacks or sheep-runs,
the factors themselves in many cases holding some of these tacks.

It is strange to think that the Border poet, James Hogg, The Ettrick
Shepherd, once nearly settled on a sheep farm on the west side of South
Harris. A last minute legal complication deprived him of the farm just
before the intended move. That was in 1804. Border shepherds were of
course employed in large numbers throughout the Highlands.

I said that *Fear Hùisinis* was only a memory now. As if to prove that he
was a real person and not a character in a folktale, one of the Hushinish
tenants of my days had a memento of him in the form of a quaich or small

drinking cup, which belonged to the tenant's grandfather, who had received it from the parish midwife. It was playfully referred to as *Cuach Fear Hùisinis*, or 'the Hushinish Man's whisky quaich', the family tradition being that he once drank three fills of whisky from it. This must have been long before the grandfather in question left Scarp in 1885, but what the occasion was is not known. The quaich was of thick china, with a decoration consisting of a red border. It had the same capacity as a wine glass, being two and a half inches in diameter and one inch in depth.

Fear Hùisinis occupies a niche in MacLeod family history, his mother having been one of the Laird of Raasay's ten daughters, who entertained Dr Johnson and Boswell so merrily during their visit to Raasay in 1773. His real name was Alexander MacRae.

Island Homes

In my early youth it was not compulsory to have a byre. The cattle shared one end of the crofter's thatched house with the poultry, no one regarding this arrangement as insanitary. In some houses the animals, though tied to the end wall, left only a narrow passage between the outer door and the inner door, and on a dark night with the inner door shut we felt terrified if we knew that the cattle had 'come home'.

In any agricultural community the barn is probably older than the byre. This was certainly the case in Scarp, several crofters having a small barn with its own thatched roof, and in at least some instances with a door leading to it from the dwellinghouse. It might even have a bed, as the one case I remember best actually had, I myself having once shared that bed with the boys of the family.

Here the corn was brought from the cornyard for threshing with the old-fashioned wooden flail which seemed so cumbersome. I well remember the flail, consisting of a long handle and a piece of smooth wood about two feet in length tied loosely to the handle with a thong of home-dressed skin. It was fascinating to watch the men wield the flail, the 'striker' circling in the air above their heads as they knelt on the floor, and descending with incredible precision on the end of the sheaf which carried the grain. When we tried to emulate the men our reward was a blow on the head or back from the striker. It had to be kept going with connecting thong at full stretch, in order to avoid disaster.

The flail has gone out of use long ago. I was surprised to hear an islander who is only a few years younger than I am, say that he had only seen a flail used in France, where he served as a Scots Guardsman during the First World War.

The construction of a house of the old-fashioned thatched type is simple, the low walls consisting of two skins of rough stones, filled in between with small stones, earth or sand, with a cope of turf laid on the top. No mortar is used. The roof, resting on the inner edge of the thick wall, is made up of wooden couples meeting at a ridge pole, with horizontal purlins tied to the couples, and light wooden laths set over these to support the roof covering. Rafters, set to a slope and resting on the end couples, make up the framework of the ends of the roof, the middle rafter at each end being long enough to show well above the roof when completed. The wood protruding in this way is known as the 'crow-stick'.

Thatch is laid, usually over a bed of turf, on this skeleton roof, and secured with rope, the ends of which are fastened to flat 'anchor stones' resting on the thatch several inches above the wall in order to keep the rope taut. These stones are sometimes so near each other that they almost touch. For securing the thatch on the ends of the house, the protruding crow-sticks are brought into use, rope being thrown round them, and the ends of the ropes fastened to anchor stones in the usual way.

Two kinds of thatch were in general use on our island, namely heather and sea-bent, heather being the commonest and presumably the older kind. One enterprising islander was in the habit of bringing fern and sedge-grass by raft from one of the islets in the centre of Scarp and using both for rethatching his house. The reason, I think, is that he was the crofter who used soot most often for his growing potato crop and he found the soot-soaked fern and sedge, especially the latter, light enough to cause no damage to the potato tops.

In thatching, the heather was carefully placed with the strong roots uppermost and the bushy heads hanging down. The bent, which is of a lighter colour and gives the roof a better and brighter appearance, was laid on in loose armfuls, with the sharp tips pointing downwards. It was secured in the same way as a heather thatch.

The rope used might be of heather or bent, or it might be a piece of gauze rope, which came into general use during my boyhood. Ropes of hay or straw, used for other purposes, were not considered strong enough. I have often watched a householder weaving a heather rope as he sat by the fireside, a heap of newly cut heather on one side and a growing coil of heather rope on the other. As heather is strong and tough, a day's work must have been sore on the fingers and thumbs.

Cutting the sea-bent was a communal activity, the bent growing on the opposite side of the Sound, above the short ferry, where there was a large tract of it known to us as *Am Baca Murain*, or 'The Bent-grass Bank', although the word 'marram' favoured by some naturalists, is nearer our native word *muran*. To the other side we repaired once a year, making a day of it and cutting with scythe and sickle the portions ascribed by lot to each holding on the island. Children contrived to scramble into the boats as usual on such occasions, and could wander about and see the rabbits that had riddled the ground with their warrens, though none has ever reached our island. The marram or bent annually cut in this way was ferried across to Scarp and used as required.

In the back to back type of houses, only the front wall had windows, one for the livingroom and one for the sleeping room. For the far end of the house, whether used as a byre or not, a small window let into the thatch, or a mere hole in the thatch, was considered sufficient. The two partitions dividing the house into three separate compartments were of wood. All doors, including the outer one, which was closed only at night, were fastened by a wooden latch or sneck, a piece of ordinary twine, passing through a hole, being used to raise it. When cattle were about, a wooden spar was placed in the outer doorway to prevent an animal from entering unnoticed.

In a typical blackhouse, as we called a thatched house, the floors were of earth – 'clean dirt', as a Glasgow girl once said – trodden hard by succeeding generations, and often uneven. The fire was in the middle of the livingroom floor, on a hearth of flat stones only a very little higher than the level of the floor. There was no ceiling. A hole in the roof, with or without an improvised chimney-pot, such as a bottomless bucket, allowed the smoke to escape. No fire was lit in any other part of the house.

Chimneys of stone or concrete have been built in all the blackhouses I knew so well as a boy, and even if they have not got the advantages of a modern range, they have at least got rid of the smoke from a newly made-up fire, which stung one's eyes and made them water so freely. These fires were never allowed to die out entirely. By the simple device of laying the half-burnt peat of the last fire flat on the hearthstone, with the 'noses' buried in the ashes, they were kept smouldering all night without burning out. *Nec tamen consumebatur!* In the morning it was only necessary to move the live embers to one side, brush the ash from the hearth, and set the embers up in a small heap with fresh peat round them. It was not necessary to apply a light. The live cinders soon burst into flame.

As pots and pans were hung on a chain over the fire for cooking purposes, it was essential that the fire should be built directly below the chain. An ingenious method, with the concentration and precision of a ritual, was used to ensure this. Before the glowing cinders were brought together, a small cinder was lifted with the tongs to the lowest hook of the overhanging chain, and then allowed to fall. Its point of contact with the hearthstone determined the centre around which the new day's fire should be built up.

The most prominent piece of furniture in every house was the dresser, with its rows of plates, a broad surface which could be used for baking, two flat drawers with round wooden knobs, and an open base in which pails of water could stand. When the guidman or guidwife was a weaver, a handloom took up a corner of the livingroom. A spinningwheel invariably stood at the guidwife's side of the fireplace.

The long bench under the window has already been mentioned as well as the seats used by children. The chairs used by adults were home-made, the seats being of handwoven heather or bent or straw, or of brown cord such as was used for long-line fishing. The better chairs, with wooden seats, were kept in the bedroom. This usually had two curtained box-beds against the back wall; the family trunk with their best clothes, at the far end of the room; a table in the centre; a large wooden girnel, or meal kist, for storing oatmeal;

and a barrel of flour in a corner. The family cream basin, carefully covered, might be seen on the table, or on a trunk, where there was least danger of upsetting it. A scallop shell, used for skimming the cream off, lay near it. Unlike the livingrooms, the bedrooms of at least some thatched houses had a wooden floor, adding greatly to their comfort, while calfskins were sometimes used as bedside rugs.

The type of brush used for sweeping the floor was either of heather or of bent, with a long handle. I have often helped to fit a handle to a brush of sea-bent. The bent was woven in one long piece, wound round the handle as tightly as possible and then secured with strong string. As a rule the heads were round, but I have also seen a brush-head of bent divided, after the handle was fixed, into three parts in such a way that it resembled the broad brooms bought in shops. For this purpose it was only necessary to tie the loose part of the head into three sections with either one row or two rows of string.

In my time the greatest revolution in household equipment has occurred in the matter of lighting. I am old enough to remember the cruisie as the only lamp in some of our island homes. This consisted of an open iron dish an inch or so deep, with a circular body and sharp beak, and with a handle of the same material for hanging it from the wall. Some cruisies had a double shell, the lower part serving to catch any oil that dripped from the upper one, which contained both the oil and the wick. Some cruisies had an iron spike attached to them by a chain, for pushing the wick further out as the flame burnt low, but in many cases a small sharpened stick was used for this purpose. At one time rushes were extensively used as wicks, but I can only remember pieces of cotton rag being used. The oil was made at home from fish liver. Even after more modern lamps were introduced, the humble cruisie was lit for the sheep smearing, for which a bright light was not required.

When paraffin oil came our way, a home-made lamp only a little better than the cruisie was used. This was simply an earthenware jampot with a tight-fitting cork top, and a narrow metal neck for burner. There was no globe. An improvised wick was still used, and the thing smoked almost as much as a cruisie, but it did not have the strong smell of the cruisie's crude oil.

The jampot was succeeded by the metal wall lamp with a proper wick, burner and globe. This wall lamp was in turn succeeded by the glass table lamp, which could stand on the dresser. Today most of the homes on Scarp are lit by Tilley lamps which do not come far short of electricity in brightness.

CHAPTER SEVENTEEN

Peat Cutting

This may be the best place for an account of how the peat used for fuel was secured.

The first step was to get the year's supply cut in the late spring, and although a family could cut small peat banks without outside help, a full day with five or even seven workers was really necessary for each home. These workers, who gave their services free on the assumption that they would be repaid if necessary in the same way, set off for the peat hags together, the men carrying a spade and two or three peat-irons, while the women had the indispensable creels on their backs, with the lunch carried in one of them.

As some families had no peat-irons of their own and as few, if indeed any, had more than one, it was necessary to borrow an iron or two for the occasion. The irons when not in use were kept in a bog, where they stood with the iron head sunk out of sight.

This implement was apparently brought over by the Norsemen, and is precisely the same as that used in Shetland, where it is known as a *tuskar*, a word identified as the Norse *torf-skeri*, which literally means 'turf-cutter'. The Gaelic word used by us to this day was borrowed in the same way, but in a form closer to the original Norse word, the letter 'r' being retained. *Turskar*, with the 'r' well rolled to suggest a short vowel sound, represents the Gaelic pronunciation pretty accurately.

Some writers wrongly regard the last part of the word as being from *sgian*, 'a knife'. This is due in some measure to the English description, 'peat-knife', but even if this form has found its way into our dictionaries, it cannot be right, both the gender and the position of the accent, to mention two objections, being against it. Another point is that when a more general Gaelic term is applied to the *turskar*, the word used is, 'iron', and not, 'knife', the size of a peat-cutting party usually being stated as, 'so many irons'. To soften my criticism, I may add that in many parts of the Highlands, including the Inner Hebrides, our familiar peat-iron is not known; an entirely different implement with a genuine Gaelic name meaning, literally, 'peat-spade', is used instead.

Peat banks were found both inside and outside the fence which divided the island, the most extensive being appropriately called *Druim na Mònadh*, or 'Peat Dale'. Every family had a share in this large peat moss. A few families cut peat even further away at *Rubha Mhànais*, or 'Magnus's Point', and one family cut a supply in a hollow at the four hundred foot level overlooking this, where several lochs have formed.

The island of Fladday at the northern entrance to the Sound, where the weaned lambs were sent, has gradually become a vast peat moss for Scarp. In my youth the practice of cutting peat on Fladday was discouraged. It deprived the lambs of pasture and also created a danger in wet weather, when a peat hag might trap enough water to drown any lamb falling into it.

Two of our island families were allowed to cut peat on the other side of the Sound opposite the South Hamlet, where an even piece of ground lay above the steep and slippery landing-place. In the same way, the missionary and schoolmaster were privileged to use a peat moss at the head of Loch Cravadale due east of us. This place went by the name *A' Bhuaile Dhubh*, or 'The Black Shieling', indicating that it had once been used as summer pasturage for our island cattle.

The same peat banks were used year by year. Only when a bank gave out was a new one opened. On arriving at the peat moss, the man entrusted with preparing the bank for the irons peeled off the turf in large sods. The others then got to work in pairs, the men cutting, and the women, facing them, catching the soft peat as it left the *turskar*, and throwing it as far out as possible on the ground behind the bank. On shallow stony ground where the peat hags were short and only one peat in depth, there was plenty of room for laying out the freshly cut peat, but when two or three layers could be cut, some of the peat had to be laid out on the low ground inside the peat hag, where water often collected. Another way of disposing of the peat of a deep bank was to build them up in a low tier on the edge of the bank as the work progressed, the peat intersecting so as to leave air holes at regular intervals. Peat dried well this way, the only drawback being that they stuck together and required to be broken up when the time came for lifting or stacking them. In the case of a newly opened peat hag, the surface of the ground on both sides was level and either bank could be used for laying out the peat. There was then no danger of the peat becoming waterlogged.

Whereas the 'turfing-spade' mentioned earlier as being used in some parts of the Highlands is used horizontally, the implement used on Scarp was held in an upright position. It had a straight wooden shaft fifty inches long, which was grasped near the top with both hands. The blade was attached to the lower end, at right angles to it. The blade, or feather, was nine inches long and two inches deep. This blade and the iron socket which bound it to the wooden shaft were of one piece and were therefore strong and secure. The blade was driven into the ground with the right foot to a depth of ten inches, a wooden step being provided for this purpose fifteen inches above the feather or blade. The peats cut in this way were rectangular in shape, and typically ten inches long, six inches broad, and two inches thick.

Apart from getting their boots smeared with the soft peaty substance, the men's job was a clean one, but the women could not escape without getting their hands and bare feet covered with the same sticky substance, which was so difficult to wash off when it dried.

The lunch carried for the peat-cutting party was the same as that for a sheep-gathering, namely oatcake and scones, with milk. My only recollection of midges on the island is associated with work among the peat banks. On one occasion when midges attacked our own peat-cutting party, getting into the milk, the oldest man present unconcernedly continued to drink his milk, saying, *Ma dh' itheas iad sinn, ithidh sinne iadsan* – 'If they eat us, we'll eat them'. A good meal awaited the peat cutters when they returned and reported on their day's work. Before they left for their own homes, my mother usually produced some tobacco she had bought for the occasion, and divided it among the men.

After a few weeks of dry weather, the peat could be raised from the ground and set up on end in small clusters. It was afterwards gathered into large stacks. If quite dry, the stacks were covered with the sods cut off the bank when the peat was cut, the grassy or heathery side being innermost; but if not quite dry, this thatching, as it was called, took place later. No special peat parties were engaged for 'lifting' or stacking. It was done by the owners themselves. The final act in securing our supply of peat, namely bringing it home, was the most difficult of all. This was a real hardship. For most of the year the daily supply of fuel was carried home on one's back, the men using bags and the women creels. There were no roads and no horses. Ponies, such as are used on some Hebridean islands, with a pannier on each side, might solve the peat carrying problem, nevertheless the island has not had a horse of any kind in my time. It was not always so. Even St Kilda, with a much smaller area of level ground, had as many as eighteen horses, according to Martin, at the end of the seventeenth century. That Scarp also had more than the solitary specimen mentioned in an earlier chapter is indicated by our place-names, there being, *Cadha nan Each* – 'Horse Pass', and either *Tràigh nan Each* – 'Horse Beach', or *Tràigh nan Capall* – 'Mare Beach'. The descriptive term, 'horse', in all three place-names is in the plural. The more I think of it, the more difficult it is to understand why our islanders developed the practice of carrying home the peat on their backs, instead of reintroducing the hardy Hebridean pony to lighten a task so difficult and so slow.

The peat was of different qualities. The top layer of a peat bank was usually of a brown colour and that of a lower level black. When it dried and was ready for the stack or for carrying home, the 'black peat', as we actually called it, was heavier than the other. It also crumbled much more quickly than the brown variety, which was fibrous and therefore held together better. As a rule the black peat took longer to catch fire and lasted longer than the brown.

To fill a bag for carrying may seem a simple matter, but it is, on the contrary, an art only acquired with experience. Care must be taken to have one side smooth, otherwise the carrier's back will be racked with pain during the long and laborious trek home.

To fill a creel was easier, the creel itself giving the required protection. There were two types of creel, the older type being made of leather and the newer, lighter type, of willow. These creels were made on the island. The creel-maker used a large thick sod, specially cut for the purpose, as a base on which to make his creel, upside down. The ribs were stuck into the sod to keep the framework firm until the creel was completed. As soon as willow was procurable from one of the island kailyards, where it had been planted, there was a decided preference for willow creels. With the arrival of the willow creel, the heaped-up load of peat, nicely balanced on the small of a woman's back, became a common sight.

I seldom recall my childhood on the island without seeing in imagination my aunt, as I often saw her in those far-off days, coming into our house with a load of peat. She always used a bag, but despised the ordinary bag used for a boll of oatmeal. Instead she used the larger and stronger bag known to us as a double-boll bag, often used as extra protection for a boll of flour, and resembling a sugar sack. As a rule it was her second trip to the peat banks, the first load being for her own home, nevertheless the big bag was always full. What we owed to her cannot be estimated.

A respite from this hard work came in the autumn and spring when all hands were busy in the fields. At such times it was customary to bring a boatload of peat from Fladday, the island mentioned earlier in this chapter, or from one of the peat mosses near the shore on Scarp itself. A calm sea and little or no wind was essential. The ferrying of our fuel by boat was however exceptional – although of course necessary in the case of Fladday – and the fact remains that for the greater part of the year, in fair weather or foul, the peat was carried home over moorland and rock, on someone's back.

CHAPTER EIGHTEEN

Island Fare

Geamhradh reòdhanach, Earrach ceòthanach,
Samhradh glas riabhach,
Foghar geal grianach,
'S le toil Dhè, buannaichidh mi aran.

A frosty winter; a misty spring;
A grey, chequered summer;
A bright, sunny autumn;
And, God willing, I shall win bread.

I have no recollection of the watermill, mentioned in the first chapter, being used, but our seniors were able to tell us of journeys to *Allt a' Mhuilinn*, or 'The Mill Stream', with bags of oats for milling.

By the time I came along, the islanders were using the manufactured oatmeal conveyed by boat from the shopping centre at Tarbert, whether bought from our island merchant or direct from one of the shops at Tarbert. Only when supplies of meal gave out was there recourse to the handquern, two of which were in use in Scarp during my boyhood.

I distinctly remember the sound of the quern, heard from outside the house in the North Hamlet in which it was being used. The quern rested on top of a high table just inside the outer door. It consisted of two round flat stones of mica-schist, the lower one – 'the nether millstone' – being fixed to the table, and the upper stone set to revolve on the lower one when turned by two women standing at opposite sides of the table. Although an aunt of mine, left with five young fatherless children, used to grind her barley alone, it is acknowledged that this was a heavy task, which only an exceptionally strong woman could accomplish. From the earliest times, as the Scripture reference in St Matthew, Chapter 24 shows – 'Two women shall be grinding at the mill' – two women commonly worked the handquern together, holding the upright wooden handle near the rim with their right hands, and shedding the grain into the hole in the middle of the upper revolving stone with their left hands. When I mention that the upper stone of the quern heard by me as a boy was twenty inches in diameter, some idea of its weight and of the difficulty of turning it on top of another flat stone surface, may be gained.

It seems incredible that the use of the handquern was forbidden by law when watermills were introduced, and that a laird could authorise the miller

1. The island of Scarp from the shoulder of Husival Beag. The village lies on the low ground facing the Sound, and Sròn Romul rises to 1012 ft. in the centre of the island. The corner of Mealasta Island in West Lewis is just seen on the right. (May 1995.)

2. A familiar view of Scarp from the slipway and jetty at Hushinish. Fladday Island and the hills of Lewis lie to the north of the Sound. (May 1995.)

3. The village, from Husival Beag, with mission and school buildings on the left near the shore. The rust-red roofed Primrose Cottage, the author's home after 1901, is the highest house in the village. The foundations of 'blackhouses' lie to the left and right, and the burial ground is to the right of the school. (July 1994.)

4. Looking north-west from *Beinn fo Thuath*—the North Peak behind the village in Scarp—with Fladday Island and the smaller *Greine Sgeir* pointing towards the mouth of Loch Resort. The land to the left of that 'long herring loch' lies in Lewis, and that to the right, in Harris. (August 1995.)

5. A calm evening view of the sheep-dotted village, taken from Primrose Cottage, with school and mission buildings near the shore. Signs of past cultivation are widespread. Husival Beag, or *Stiamar*, as it is called by *Scarpachs*, rises to 1004 feet across the Sound. (May 1995.)

6. The schoolhouse (left), the author's home from 1889 to 1901, and school, opened in 1879 and closed in 1967—fine buildings which replaced an earlier thatched school—were later converted into a single dwelling house, but are now sadly derelict. The long axis lies due north and south. (May 1994.)

7. The mission-house (left) and mission-hall were built around 1891 for The Glasgow and West Coast Mission. In 1950 the Church of Scotland adopted the Scarp mission. The last resident missionary left in 1966, but the mission-hall was in use for worship until the last families left in 1971. (May 1994.)

8. The *Mol Mòr*, or 'Big Shore', exposed to the south-westerly winds, attracts driftwood logs and modern flotsam and jetsam. No 'Barra Beans'—acacia nuts or 'sea-hearts'—as found there by the author, were seen during this visit. Gasker and Gasker Beg just break the horizon on the right. (May 1994.)

9. The big sheepfold at Islaca is built against a rock face. It is still used once a year in May, when the lambs from the centre and back of the island are 'marked'. Chapter 6 describes the children's excitement during a sheep-gathering here around the turn of the century. (May 1994.)

10. *Clach a' Chomharra*—'the marker stone' or 'asbestos rock'—lies in the west of the island, where its ice-moulded shape and slightly darker colour help to pick it out. A metre-stick leans against the glacial erratic which tops it. Typical outcrops of light grey gneiss are in the foreground. (May 1994.)

11. The high ground and lochs in the centre of Scarp. 'The Little Mill Loch' is on the left, and the end of Loch Uidemul, with its islands, is on the right. The signs of old 'lazybed' cultivation, to be found throughout Scarp, can be seen here. Sròn Romul lies beyond the ridge on the skyline. (May 1994.)

12. Wool and lambs are the main 'crop' of the island. A flock of rams and lambs in the fank, each bearing its owner's markings. The lambs were dipped and released in the village, the ewes having been driven beyond the fence. The rams were taken to Fladday, where they would remain until late November. (August 1994.)

13. Crofters' boats lie on the slip at Hushinish, while a modern 'inflatable' rests on the beach. The twenty-two foot long—eighteen foot keel—green boat *Uilleam Dubh*, built in the early 1930s, is typical of the craft which served Scarp well over the last century, albeit now using an outboard engine in place of oars and sail. (July 1994.)

14. The south sands of Hushinish. 'The North Port' and jetty lie across the isthmus to the right. The cottages on the left were built for three families who moved to Dirascal in 1885, at a time of great overcrowding in Scarp, and in 1900 were re-settled here. Two old burial grounds lie beyond the houses. (July 1994.)

15. In 1890 W.S. Duncan, a keen amateur botanist, collected a new microspecies of Hawkweed in Scarp. It was later given the botanical name *Hieracium scarpicum* in honour of the island. It is found only in North Harris and Lewis. (Specimen photographed at Mealista, Lewis, by Dr R.J. Pankhurst, Royal Botanic Garden, Edinburgh, July 1984.)

16. The dogs 'Boy' and 'Queen' take a lively interest as the lambs are sorted out and marked. (May 1995.)

17. An unusual Scarp lamb with her brown-collared mother. The ewe may have a trace of the old Hebridean breed in her genes. (May 1995.)

to search out and destroy any handquerns found by him. The tradition still persisted in the southern end of Harris that a certain laird sent his factor on such an errand, openly carrying a hammer for the purpose. The watermills, generally speaking, were the laird's property, and toll was exacted for their use.

As with the watermill, so also with our island cornkiln. Its use for drying or parching grain was apparently discontinued when the regular use of the watermill ceased. Only the stone foundation of the island kiln now remains, but fortunately the circular cavity at one end, over which the grain was dried, and the 'funnel' or vent leading to this cavity, are clearly marked. The dimensions of the kiln are roughly thirty-six feet by twenty-four.

I remember only barley being ground by the handquern in Scarp, not oats. After being threshed and winnowed in a light wind outside the house, the grain was parched in an ordinary iron pot placed on red-hot cinders beside the fire. It was continuously stirred with a wooden spurtle to prevent burning. The Gaelic name for this process has given writers the word, 'gradan', as in gradan-bread or graddan-bread. In some parts of the Hebrides, both north and south of us, the barn serves the purpose of a kiln, being fitted, like a kiln, with a furnace, called *sorn* in Uist, and *surrag* in Lewis. We had only a few barns on our island and I cannot recollect that any of them was used in this way.

In our special circumstances it was inevitable that supplies should often run short. As a rule only one boat went to the shopping centre at a time, and even if one of our larger boats was taken, as was usually the case, it was not possible to bring back a whole boll of meal for every family. A sack of meal had to be shared by two families and sometimes by three or even four. The work of sharing out a boll of meal, using a pail at first, then a basin, and finally a bowl, until the last grain was measured out, was a very common spectacle every time an island boat returned from Tarbert. Very often the cargo suffered a wetting in the open boats, in which case the meal next to the canvas bag stuck to it in lumps and could only be used for feeding to cattle or hens. Fine meal was preferred to coarse meal, the former being, as we said, bread meal and the latter porridge meal.

When stocks began to give out, recourse was had to borrowing. 'My mother wants a loan of meal!' Even if the anxious mother had the resources of a Carnegie, her request would be unavoidable on 'an island of the sea', as we called Scarp when its isolated nature was uppermost in our thoughts. But the loan was always scrupulously repaid in good measure, pressed down, shaken together, and running over.

Very little flour reached our island in my boyhood, and when it ultimately appeared, the quantity had a certain definite ratio to the quantity of oatmeal carried into one's home.

Potatoes provided the midday meal in the crofters' homes. A potato board, such as that described by the early nineteenth-century traveller, MacCulloch, was used in the house I myself frequented most, namely my aunt's house. Potatoes were cooked unpeeled, 'in their jackets', and no objection could therefore be made to the use of a clean board not unlike the board fishermen used for baiting their lines, but smaller, instead of a basin or plate. As a whole potful of potatoes was usually cooked for a family, those left over going to some animal or other, a mere plate would be too small. The metal basin, so light and so handy for many purposes, superseded the potato board, which must have been in general use at one time. Only rarely were the potatoes mashed. When this happened it was an event indeed for the children, for it was done at night, when it took the place of the usual supper of porridge. Our islanders supped and bedded late, but the visiting children held on grimly until they saw the potful of peeled potatoes mashed with a heavy wooden masher. They then got their spoons into the smooth and succulent heap in the basin. Milk, served in bowls, was usually available on such occasions.

In the autumn it was usual to kill our own mutton, either a three-year-old or four-year-old wedder being chosen from our own flocks. Two, or even three, might be killed at intervals to provide meat for the winter. Lammastide, when the animals were regarded as ready for the butcher, was thus a happy season for the children of an island household. In this connection, my father used to tell visitors a joke at my expense; but the greatest joke of all, had he realised it, was that the thing had grown hoary with repetition before I myself saw through it. Using the various animals seen from a back window, for a simple lesson in nature knowledge, he asked what a hen gave us. 'Eggs', I stated correctly. 'What does the cow give us?' 'Milk', I said. 'And what does the sheep give us?' '*Maragan!*' – 'Puddings!' – I cried, clapping my hands. I thought the joke lay in my excitement at giving the only possible answer.

One of my cousins butchered our beasts for us, and after an interval even the youngest was allowed to watch. Other island boys would have gathered, waiting in expectant mood for the breast-strip and the tail-strip to be thrown to them. These were cut from the skin and taken home by the boys, who cut or plucked the wool, singed the strip, and cooked it on the cinders, by which time it had curled tight, in shape resembling the sealskin tobacco pouches used by the older men on the island. It made very tough chewing, and being as black as charcoal when fired in this way, gave all who dug their teeth into it a very black mouth. As shown later in the boys' Hogmanay rhyme, these strips were once treated as charms, the ritual associated with them being observed only at Hogmanay, or Old New Year's Eve.

The most interesting part of the butcher's duties was the making of the ropy pudding, the long intestine used for this being first turned inside out without severing it from the carcass. When this was successfully done, the butcher quickly cut up the kidneys and liver and some suet, and began filling the pliant rope, working the stuffing with his left hand to the very end, where it was narrowest. He then called for meal, and mixing it with some of the congealed blood from the basin, and adding suet, stuffed it into the rope, which was then cut away. Woe to the person who opened the door even for a split second while this was going on! A whiff of cold air might render the whole material stiff and unyielding. When my mother's ashet was brought in, the butcher, with an air of triumph, raised the long rope with both hands and laid it in glorious coils on the large oval dish. But I have seen him fail. If the rope tore while being filled, the part filled could be used, and the rest cut away, but if it tore while being turned, the whole pudding was lost and the butcher, even before our keen eyes saw the rent, would throw the whole thing down with a gesture of disappointment and disgust.

'Have you made a ropy pudding?' was either the first or second question asked by my mother on emerging from her retreat – for no woman was ever present at a kill – the only competing question being, 'Was there suet in it?' that is, in the sheep. The ropy pudding, in popularity rivalling Burns's haggis, was ready for the pot as soon as it left the butcher's hands, the rest of the sheep's entrails being cleaned out the following day, to provide us with mealy puddings of different shapes and sizes. The suet was melted and a little salt added, and then when the feast of fat things was forgotten, my mother would make a rich roly-poly, embellished with raisins and currants, and securely tied with string in a cloth. Puddings? Surely! What else was a Lammas sheep for?

A favourite substitute for mealy pudding was made in a small pan in which dripping was melted, with oatmeal added. This concoction, which was known to us by the picturesque English name, 'scream pudding', had to be stirred all the time it was cooking, to prevent it from singeing. The Scots name for it is 'skirlie'.

The crofter families did not trouble to lay in a supply of either rice or barley, and as few families grew either carrots or turnips, far less leeks and onions, the only vegetable in the broth was cabbage. Their broth was literally kail, as such broth is called in Braid Scots.

Beef was not popular as food. Occasionally a cow was butchered and shared by either two or four families. No island boy is likely to forget this, for it was the occasion for some trouble, the boys stealthily taking some of the blood and using it after dark to make any cattle found loose about the village bellow and stampede. The cattle were quick to smell blood, and if more than one animal was abroad they quarrelled with each other, bellowing horribly.

I am not going to pretend that we always had fish, or flesh, or milk, or butter, with our potatoes. Just as Hugh Miller saw ground salt taken with potatoes in Gairloch a hundred and twenty years ago, I myself have seen salt as the only accompaniment of potatoes at the midday meal. A jug of water stood on the table or on the broad stool used as a fireside table, and the kettle was put on for tea before the meal began.

Although *ceann cropaig*, or 'crappit heids', were known in Scarp, I do not remember it as a meal, but I have enjoyed it several times in a crofter's home in Coll, near Stornoway, where my mother-in-law was brought up. It was made from the stuffed heads of fresh haddock from Broad Bay.

In summer most families had a good supply of milk and were therefore well provided with butter and crowdie, the latter being made with the skimmed milk that had set like junket without going sour. No rennet was needed. The whey left in the pot after the crowdie was taken out and pressed, was used for baking, in the same way as buttermilk. While fresh, whey made a good drink. Children were fond of the custard-like dish made from the first few milkings of a newly calved cow, but it could not be used for ordinary purposes.

Natives on holiday on the island were often given a bowl of crowdie and cream in the homes they visited. It was rich fare – indeed rather too rich – as was full cream with a little oatmeal added. As a change from porridge a housewife sometimes made sowans for supper. This dish was made by boiling oat husks for several hours. My recollections of sowans are that it was greyish in colour, with the consistency of thin porridge without any grains, and that it had a pungent taste. As in other parts of the country, thin gruel was often taken to ward off an approaching cold.

Bread, the staff of life the world over, was made in large bannocks, whether as scones or oatcakes, on a hanging girdle, fired before an opening made in the peat fire. In the case of oatcakes there was also a quick way of baking it, a small thick bannock being kneaded between the guidwife's palms and fired without bringing the girdle into service. This bannock, usually showing the guidwife's finger marks and in shape resembling a shallow saucer, though larger than a saucer, was known as a *bonnach boiseadh*, or 'palm bannock'.

CHAPTER NINETEEN

Harris Tweed

As our parish has given its name to a popular handwoven cloth, it was inevitable that Scarp should have shared in the development of what has now become a great industry.

Its rise was due to the interest and foresight of two ladies, the Countess of Dunmore, wife of the Earl of Dunmore, and Mrs Thomas, wife of Captain F. W. Thomas, RN, who saw the possibility of placing the handwoven tweed on a commercial basis. The walls of the house in which the first tweed was made for the market are still pointed out.

In my youth a distinction was made between a web of cloth made for family use and one made for the market, by calling the first a *clò beag*, or 'small tweed', and the other a *clò mòr*, or 'large tweed', the exigencies of trade demanding that a tweed offered for sale should be of much greater length. The process of manufacture was the same in each case, but special care was taken in dyeing the wool for the marketable article.

The wool of our own Blackface sheep was used for both. It was first washed, then dried on a wall or on large stones. It was then dyed in a huge boiler owned jointly by the crofters, and afterwards spread out to dry once again. Then followed the teasing – *cìreadh* or combing as we called it in our language – and carding, the result of the carding being light rectangular rolls, quite unlike the long thin rolls made in the carding mill at Tarbert. The wool was now ready to be spun. Every house had a spinningwheel of the old type, probably Dutch in origin, or the newer Norwegian wheel which was smaller and lighter. Three of these were brought to Scarp in my youth and my own aunt got one of them. These were easier to drive, but the pirn, or reel, round which the wool wound in the process of spinning, could only hold half that of the older wheel.

A hundred and fifty years ago the spinningwheel was practically unknown in the Highlands, all spinning being done on the distaff. Although the spinningwheel was in general use in my boyhood, the distaff was sometimes brought into use, for example, when very finely spun wool was wanted. Older women too, whose days at the wheel were past, or who had never become accustomed to it, plied the distaff and spindle, a woman living behind the school garden using them as she sat by her own fireside. No boy of the period is likely to forget this grey-haired lady, with whose distaff we had to reckon when we invaded her house for drinks of water at playtime. It was not uncommon, either, to see some woman spinning on the distaff as she went from house to house in her own hamlet, while a few took their distaff, with the end tucked under a waistband, when they went to the moor for peat or to do the milking.

The distaff was not merely a wooden stick. The head, about half the length of the round handle, was thicker at the base, four cornered, and tapered to a point. It was knife-carved, apparently to keep the wool in position, the mass of wool being tied to the head of the distaff with a short string. The wool was spun by drawing it out carefully with the left hand and twirling the spindle, with an action like that of spinning a top, with the right hand. When as much as could comfortably be held between the fingers of the right hand, extended at full length, was spun, the two loops on the spindle – one on the sharp notched point and a larger one on the heavy end – were released. The length of spun wool was then wound round the spindle and secured by two loops as before. The spindle was used by itself for twining two threads of yarn into one.

When the wool was wanted in hanks, a simple *crois-iarna*, or 'hank-cross', held in one hand by the middle, was used. A hank, on the other hand, was turned into a ball by laying it on a horizontal winding-reel which spun round on a heavy wooden stand with a swivel-pin in the top. The four arms of this winding-reel had graded holes in which round wooden pins were put to keep the hank of wool from slipping off.

As the process drew nearer the loom it became more intricate, the yarn used for the warp being laid out on a heavy upright frame, as many as eight balls of yarn being used simultaneously. It was comical to see the variety of household utensils and other articles, including three-legged pots, metal and wooden basins, baskets, and upturned stools, used for holding the large balls of yarn during this operation. Then followed the last and most difficult work of all, namely the transference of the warp from the warping-frame to the handloom, with the loose ends being put singly through the reed and heddles, ready for the actual weaving to begin, but not until the whole of the yarn used for the warp was passed through in this way and wound round the yarn-beam at the back.

In my youth only the old handloom was known on our island. The yarn for the weft was wound on bone bobbins, or spools, dark yellow with age and use, the bobbins being filled on a bobbin-wheel or spool-winder held on one's knees. One bobbin at a time was fixed in the shuttle, which was thrown across alternately from each side of the growing web, the wooden treadles being changed by foot after each throw.

A good detailed account of the whole process up to this point is given by Margaret Leigh near the end of chapter 18 in her book *Highland Homespun*. Those who would like to know the different parts of a handloom and of a spinningwheel, with the Gaelic and English names for each part, should consult *Dwelly's Illustrated Gaelic Dictionary*, which contains diagrams and sketches by the Stornoway artist, Malcolm MacDonald, whose mother was a native of Scarp.

When *a' bheairt mhòr*, or 'the big loom', was introduced, the slowness of *a' bheairt bheag*, or 'the small loom', was apparent. Very often the shuttle thrown by hand stuck half-way and required to be helped along with the weaver's fingers, the weaver then pulling out enough wool to allow the shuttle to run freely before throwing it back. There was none of this difficulty in the case of the new loom, the weaver simply slinging the shuttle from side to side with a belt suspended in front of him, and without a pause until the shuttle was empty, both the spools and shuttle being larger than those used for the old type of loom. There was only one drawback. Weaving on the big loom was considered too heavy for a woman. The result was that the only big loom on Scarp for many years belonged to one of our crofter-fishermen, while the women of the island stuck to the old and much slower loom. A still newer loom is now extensively used in the Outer Isles, one of them being at Hushinish.

Modern improvements in transport, as well as the increased trade in Harris Tweed, have made the preparation of the yarn a much lighter task for the women of the isles. Spinning mills as well as carding mills are available, and not only so, but the yarn comes back dyed any colour, or mixture of colours, required. Mixing the colours, which was done during the carding, was a tricky job, it being essential that the whole length of tweed should be of a uniform shade. These modern methods have relieved the women of the labour and time involved in gathering and preparing vegetable dyes, such as green from heather, yellow from sorrel, and grey from groundsel, as well as the popular brown from lichen scraped with an old iron spoon off the big stones on the moor. Indigo was generally used for blue.

When the tweed was woven and cut away from the loom, it was waulked on a heavy grooved board which went the round of the village as required, a short board being used for a 'small tweed' and a long board for a 'large tweed'. Round this board, known as a waulking hurdle, sat a panel of young women brought together for the waulking of the cloth, the board being placed waist high or lower.

The waulking of the cloth, although necessary routine work connected with tweed making, whether for sale or for family use, has always been regarded as a social occasion, the chief reason being that the young women taking part lighten and speed the work by singing favourite waulking-songs. A typical waulking-song consists of two-line verses and a lively three-line or four-line chorus, one girl singing the verse, and all joining in the chorus. Both Alexander MacDonald and Duncan Ban MacIntyre, the great eighteenth-century bards, composed waulking-songs, but anonymous traditional songs of this class are also numerous. In addition, local poets used the model. One of the liveliest

of many waulking-songs used on Scarp in my youth, set forth, verse by
verse, the characteristics of the young men of the various villages in the
parish to the north of us. Then when their repertoire was exhausted, some
of the girls were capable of improvising verses, such an effort always causing
great merriment.

But today, those who once sat round the waulking hurdle and joined in a
merry chorus, send their newly-woven tweed to a fulling mill in Stornoway
to be finished there. Shades of Don Quixote, who spent an anxious night,
along with his squire Sancho Panza, within sound of a fulling mill, which
seemed to promise a great and hazardous adventure when morning came!

And just as the watermill for grinding corn put an end to another class of
work songs, namely those of the handquern, the finishing mills will banish
the songs one has often heard rise sweetly and merrily above the thump,
thump, of the fulling hurdles on many a quiet starlit night.

There was no ready market for our tweed in my early youth. A tweed,
packed in a canvas bag, often stood for a long period at one end of the long
bench, or in a corner of the room used as sleeping quarters, and when a boat
returned from a trip to Tarbert, the question, 'Are they accepting tweeds just
now?' was often asked, the reference being to the many shopkeepers there.
Organisations such as The Crofters' Agency, and Highland Home Industries,
have done much since then to encourage production, and to find markets for
the sale of tweed, while the Harris Tweed Association now keeps a watchful
eye on all phases of the industry.

We had two self-taught tailors on our island and to these the family tweed
was taken to have suits, or more frequently trousers, made, the men using the
familiar home-knitted fisherman's jersey for daily wear, instead of a jacket and
waistcoat. I, however, remember one itinerant tailor visiting Scarp and moving
from house to house for some weeks, as he cut, sewed, and pressed, using a
tailor's board and a heavy pressing iron. In olden days the itinerant tailor was
welcomed in country villages, for he brought news of the outside world. He
also entertained his host and hostess, as well as the neighbours who turned
the house in which he worked into a ceilidh-house, by recounting traditional
folktales. One wonders if he told those tales that make fun of his own class,
halt, lame, and maimed as many of them – in the tales at least – seemed to
have been.

Those were leisurely days, when the family tweed, alternating with heavy
double-width blankets, made its slow appearance. The popularity of Harris
Tweed as a marketable product livened things up considerably, and when trade
was brisk, all the women of a household might be engaged in some activity or
other connected with tweed making, This was sometimes too much for the
men, who could scarcely get the members of the other sex away from the
work except when they were in bed. One household, for example, not on
our island, but near enough to be well known to us, often had two or even

three women busy spinning, while another sat all day at the loom. One of our island wags used to mimic the grace said by the head of this particular family, consisting as it did of short quotations from the metrical psalms. But the first words, as remembered and repeated by our island wag, were always, 'Put away the wheel!'

A recent writer on the Western Isles says that drugget is woven in the isles. I have never heard of this. Some of our islanders sent their wool to a firm in the Borders, receiving in return fine good-wearing Border tweed for men's and boys' suits, and either grey or russet drugget, as strong and durable as sail-cloth, for women's skirts.

For Sunday wear most of the men wore navy double-breasted serge suits, some jackets having velvet collars. Women wore tweed skirts and blouses on weekdays, pulling on a short bodice when going out to work in cold or wet weather, and often wearing a thick shoulder plaid, laid loosely over their backs and shoulders, when carrying a creel. On Sunday they wore black, the married women wearing a dolman or cape, embroidered with ribbons and beads, and a neat bonnet covered with bows and feathers and beads. The older women wore a black knitted mutch, with a white lace frill, dressed on a goffering iron. I often saw the latter in use on a Saturday in my youth.

Warehousemen's catalogues were even then known in Scarp and from one of them my own first Eton suit was ordered. The firm may have been that of Ogg and Hodge, Glasgow, sometimes known by the islanders as 'Ogan Hodge', or 'Ogan Todge', or, following the retiral of Mr Ogg, from its successor firm, Thomas Hodge & Co. When news of the death of Mr Hodge reached the island, some neighbours called on an elderly woman in South Hamlet and asked, 'What will you do, now that Mr Hodge is dead?' But the old lady was too clever for them. 'Shall we not have Ogan himself?' she said.

CHAPTER TWENTY

The School

As Scarp is on the western fringe of a parish twenty-one miles in length and at the northern end twenty-one miles broad, we may safely assume that it never had a parochial school, for only one parochial school was reported in the whole parish when the Statistical Account of 1794 was compiled. This school was at Rodel in the southern end of Harris. The Society for the Propagation of Christian Knowledge – the SPCK – which opened its first school in St Kilda in 1701, had also set up a school in our parish by 1794, as well as a 'seminary of female industry', in other words a sewing-school, although knitting, spinning and dyeing were taught in these schools. By 1841 the parish had four schools, one being parochial and three being 'Gaelic Schools'.

Scarp's first ever school was opened in the year 1821 by The Society for the Support of Gaelic Schools, which was formed in Edinburgh in 1811 for the express purpose of teaching the people of the Highlands and Islands to read the Scriptures in their own language. An account of the Society and its 'circulating schools' is given in the next chapter.

The first Gaelic teacher, John Shaw, remained for two years, when he was transferred to another Gaelic School in the same parish, leaving our island without a teacher until 1830, when Murdoch MacDonald was appointed. Mr MacDonald, whose Gaelic name, *An Dòmhnallach Ruadh*, is still remembered, remained for five years. The island was again without a teacher until 1837, when Angus MacLean arrived. Mr MacLean remained for four years and was succeeded, after a lapse of three years, by Malcolm MacKenzie, who left the service of the Society for some untold reason in May 1845. After a further lapse of four years, the fifth and last Gaelic teacher was appointed in 1850. This was Donald MacDonald, who was left in Scarp for three years, after which he became Gaelic teacher in a small village a few miles south of Tarbert.

Scarp was then without a teacher until the year 1856, when The Ladies' Highland Association of the Free Church sent a teacher who took over the school and dwellinghouse which had been occupied by the Gaelic School. So anxious had been the heads of the island's twenty-four families, that they told a delegate who visited the island in 1855 that if he got a teacher for them, they would gladly row him not only to Tarbert, where they took him after his visit, but as far as Lochmaddy, forty miles away! That LHA delegate was the Rev Lewis Hay Irving, Free Church minister of Falkirk. A third of the island's population, including married men – as was customary in the Highlands a hundred years ago – attended this Ladies' School, the instruction consisting chiefly, if not entirely, of reading and arithmetic.

I have seen it reported that Scarp had the last of the Ladies' Schools, but this is not so. The LHA was founded in 1850, and opened as many as one hundred and sixty schools during the next seventy years. The school at the head of Loch Resort, where one of my aunts lived, was a Ladies' School. It was visited every year by the secretary, Miss Christina Rainy, who not only brought school prizes, but also distributed sweets, made up in separate bags, to all the pupils. On an island to the south of us, namely Taransay, there was also a Ladies' School, and to this one belongs the distinction of having been the last Ladies' School in the Outer Isles. It was taken over by the School Board in 1921.

By the time I came on the scene, our island school was fully established as a public school, a modern school and schoolhouse built by the School Board having taken the place of the thatched building formerly used. It was opened on 2 June 1879, with John MacDonald, one of the Cravadale shepherd's sons, as schoolmaster.

Our first public school teacher was succeeded by a master who stayed only ten months, this man's successor staying only two or three days! The reasons given for the latter's precipitate flight were that he could not occupy the schoolhouse and could find no suitable lodgings, but as his first question on landing was: 'Whereabouts is the hotel?', the real reason is not far to seek.

Another of those early schoolmasters taught in the island for three years, but died in mysterious circumstances. He had been found dead in bed. The cause of death was said to have been poisoning. Although our islanders were reticent about this tragedy, the children got to know about it and imagined all sorts of queer things, which they repeated to each other in school. A desk inkwell with its sliding lid stuck fast, or some hairs seen in the wall plaster, was enough to set us reconstructing the sombre event.

The old thatched school was at the south end of Mid Hamlet, but the modern school was built on a new site on higher ground some distance in front of it. It had a large kitchen garden and two playgrounds, enclosed within a good stone wall. The wall, curiously, was usually referred to as, *Gàradh Chluichein*, or 'Cluichean's Wall', after the mason who built it.

My own first teacher, W. S. Duncan, took up his duties on 7 August 1889, having however been in charge of the school for a period of over two and a half years up to the summer of 1886, when he was transferred to the public school in Obbe, at the southern end of Harris. This last fact explains how he could tell one of our island pupils, who still remembers the remark: 'You do not seem to have made any progress since I left!' Like Dominie Sampson in Scott's *Guy Mannering*, he had a favourite ejaculation, which he used in appreciation or depreciation. This was: 'Most extraordinary!', pronounced as deliberately as Dominie Sampson's 'Pro-di-gi-ous!' We often heard this exclamation in school when he had occasion to find fault with anyone's behaviour. A strict disciplinarian, he tried to soften his severity by telling offenders: 'I'll have to punish you in spite of myself', but his pupils thought this highly illogical and consoled each other by pointing out that he was doing it, as it seemed to them, against his better judgment.

A pupil-teacher or monitor assisted, taking the younger pupils in a small room off the main schoolroom, with a door leading to the girls' playground. In this small room the weekly sewing class was also held, the schoolmaster's wife coming in to take it, but I also remember that class meeting round the school fire in the principal classroom. In those far-off days, no fuel was provided for the school, each pupil having to carry a peat to school every morning and dump it in a corner beside the fire. Before I left the school, an isleswoman was engaged to deliver a few bags of her own peat every week in winter, so the custom of carrying a peat to school under one's arm went out of fashion, no one regretting the change.

The school's eight-day clock, hanging high on the front wall of the classroom, was often checked by the schoolmaster at noon, as was his own watch. The long axis of the school and schoolhouse lay due north and south.

Even if our schoolmaster did not come up to the standard of Goldsmith's village schoolmaster in *The Deserted Village*, he was nevertheless master of many subjects. He excelled as a naturalist, giving us object lessons, as they were called, on the heavy blackboard set in the high wooden frame in which it could be moved up and down. As he was an excellent draughtsman, we could at least admire the animals he drew for our instruction. He was also an accomplished musician, with a good tenor voice, and taught us many songs, especially Scots songs and English patriotic songs, the preliminary to all singing being the production from a vest pocket of a tuning-fork, which he struck on his raised knee and put to his ear.

Himself a good calligraphist, he strove to produce good writers, with the result that his former pupils, as I have often heard said, could be recognised by their handwriting. He also gave us a 'prodigious' amount of spelling, as we stood back to back and face to face with slate and pencil in hand. The slates were afterwards taken home by him and corrected, a pandrop being awarded for the best results, handed to the pupils on top of their slates the next day. Slates and slate pencils took the place of the more up-to-date jotters and lead pencils. When any one of us lost our slate pencil, we could carry on for a while with a pencil made from some broken piece of slate off the roof, the large smooth stone in the boys' playground being used to grind it.

As some of his pupils were sure to follow a seafaring career away from the island, he prepared them for this by giving all senior boys lessons in navigation. As it was of a less formal character than the ordinary class subject, he sometimes unbent so far as to crack a joke while teaching a navigation lesson. Once as he stood with pointer in hand in front of the big blackboard, on which he had drawn the diagram of a compass, he said, 'I once knew a lady who could box the compass'. The joke was of course in the double meaning of the word, 'box', and he himself seemed to enjoy it. His pupils were taught to box the compass in both Gaelic and English. He was also in the habit of taking the highest classes to the schoolhouse in the evening for lessons in Latin.

Knowing Pitman's shorthand, he made extensive use of it, with the result that the most inquisitive pupil could not read his desk notes. As we grew older some of us learned to distinguish the outlines of our own names, and could ascertain during his temporary absence whether we had done well in a test. He never fully mastered Gaelic, but he made a close study of *Stewart's Gaelic Grammar*, and he translated English reading lessons for the benefit of the infants, although his pupil-teacher could probably have done this better!

Our school opened at ten o'clock, when the dominie's whistle with its long modulated tone summoned us, but an hour earlier his 'nine o'clock whistle', as everyone called it, was heard all over the village, as a warning that it was time the children were stirring.

The only time we dressed specially for school was the day the inspector paid his annual visit. That was a day to be remembered! As it usually coincided with the closing of the school for the summer holidays, we threw off the nervous tension as soon as the inspection was over and we were dismissed, class by class. Everyone we met on the way home asked, 'Did you pass?' Those were the days of the Merit Certificate for which senior pupils strove.

The schoolmaster's Aberdonian origin could scarcely be guessed, the Braid Scots he knew so well being kept in the background and never used in ordinary conversation. His place of origin, however, showed up in other ways. He never bade a visitor goodnight, for example, without adding the words: 'Haste ye back!' just as he would have done had he never left his old home. Once indeed his upbringing in an Aberdeenshire farming community declared itself in a startling way. The occasion was a present of bottled ale sent him by the nearest hotel keeper, who did not know him personally. As he was a total abstainer, as became a former Free Church teacher, his family wondered how he would act in the circumstances. They did not have long to wait. When supper was ready and they all sat down to the porridge usually taken then, but never for breakfast, he fetched one of the bottles and drew the cork, while his family watched in horror. He then poured half of it into a bowl and after saying grace as usual, began to sup his porridge, dipping the spoon in the ale as if it was milk, or buttermilk, of which he was very fond. This was a custom in Aberdeenshire, where farmers brewed their own ale when milk was scarce, and took it with their porridge. And who has not heard of harvest ale, with malt or yeast being used to produce fermentation?

The schoolmaster was a good astronomer and always watched an eclipse, whether it took place by day or when others were asleep. His oldest surviving son remembers being awakened at some unearthly hour to watch the sun emerge from an eclipse. As his father held him up in his arms at a front window facing east, the light played tricks with the boy's eyes and he imagined the sun was turning a green colour, whereupon he began to scream.

Keen naturalist as he was, his chief interest lay in botany, and being a great walker he often traversed the wide deer-forest opposite Scarp for a thorough botanising of the locality. He sometimes hired a guide to help him reach the highest peaks. For those journeys he used an Ordnance Survey map with the contour lines at one thousand feet and fifteen hundred feet marked by him in red ink, and with all the summits, some of which are over two thousand feet, carefully marked in red. This map has since been donated to the British Museum. He of course botanised our own island, his figure taking to the hills early on a Saturday, with walking-stick in hand and a botanist's vasculum slung across his back, being a familiar sight. On such expeditions he carried a small folding magnifying glass of three lenses, with which to examine plants where found, and he spent a busy evening at his microscope when he returned home.

His own collection of plants, pressed in books and described in shorthand notes in blue pencil, has sadly not been preserved, but some of the many specimens he sent to a correspondent in England form part of a collection now housed in the British Museum.

While he lived, this schoolmaster, whose full name was William Smith Duncan, served as a link between two educational epochs, having been a Free Church teacher in his native county before the advent of the public school. A few years after his death in May 1912, his widow was granted a pension from the fund for former Free Church teachers, so this link was in a sense restored. That pension continued until her own death in December 1938, when she was eighty-four years old. The schoolmaster was seventy-eight years old when he died. [*Note*: W. S. Duncan was the author's father.]

The Mission

By the time I was born, the organisation known as The Glasgow and West Coast Mission had established itself in Scarp and had a full-time agent at work there. This organisation was formed in the year 1856, and throughout its life maintained mission stations in the West Highlands, from Lewis in the north to Jura in the south, the maximum number being thirty.

Even as late as 1845, the northern half of Harris had only one missionary, namely the one and only missionary supported by the Royal Bounty, as mentioned in the first Statistical Account fifty years earlier.

The West Coast Mission came to our island in 1878, when the first missionary, Donald Murray, was appointed. He was succeeded by two agents, Alexander MacLeod and a Mr MacKenzie, neither of whom I remember, but I saw the first missionary at least once, when he paid us a visit during my boyhood. I still remember his appearance. Three of his family, a minister, a minister's wife, and a nurse, were personally known to me.

Like the school buildings, the mission buildings, consisting of a mission-hall with dwellinghouse attached, occupied a central place on the   island machair, which was bright with buttercups and daisies in summer. Unlike the school and schoolhouse, there was no surrounding wall. These mission buildings were erected in or about the year 1891. The school and schoolhouse, built in 1879, were slated, but the mission buildings, although modern stone and lime structures, were at first roofed with felt, which needed a fresh coat of tar periodically. I still remember a large pot of tar catching fire as it was boiled behind the mission-house. The tar was heated before being applied to the roof with a heavy mop. The felt gave way to slate about 1900, when two slaters came to deal with the hall and dwellinghouse. Everyone on the island, including the children, helped to carry the heavy slates from the shore.

The earliest missionary I remember on the island was Donald MacLeod, the fourth successive West Coast agent, who came to us from Coigach, in Wester Ross. He had three sons whom I remember perfectly. Alexander, the eldest son, had had a leg amputated at the knee and always used a crutch, but in spite of this handicap he was as active and agile as a roe. He was a good swimmer, my most vivid recollection of him being that he swam well out into the Sound, opposite South Hamlet, then turned on his back and floated with his stump of a leg held upright in the water. The youngest son, Colin by name, became a noted Gaelic singer. As a regular soldier serving in a Highland regiment, and quite unknown to concert audiences, he appeared at the National Mod held at Dundee in 1913, and carried off the principal prizes, including the gold medal for male voices.

Changes must have been frequent in those days, for this missionary was succeeded, while I was still a boy, by the fifth West Coast agent, Edward MacKay, a native of Easdale, near Oban. He had a large family of boys and girls, some of whom were born in Scarp.

This missionary was remarkable in many ways. Before he became a preacher, he served as a Sergeant Instructor in the Argyll Volunteer Regiment, and had attended the famous Wet Review in 1881, when 40,000 Scottish Volunteers, watched by 250,000 spectators, were reviewed by Queen Victoria in the Queen's Park, Edinburgh. He was every inch a soldier, broad-shouldered and deep-chested, though a small man, and as strong as a horse. From his pulpit style, one would say that he fancied he was on a parade ground as he shouted and gesticulated, often threatening, like John Knox, to 'ding the poopit in blads'. Someone once claimed to have heard him from the other side of the Sound.

The old volunteer was a family man who sought no other company and even seemed to avoid it whenever possible. An incident I recall reveals the man. When the first of our islanders who had served in the Boer War came home, the missionary was the first to shake hands with him as he was carried ashore from the boat, almost getting his feet wet in his anxiety to be first. He simply asked the returning soldier if he was well, and receiving a favourable answer, went away home at once using the unfrequented route by which he had come.

Once at least he must have felt the urge to take charge of a parade, and I have often regretted that he did not do so. A young man from the mainland, who had picked up some knowledge of military drill, got as many boys as possible together near the end of the mission-hall and was soon busy putting us through our paces. Quite unknown to any of us except our instructor, who must have seen what was going on, the old soldier slipped out of the house, and making his way in our direction behind the buildings, came and posted himself in our rear. We knew nothing of this until he came noiselessly behind his own oldest boy and without uttering a word, squared the lad's shoulders for him. He then went in front, where he stood with his hands clenched and every muscle taut. When our amateur instructor hesitated, the old soldier encouraged him to go on, saying: 'You are doing very well!' He quite obviously wanted more.

The missionary held two services every Sunday as well as Sabbath-school. Scarp children first learned to read Gaelic at the Sabbath-school. There was a weeknight meeting every Thursday, when a bottomless bottle was used as a horn to call the people together. I also remember this same missionary conducting the singing-school, as we called the weekly class at which we were taught the common Psalm tunes, a small blackboard being borrowed from the public school for the occasion. The older lads had only one objection to the singing-school. The girls were let out first, and the door was closed for a considerable time before the boys were released!

I have written at some length about this missionary because he was the one of my boyhood and of my Sabbath-school days. I still remember his annoyance when I showed him the form of my Christian name written in a Bible received as a Sunday-school prize. The Glasgow folk had given me the girl's name Agnes.

Although dependent on a voluntary, undenominational mission to such an extent, our islanders belonged to the Free Church congregation formed in 1862 for the northern half of our parish, with the scholarly Dr MacIntosh MacKay as its first minister. Before a missionary was settled in Scarp, the islanders frequently went on Sunday by boat all the way to Tarbert, where the new church and manse had been built.

A visit from the minister was an event of great interest. With his coming on Saturday, those parents who wanted a baptism, visited him on the Saturday night, and the first service next day might be enlivened by the crying of several infants, the minister remaining in the low pulpit for the baptismal ceremony. The minister's occasional appearances in this way brought many visitors to the island. While the islanders went about their Sunday morning preparations in a leisurely way, boats under sail might be seen in the distance, one from Hushinish, and two – prior to the clearing of Dirascal in 1900 – from Loch Resort.

At *Am Port a Tuath*, or 'The North Port', as we called the landing-place for the long ferry at Hushinish, men and women from half a dozen villages could be seen arriving in small groups, a few coming from as far away as Soay Island, having left their boat in Loch Leosavay at Amhuinnsuidhe, and walking the five miles to the ferry in the best of Sabbath company. When the Hushinish tenants, after their settlement there in 1900, had no boat at The North Port, their regular fishing-boat being berthed on the south side of the peninsula, a Scarp boat set off to bring the pilgrims over, finally collecting the shepherd's family living at Cravadale due east of us. They would first have crossed Loch na Cleavag at Cravadale in their own cobble.

Unless a break in the weather was feared, the visitors waited for the evening service, which was held at an early hour, but it would be nothing short of a miracle if they were never trapped. Once at least, the boats from Loch Resort were stormstayed on the island for several days, leaving only the old folk and the children to carry out the duties of home and field as best they could. When the first of the boats returned home and those on board saw one of the older men awaiting them at the landing-place, they wondered what his greeting would be. Silently they approached him and when the boat was within hailing distance, he spoke and said: 'Even if Dr MacKay were preaching at the gate up

yonder, none of you will ever attend the sermon again!' As a matter of fact
Dr MacKay had been in his grave for at least twelve years, but his name,
cleverly used in this way, still carried weight. Dr MacKay died in 1873, and
was buried in Duddingston Kirkyard, Edinburgh.

That the minister's visit was regarded from the beginning as something of
an event is shown by what a woman who was old enough to remember the
formation of the congregation once told me. Suspected of having been in
contact with measles while on a visit to another part of the parish, she was
compelled to live alone in a shieling type of hut for some days, food being
brought to her and left at a safe distance. She remembered that the minister
visited the island during her term of isolation and to my surprise she was able
to repeat his text, which she had heard from those who brought her food.

As our island graveyard was known to us as *An Teampall,* or 'The Temple',
it is obvious that Scarp had a Christian settlement and a place of worship
many centuries ago. The term 'temple', borrowed like the English word from
Latin, simply means a church. We have one record of such a place of worship
in an early manuscript which says that the 8th Chief, Alexander MacLeod,
known as Alasdair Crotach, not only restored the twelfth-century Church of
St Clement in the southern end of Harris and endowed it, but also: 'built
two other beautiful small churches', one of them on Scarp. As this happened
some years before the Chief's death in 1547, Scarp can claim to have had a
place of worship more than four hundred years ago, and therefore before the
Reformation was consolidated and the Protestant Church legally established
in Scotland in 1560.

Indeed our seniors used to tell us of a stone building that once stood in
the burial ground, and I myself cannot dismiss the impression that I have
seen the ruins of this building, as if it were of red sandstone and unlike the
walls of any other island building in colour. This impression may, however,
be due to the tales heard around the peat fire of some ceilidh-house. We were
told, for instance, of how a certain Gaelic School teacher took some of The
Temple stones to build a chimney-stack for his own dwellinghouse, and how
he was haunted by ghosts until he took the chimney-stack down and returned
the stones to their old site. As the mere mention of The Temple or graveyard
filled us with superstitious fear, we accepted such a tale without the slightest
hesitation.

The island, like the country generally, must have passed through periods
of spiritual darkness. This seems to be reflected in the numerous stories
illustrating individual ignorance, as when a minister, amazed at the answers
he received when catechising, at last said, 'O man! Are you not in great
darkness?' 'You should have seen it', said the other, 'before the window
was put in!' Such a story may have floated to our island from the Scottish
Gaelic-speaking mainland, or Continent, as it was called two hundred years
ago. It can be capped by one which, if authentic, must apply to Scarp and

indeed is attributed to a certain islander, the idiom, not to mention the humour, being typical of our people. The islander was railing at womankind, when someone reminded him that transgression entered the world through a woman's action. He replied, *Tha mi 's a'bhad an cuala mi e, ach tha mi a' cur mo làn aonta ris!* – 'I have only now heard of it, but I entirely agree!'

There were those on the other hand who were bright and shining lights and whose piety and wisdom became proverbial. I often recall a saying of my grandfather, who was usually referred to as *An Deucon*, or 'The Deacon'. On occasions when there was no one on the island to conduct public worship, he used to insist that even when there was no Sunday service, everyone should wear his or her best clothes on the Sabbath. This was good practical counsel.

Dòmhnall Og, or 'Young Donald', another islander of a former generation, must have been a remarkable man. Once when I was home on holiday, his grand-daughter entertained a houseful of evening visitors with anecdotes about him, culminating with an account of the advice he gave a young teacher who had come to Scarp. Replying to a request for advice on taking up his duties, the islander told the young man that the first rule was humility, the second rule humility, and the third rule humility. This was really a quotation from St Augustine and was probably heard in a sermon, our islanders past and present having a grand memory for sermons, and especially for illustrations heard in sermons. Although our islander did not originate the saying, he was well able to make an original application of it when the occasion arose.

Some of the older women, my own aunt among them, seemed to know the whole of the Gaelic Psalter by heart. I remember being told as a boy that a certain old lady whom the minister visited in her small cottage, repeated from memory the chapter the minister wanted to read with her, but which he could not read in the bad light.

When I began attending the mission services, the hall was lit rather dimly by a few metal wall lamps with single wicks. These gave way to two large brass hanging lamps with circular wicks. This was a great improvement. There was no heating of any kind. Today there are three Tilley lamps hanging in the mission-hall, as well as two paraffin heaters for use in winter.

The old-fashioned wooden ladle, with a long handle, was used for taking up the collection at one of the Sunday services, usually the second service, and there was a spare one, which was brought into use when there was an extra-large attendance. A precentor always led the singing, chanting each line in slow time, to some well-known psalm tune.

It only remains for me to say that the directors and subscribers of The Glasgow and West Coast Mission decided on 19 May 1939 to hand over their six remaining mission stations to the Free Church and the Church of Scotland, one to the Free Church and the other five, including the Scarp mission, to the Church of Scotland. The transfer of all property and other assets, including accumulated funds of about £20,000, took effect on 1 January 1950.

Our island has good reason to remember the West Coast Mission with pride. During the period of seventy-two years in which the Mission served us, this small island produced no less than eleven ordained ministers, six lay missionaries, and twelve school teachers.

CHAPTER TWENTY-TWO

Charms and Superstitions

Scarp was on the whole remarkably free from superstitious faith in charms and amulets. And yet I myself as a child wore a charm.

As I was troubled with nightmares, and troubled others with my screams, someone suggested to my mother that I should wear a string of the metal roves or washers used in boatbuilding for clinching nails. A request for a dozen or so of these was made to an islander who was a self-taught carpenter and joiner. He sent the smallest he had, including some copper ones. The roves were then strung like a set of girl's beads and for some time – how long I do not now remember – this charm against the terrors of nightmare was put round my neck at bedtime.

At one time it must have been common throughout our parish to charm away all sorts of ailments, but the Church discouraged such practices, and only a few people were known to resort to charms in my time, confining them to such simple ailments as toothache or a stye on one's eye.

An interesting spell for toothache, used in Harris, is given by Dr George Henderson in the book entitled *Leabhar nan Gleann*. It must have been one of many used for this common complaint. The performer's method was to give the sufferer a tiny piece of wood to put in the aching tooth. He then searched for the tooth that held the chip of wood, repeating at the same time the following rhyme:

EOLAS AN DEIDIDH

> Chunnaic mi Tàbhart (sic!)
> 'Siubhal air beanntaichean Nabot
> A' chnei(mh) 'na dheud
> Gun tuigse 'na bheul
> Dhianag leigheas dha dheud
> Ach tha mise gad leigheas
>   An ainm Mhic Dhe
>   (An t-ainm.)

I saw an apparition
Walking the hills of Nabot;
The ache in his teeth,

But no skill on his lips
To bring relief:
But I heal thee
    In the name of God's Son!

The Gaelic is taken direct from Dr Henderson's book. The English translation is my own but I have left the word *Nabot* in its original form.

Those who possess the second volume of Dr Alexander Carmichael's *Carmina Gadelica* will find another toothache charm there. The first verse, as given by Dr Carmichael in Gaelic and then English, is:

Ob a chuir Bride bhòidheach
Romh òrdag Màthar De,
Air mhir, air lìon, air chorcraich,
Air chnoidh, air ghoimh, air dheud.

The incantation put by lovely Bride
Before the thumb of the Mother of God,
On lint, on wort, on hemp,
For worm, for venom, for teeth.

In the island charm for a stye, the performer took a silver coin, such as a sixpenny piece, and rubbed the affected eye with it as she repeated the following words:

CHARM FOR A STYLE

Who put one there, and did not put two there?
Who put two there, and did not put three there?
Who put three there, and did not put four there?
Who put four there, and did not put five there?
Who put five there, and did not put six there?
Who put six there, and did not put seven there?
Who put seven there, and did not put eight there?
Who put eight there, and did not put seven there?
Who put seven there, and did not put six there?
Who put six there, and did not put five there?
Who put five there, and did not put four there?
Who put four there, and did not put three there?
Who put three there, and did not put two there?
Who put two there, and did not put one there?
Who put one there, and put none at all there ?

Having arrived in this roundabout way at the word 'none', the spell for the eyes was completed and a cure confidently expected. This resembles a charm given by Dr Carmichael in the volume already quoted. It begins:

> Why came the one stye,
> Without the two styes here?
> Why came the two styes,
> Without the three styes here?

and goes on up to nine, after which it concludes with the lines:

> Why came the nine,
> Or one at all here?

The well-known folklorist got one charm in Scarp. It is a charm for 'the rose'. This does not mean that the islanders at that time either believed in it or used it, but one of the isleswomen, Ann MacLeod, still remembered it. Here it is in Gaelic, followed by Dr Carmichael's English translation:

EOLAS NA RUAIDH

> A ruadh ghaothar, atar, aogail,
> Fàg an taobh agus an tac sin,
> Sin an càrr 's an làr,
>   Agus fàg a chìoch.

> Seall, a Chriosd, a' bhean
> Agus a cioch air at,
> Seall fèin i, Mhuire,
>   'S tu rug am Mac.

> A ruadh ghaothar, aogar, ìota,
> Fàg a chìoch agus am bac,
> Agus sin a mach,
> Slàn gu robh dh'an chìch,
>   Crìon gu robh dh'an at.

> Teich a bhradag ruadh,
> Teich gu luath a bhradag,
> At a bha 's a chìch,
> Fàg a' chàrr 's a chìoch,
>   Agus sin a mach.

CHARM FOR ROSE

Thou rose windy, swelling, deadly,
Leave that part and spot,
There is the udder in the ground,
    And leave the breast.

See, Christ, the woman
And her breast swollen,
See her thyself, Mary,
    It was thou didst bear the Son.

Thou rose windy, deadly, thirsty,
Leave the breast and the spot,
And take thyself off;
Healed be the breast,
    Withered be the swelling.

Flee thieving red one,
Flee quickly thieving one,
Swelling that was in the breast,
Leave the udder and the breast,
    And flee hence.

The glandular swelling known by the old-fashioned name, 'the king's evil', was believed to yield to magic treatment from the seventh son in a family. Only one person answered to this description on our island in my youth, and as he was himself but a lad and could not take the matter seriously, his services were not much sought. The influence of the Church in combating this practice was perhaps reflected in the attitude of one of our old saints, who mocked at anyone repeating the name, 'the king's evil', saying, 'Only the king himself has the king's evil'.

In the treatment of animals a few traditional cures were still resorted to. As a boy I once spent several hours at the freshwater Loch na Cleavag across the Sound, with an islander who wanted brown trout for an ailing cow. What was wrong I do not know, but the traditional cure was a brown trout swallowed whole and if possible alive. Cases of the cure mentioned by Martin Martin, namely a black cockerel's kidneys, while the cockerel itself was buried alive, presumably before its kidneys were removed, were known in the Outer Hebrides, but the vast majority of the people regarded this as crass superstition. The Aberdeen periodical, *Scottish Notes and Queries*, for April 1900, referred to a cock having been buried alive in Caithness as late as 1850, as a cure for epilepsy.

Since the people depended so much on their cattle, it is not surprising that the animals should be thought highly vulnerable and therefore in need of special care and attention. Hence the fear of the 'evil eye', the malignant power by which a beast can be injured and rendered sterile and milkless. One man in Scarp was thought to possess this power, and an uncle of my own, whom I barely remember, mentions him by name in a homely pastoral song composed by him. Addressing his milch-cow as he drove or led it to pasture, he tells it where he will take it and where he will not take it, adding his reasons. One verse says:

> I will not take you to the Potato Knoll,
> Lest (the named man) meet us;
> Knowing him to be an enemy
> Who will cut and injure you.

Witchcraft, or rather belief in it, must have been rife on the island once upon a time, as indeed it was all over the country. 'What witchcraft you have!' was a common way of addressing anyone who had correctly foretold an event, even such an insignificant event as a neighbour's visit. In the same way I have heard my aunt, who knew and used many old words and phrases, say to a fast walker, 'A charm on your walking!' suggesting that such walking was unearthly and uncanny.

We had only one 'witch' on Scarp in my time. This was the common fieldmouse. When it crossed the milkmaids' path as they went to the moor for the milking, its appearance gave rise to speculation as to whether it meant good or ill for the cattle. Old folktales in which witches undergo certain metamorphoses, assuming the forms of animals at will, were no doubt responsible for this apprehension at the sight of a tiny mouse.

Our island children had implicit faith in fairies. Above North Hamlet stood *Cnoc an t-Sìthein*, or 'The Fairy-knowe', and among the summits far from the village was *Aird nan Sìthean*, or 'The Big Fairy-knowe'. It is true that the word *Sìthean*, used for a fairy knoll, though very seldom heard now except in place-names, can be applied to any green knoll and that this may be the significance of our island's 'fairy hills'. Houses stood on the nearer knoll but we had no difficulty in believing that fairies lived among the green hillocks behind it – their dwellings had merely been pushed back a little! We did not regard the fairies as either friendly or hostile. They were neutral, keeping to their own company and not likely to interfere with us unless taken by surprise. They might however be near without our knowledge, unless a dog happened to be with us. The dog seemed to perceive their presence and would show unmistakable signs of alarm.

Both young and old believed in portents and apparitions. How often have I heard my mother exclaim all of a sudden: 'Dear me! The tinkling I have in my ears!' This merely was the noise one sometimes has in the head but to her it portended bad news. And when bad news actually reached us, I have sometimes heard her say in our own idiom: 'That is the tinkling I had in my ears!' meaning that the news explained the mysterious noises in her head. The younger generation, largely free from such physical symptoms, was inclined to be impatient with this particular portent. I have seen my sister trying to humour her mother on such occasions and asking at intervals: 'Is that tinkling still in your ears?'

In the poem *The Pedlar*, James Hogg, the Ettrick Shepherd, refers to 'the dead-bell' – 'O lady, 'tis dark, an' I heard the dead-bell.' – and writes in a sub-note that country folk regarded the tinkling in the ears as secret intelligence of a friend's death. His friend Sir Walter Scott makes use of the same portent in the long narrative poem, *Marmion: A Tale of Flodden Field*, Third Canto, XIII.

Portents from dreams were common, and like the last-mentioned were confined to the older members of a family. Very often when my mother got up and was dressed, she would say: 'The way I myself was seeing so-and-so in my sleep last night!' Her dream was then related, to the last detail, and the implication adduced that something was about to happen to the person named. In a community such as ours everyone was interested in everyone else, and those seen in a realistic dream might have no close connection with the dreamer. Whenever one member suffered, all the members suffered with him, and my mother worried almost as much about any islander seen in her sleep as she would have done in the case of any of her own children. When some crony called and someone was mentioned by name, my mother would frequently recall a recent dream about the person in question, and proceed to tell her dream in all its colourful detail, the other woman listening with rapt attention and evident interest.

Many of the recognised portents and auguries had reference to someone's death, and in this connection superstitious belief held its own in spite of bell, book and candle. I remember being told by another lad that a certain islander, otherwise very like the rest of us, 'had the second sight'. This meant that the person referred to, a woman, could predict future events, especially events connected with one's individual life. Such a gift or endowment was not however considered necessary in order to see apparitions and other omens foretelling the death of someone. These were objective realities, we thought, which could be seen by anyone who happened to be out at the time and favourably placed.

I remember my aunt, whom I have already mentioned in this chapter, discussing the matter in our house and telling my father how an islander had seen one of our isleswomen pass him as he went along some path. She was wearing a white mutch and though spoken to, made no reply, but quickly disappeared. The significance of the apparition apparently lay in the mutch worn, this article being part of the grave-clothes used for a woman. My father, I remember, tried to show that the whole thing was an impossibility, but my aunt held to her conviction. She knew many other instances of the same kind!

A meteor or shooting star of exceptional brightness was thought to presage death, its direction indicating where the death might occur, while a light seen travelling along the ground, being of a more mysterious nature, was a sure sign of death, its course marking the route the funeral procession would take.

Sounds as well as visions played their part in this occult business. One of the large wooden trunks found in every house might be heard to close with a bang, and the person hearing or imagining such a thing would afterwards remember it if the trunk was opened to get some article, or one's Sunday clothes, for a funeral. That was the precise sound heard when no one was anywhere near the trunk! The sound of hammering in the dark, when investigation showed that no one was using a hammer at the time, could be associated with coffin-making, coffins being made in the village as required, only the fittings and cloth for covering them being brought from the shopping centre. In the same way, the sawpit mentioned in Chapter 9 had its ghostly associations. As the first step in making a coffin was the sawing with the great saw of a plank or log into lengths of a certain thickness, it was inevitable that someone with sharp ears would hear the 'swish-swish' of the great saw some weeks, or even months, before the event. This made the sawpit, situated above the main harbour, a place to be feared and avoided, especially when it had in position the cross-planks that served as a platform to keep the wood in position. With such associations, the saw itself assumed spooky qualities, even while hung horizontally on the wooden partition of a house. I have seen nervous glances cast at it as some vibration made it ring slightly, and to hear the death-watch beetle in the silence of the night, ticking away like a watch, was a sure sign of someone's death.

An Teampall, or 'The Temple', as we called the graveyard, was always an object of fear in the dark. As already shown, some of the traditional tales told round the peat fire of a ceilidh-house had much to do with the development of such dread in our minds. Another circumstance aggravated the trouble in my own case and in that of my contemporaries. This was the discovery by one of my cousins, at that time a big lad, of a drowned man in one of the coves on the south coast of Scarp. The body was brought to the village and taken to the unenclosed graveyard, where it was watched day and night by relays of men until a boat came from one of the islands further south, and outwith our parish, to claim it. My recollection is that the body lay in the open among the gravestones, covered with a tarpaulin or a brown sail. It could even be seen at night in the light of a lantern used by the watchers.

The old graveyard at Hushinish supplies a modern instance, and as four of the five men involved in the incident about to be related were either natives of Scarp, or the sons of natives, no apology need be given for recounting the incident here. Following his discharge from the regular army some time after the First World War, one of our islanders was engaged to repair the wall of the Hushinish graveyard. While engaged on this work he found a large hollow stone, which may have been a baptismal font in a former chapel there, or perhaps, although I have not personally seen it, a quernstone. Only the flat handquern is known in our island, but in Galloway old stones of this kind and of varying sizes have been found, going under the name 'quern', or 'quernstone'. The Gallovidians, indeed, tell a joke against themselves, to the effect that at one time whin bushes were ground in these, and fed to the Galloway ponies, or Galloway nags, as Shakespeare calls them.

The use to which the Hushinish stone had been put is immaterial, the salient point being that it was found in the old graveyard. A native of the parish, living at Tarbert, where he held a number of public offices as well as some business appointments, sent for the stone, so that it might be identified. It was duly sent to him, one man lifting it onto another man's back and this man carrying it to the road-end, where the driver of a car – or a small bus – took charge of it. All three men suffered for their share in such sacrilege. The driver of the car fell and broke his leg, the big man who carried the stone to the car developed a cyst in the small of the back, and the man who lifted the stone onto this man's back had a kink in one of his little fingers ever after.

I heard the story direct from the last-named man, who laughed as he told it, as if to show that he attached no occult significance to this series of mishaps. However, it may be that he laughed because he got off so lightly!

Social Occasions

At the homely gatherings in a favourite ceilidh-house the children looked to their seniors for entertainment, but twice a year, at Hallowe'en and Hogmanay, the children had the stage to themselves. In each case the old style was observed and the celebrations were held on the evenings of 12 November and 12 January respectively, the celebration of Hallowe'en being left entirely to the girls and Hogmanay to the boys.

I shall deal with Hogmanay first. A house having been selected as the venue, the boys gathered there at dusk and began their preparations. These preparations were chiefly concerned with the company's round of the village homes, which began as early as possible. One lad was selected to lead the others when they entered a house and, as it was a family's privilege to strike the leader as he ran three times round the fire, a dried calfskin or sheepskin was fastened to his back. Two of the other boys were each given an empty flour bag in which to carry gifts received in their house-to-house foray. Some of the older boys would then practise the Hogmanay Rhyme that must be repeated before gaining admission to a house, and when satisfied that all was in order, they trooped out in a body and began the Hogmanay celebrations in earnest.

On arriving at a house the whole company halted at the outside door, which usually stood open. The boy detailed to repeat the Hogmanay Rhyme was then pushed forward until he was about halfway between the outer door and the inner door that led to the livingroom. When those inside heard the procession arrive they kept still, listening for the rhyme, but the boys themselves gave no warning.

Whether the house was still or noisy, the reciter raised his voice and repeated the rhyme, here given in a literal translation. The word 'Calends' is used instead of 'Hogmanay', because it resembles the Gaelic *A' Challainn*, which is derived, like the English word, from the Latin *Kalendae*.

> Here we come approaching you
> To renew for you the Calends;
> We do not need to tell you this,
>   It has been known since our grandsires' day:

Going sunwise past the lintel-stone,
And descending at the Entrance,
I will say my rhyme, well-mannered, calmly,
  Behind the door of every household:

A wee bit skin is in my pocket,
And good smoke will issue from it;
No one feeling its smell
  But will be healthy ever after:

The guidman will get it in his hand
To place its end in the fireplace;
The guidwife will get it, and deserves it,
  While she serves to us the Calends:

With such a drought throughout the land
A dram we do not look for;
But if you have some Summer produce,
  We do like it with the bread:

And if it is in your possession,
  Hand it over, and do not delay us!

The boys then burst into the room, the lad with the hide plunging round and round the fire, while those sitting near rained blows on the hide with the tongs or a stick. When the excitement caused by all this had died down, the boys produced their bags, expecting the guidwife to put a whole bannock of oatcake or a girdle-sized scone into one, and either a piece of home-cured mutton or some butter into the other.

Although not insisted on, a benediction in verse was sometimes uttered by the boys before leaving. It was as follows:

My blessing on the present house,
On its wood, and stone, and child;
Sufficient clothes, and ample food,
  And Health may all its folk enjoy!

The visits were repeated throughout the entire village, unless there happened to be two companies, representing the two ends of the village, that is, the North and South Hamlets. Even when a company of younger boys kept Hogmanay by themselves, both companies visited all the houses, thoughtful housewives having baked extra bannocks and scones for the raiders.

The boys duly returned to their quarters, where they spent the night.

A royal supper was enjoyed before the family retired, further meals being prepared by the boys themselves, or by a young man who undertook to do the cooking for them. Tea and sugar, as well as jam, was bought with the pennies the boys had received for the great occasion from their mothers or from some relative.

Much of the night was spent making shinty sticks so that a game could be played the following day, Old New Year's Day, either in the school playground or on the long sandy beach in front of the village. This occupation kept the boys awake and interested until daybreak.

Once or twice during the night they sallied forth to raid the kailyards. This practice was not confined to Hogmanay, but when so many boys were together and all in high fettle, the kailyards were not likely to escape. Our kailyards were well-protected against cattle and sheep, but the boys found a way over the stone wall, and choosing a cabbage with a thick stock, cut through it near the ground and stripped it of its leaves. They then left the kailyard as quickly as possible lest they should be discovered. A cabbage stock was peeled with the teeth, beginning at the thickest and hardest end where the knife left a circular edge. It is quite safe to say that no city or town boy ever enjoyed an apple or a pear more than the island boys enjoyed a raw cabbage stock, whether carried off in a night raid or not.

A comparison of Hogmanay customs in different parts of the Highlands reveals a fairly wide divergence in the Hogmanay Rhyme, but I have here given in translation the version used in Scarp, as I recall it. The obscure lines about the wee bit of skin refer to the custom of singeing a sheep's breast-strip on Hogmanay as a charm against illness during the New Year. As I cannot recall such a charm being carried, or put to use by a Hogmanay party on our island, I conclude that the custom had been dropped, only the eight lines of the rhyme remaining to remind us of it. The boys, as has been shown in an earlier chapter, had a more practical interest in the strip of skin cut from a butchered sheep's breast.

Hallowe'en was celebrated by the girls on 12 November, the night preceding the Festival of All-Hallows, or All Saints' Day, according to the old reckoning. Like May Day and Lammas, All-Hallows was a well-known date, still used in ordinary conversation by everyone. Hallowe'en itself was perpetuated in a rhythmical line reminding us that, *Oidhche Shamhna, theirear gamhna ris na laoigh* – 'On Hallowe'en the calves are known as stirks'.

As already mentioned, Hallowe'en celebrations were left to the girls, just as Hogmanay was left to the boys. Both sexes were very jealous of this privilege, and any spying by boys on Hallowe'en, or by girls on Hogmanay, was strongly resented and visited with dire punishment if discovered. Although the boys made no attempt to dress for Hogmanay, the girls were more particular and looked splendid in short pinafores and small kerchiefs, for which they used the English word, 'head-dress'.

Unlike the boys, they made no systematic round of the village and had no rhyme corresponding to the boys' Hogmanay Rhyme. I can recall their merriment as they set out about bedtime for the upper part of the fields above the village. There, in the black loam near the foothills, each girl dug a hole which was left uncovered until daylight, when they returned to examine the results. This ritual had to do with the girls' matrimonial prospects, an empty hole being regarded as a bad omen and one in which an earthworm was found, as a good omen.

A more elaborate way of foretelling their fortune was tried back inside their den. For this, four saucers were laid on a table – one was empty and the others contained respectively, oatmeal, salt, and water. Each girl was in turn blindfolded, then the saucers were mixed round and made ready for use. The blindfolded girl put her finger or hand into one to discover her own future: the oatmeal signified wealth; the salt, widowhood; the water, marriage; and the empty saucer, spinsterhood!

The girls, like the boys, sat up all night entertaining one another with songs and games. They also feasted well, bringing food from their own homes and the homes of relatives. They even raided the kailyards in their curiosity about their future, taking a cabbage stock home with them in the morning and putting it under the pillow when they went to bed. By this means a girl was sure to dream of her future husband. In other parts of the parish, as we were reminded by incomers at such a time, a girl would go eavesdropping on some house until she heard a boy's name mentioned. She then ran away excitedly, believing that the name overheard in this way would be her future husband's name. As she was obliged to have a mouthful of water while listening, she could not wait very long at a single door. The sound made when she was no longer able to breathe properly, and had to get rid of the water, would often betray her.

The greatest of all social occasions in Scarp was a wedding. In a small community such as ours, there could be long intervals between marriages, but both young and old made the most of the occasion when it arrived.

The traditional custom of having an Espousal Feast was kept up on our island. This was held in the bride-to-be's home, with the future bridegroom present, a fortnight before the date of the marriage. In the course of the evening, speeches were made in praise of the contracting parties, and the bride's father was formally asked by the best speaker for his consent to the marriage. As we regarded this function as a private affair, more or less, the children kept away from it, but from the accounts afterwards circulated, it was apparent that it provided good entertainment for those present.

I can only recall one marriage being solemnized on the island itself. A native of Scarp, home on holiday at the time, officiated at the ceremony, which was held in the mission-hall. As a rule the bride and bridegroom, attended by the best man and bridesmaid, and accompanied by the young men and young women of the island, went to Tarbert, seventeen miles away, where our minister lived, or to Amhuinnsuidhe, five miles from the long ferry, where he met them. When they returned and came ashore on the island after being ferried back, a salute from someone's sporting gun was fired in honour of the newly-wed couple.

The boys of the island came into their own in the evening, when the wedding guests assembled in the bride's home. They cared little for food, though there was plenty of it, but lost no opportunity of slipping under the tables to forage for the sweets that were thrown about. The favourite sweet in such company was of course the conversation lozenge, and these at least rattled across the tables and sometimes fell on the floor.

I have many happy memories of boyhood weddings on Scarp. Familiar songs were sung, one person leading and singing the verses, while the others joined in the chorus. Some of the men knew humorous songs, which they were urged to sing, but it was difficult to get them started on a solo. The song with a chorus was the thing, especially when it dealt, as most of them did, with the tender passion.

Being in simple language and set to simple music, these songs were easily imitated and even parodied. I well remember a confirmed bachelor, who lived with an equally confirmed spinster sister in the North Hamlet, enjoying himself at his niece's wedding in South Hamlet. As the night wore on – for boys were allowed to stay out on such an occasion until slumber drove them home – and he warmed up after a few drams, it was amusing to see him capering outside and singing without any variation, the two lines:

> Going to Taransay this year,
> To swagger, and to seek a wife there.

Rightly or wrongly, we regarded the couplet as an extempore effort of his own, and although the word 'I' did not occur in it, we thought he himself was the swaggerer, seeking a bride on an island not very far from Scarp.

I remember another incident from the same wedding and connected – to his credit! – with the same man. After he opened his bottle and had passed it round the wedding guests, he sought out the boys and insisted on their having a taste from the bottle.

Spirits were not provided for all by the host and hostess, but most of the male guests brought a bottle for the occasion and served the guests at intervals.

Traditional customs were observed when putting the bride to bed. While undressing, one of her attendants pulled off one of the bride's stockings and threw it high over her shoulder. The girl struck by the flying stocking would be the next island bride! In the morning the married islanders, both men and women, 'came to get the bride up', as we said, and after breakfast a procession was formed, and bride and bridegroom were escorted to their new home.   A second wedding feast, called the 'House Wedding', followed the homecoming, and to this reception the married men and women of the island were invited, as well as the previous night's guests. Stories are still told of how the married folk danced, and of the tricks they played on each other, in the spirit of the happy occasion.

EDITOR'S NOTE

This Gaelic version of the boys' Hogmanay Rhyme has been provided by Morag MacLeod:

Tha sinne 'n seo a' tighinn gur n-ionnsaigh
A dh' ùrachadh dhuibh na Callainn
Cha ruig sinn leas a bhith ga innse
Bha i ann o linn ar seanar

A' dol deiseal aig an àrd-doras
'S a' teàrnadh aig an trannsa
Canaidh mi mo dhuan gu modhail ciùin
Air cùl dorais gach fàrdaich

Mìr de chaisean-uchd nam phòcaid
'S math a' cheò thig as an fhear ud
Chaneil duine gheibh àileadh
Nach bi gu bràth dheth fallain

Fear an taighe gheibh na làimh e
'Son a cheann a chur dhan teallach
Gheibh bean an taigh' e, 's i 's fhiach e
'S i riarachadh dhuinn na Callainn

Leis an tart a tha 's an dùthaich
Cha bhi dùil againn ri drama
Ach beagan de thoradh an t-Samhraidh
Tha sinn an geall air leis an aran

'S ma tha e agaibh
Sìn a-nall e, 's na cuir maille oirnn!

*   *   *

BEANNACHADH

Beannaich an taigh 's na bheil ann
Eadar fhiodh is chloich is chlann
Pailteas bìdh 's pailteas aodaich
'S slàinte dhaoine gu robh ann!

CHAPTER TWENTY-FOUR

Island Characters

As I glance back through the years to my early schooldays, I recall my encounters with the man whom I afterwards visited many a night for the sake of the stories, both old and new, that he could tell so well.

He was a great tease, often intercepting the children on their way home from school, and asking them more questions than they were able to answer. The opening question usually was: 'Were you in school today?' When we answered in the affirmative, he would say: 'Spell cat and begin at its tail'. This form of the question puzzled us so much that we did not think of spelling the word backwards, which might have satisfied him. We merely stared at him, while he beamed at us, as if to show that he knew how it was done. Sometimes the opening question was: 'Do you know English?' and we, who often heard the saying: ' Yes and No, the greatest part of English', and confident that we at least knew these two much-worked words, would happily answer: 'Yes!' He would then test our knowledge of the Saxon tongue by asking: 'What is the English translation of . . .?', repeating an impossible Gaelic word of five syllables, that sounded like a place-name. The unwary boy or girl would say in Gaelic: 'I don't know', whereupon Rory would shrug his shoulders and walk away, saying: 'Oh! It is not!'

Rory's victims were not confined to children. He loved to tease his near neighbours, especially those he could use as a butt for his wit and banter. As I was once visiting a certain house, the guidwife, in an effort to make him desist, asked him to make up the fire, the Gaelic phrase literally being, 'lift the fire'. Rory obediently took the tongs she passed him and picking up a small cinder with it, raised it high above the hearth and said: 'I have lifted it!'

He knew many quaint sayings which he interjected into any conversation he overheard from children. We often used the word 'almost' or 'nearly', for example, as in the expression: *Theab mi tuiteam* – 'I almost fell'. Whenever he heard this word used, he was sure to quote: *Chaidh Theab ri creig 's theabar a bhàthadh* – 'Almost fell down a crag and was almost drowned'. This was our island equivalent of the old English proverb: 'Almost was never hanged'. It was said, and I can well believe it, that when Rory himself slipped and fell into the sea while helping to round up a bull, and was pulled into a waiting boat, his first words were: *Chaidh Theab ri creig 's theabar a bhàthadh.*

Rory was by no means the only humorist on the island. Of one man, indeed a much younger man, it might be said that he never spoke in company without uttering a witticism. It was his common conversational style. Many of his witticisms were in the form of puns, which cannot be reproduced in another language, and although punning has been described as the lowest form of wit, it can be very amusing. It also shows an enviable feeling for words on the part of those who indulge in such word-play.

It says much for the general good humour of our islanders that a joke was remembered and repeated over and over again in company. Even plain men, not naturally endowed with a sense of humour, often said witty things, as when a man said of his own boat during a discussion on sailing-boats that, since a certain alteration had been made, it could win any part of the land to which one could point. I once heard a man of the same type say of another man, that he walked the street with his head in the air, like a man in attendance on the moon! Have any of the world's literary geniuses thought of that figure? If so, I do not know of it.

Jokes and sallies at the expense of the unmarried, whether spinsters or bachelors, were numerous. I once asked permission in a University Celtic class to tell a humorous story illustrating our use of the adverbial phrase, *a chaochladh*, used in the same sense as the English phrase, 'the contrary'. Had I then known the following story, which is shorter, I would have told it instead. A spinster, in whose name the family croft had been entered, received an official letter addressed to, 'The Proprietor'. Adverting to this when a neighbour, himself a bachelor, called, the crofter's brother, also a bachelor, turned to his sister and said, 'They think you are a male!' 'She has not proved the contrary!' said neighbour Roderick, who had known her all his life.

As might be expected of people who knew the Bible well, an apt use of some Scripture passage was often heard in ordinary conversation, the cleverest example within my recollection having been used by a man whom I have not hitherto mentioned, but who was naturally clever as well as being well educated. Friends of his own, nicknamed 'the Egyptians', because one of their forebears had served with the army in Egypt, had been ferried across the Sound after a visit to Scarp. As we watched them make their way along the steep path towards Hushinish, a mist came down, hiding them from us, whereupon Angus, who had been watching with shaded eyes, turned to the rest of us and said: *Na h-Eiphitich a chunnaic sibh an diugh, cha-n fhaic sibh iad a chaoidh tuilleadh* – 'The Egyptians whom ye have seen today, ye shall see them again no more for ever'.

Good humour prevailed in this way from day to day and there was no lack of entertainment. One circumstance, however, could interfere with it, making the best tempered men either crabbit or morose. This was a tobacco famine, one of the concomitants of life on an island which was sometimes isolated by stormy seas. To see a man scrape the inside of the bowl of his pipe, or turn out his vest pockets looking for bits of tobacco sometimes put

there to chew, was a bad sign. The man who was fortunate enough to have a
little in reserve during a tobacco dearth, was the most popular person on the
island for the time being, his company being much sought after. I imagine
I can see my old friend Rory laying siege, in a good-natured way, to such
a man. 'Have you baccy?' he would begin. If the answer was: 'Yes!' Rory's
gloom would change to smiles and chuckles, and he would withdraw a little,
as if he had no further interest in the matter. He would then return and ask:
'Have you pipe?' If the answer was still favourable, Rory's pleasure was even
more apparent than before. His third question was: 'Have you knife?' – that
is, a pocket-knife for cutting the black-twist tobacco used by our men. If the
answer was: 'Yes!' Rory's satisfaction mounted visibly, and after the usual
theatrical pause he would finally ask: 'Have you match?' It was difficult to
refuse him a smoke after such entertaining capers.

I have only seen snuff taken on the island when there was a tobacco famine.
Such scraps of tobacco as could be found, for example in a sealskin tobacco
pouch, were dried on the hearthstone and ground between the palms.

A cousin told me of an incident that shows the men's attachment to the
weed. My mother had bought a load of peat from one of the two men who had
succeeded our own islander on Soay, and my cousin, then a lad, was allowed in
the boat sent for the peat. After a meal on Soay, Big Findlay, who supplied the
peat, and who was distantly related to my mother and to others on our island,
stood in the doorway and said: 'Not a soul will leave this house today until I
get the food for which there is room on top of every other food!' My cousin
remembered that another cousin, who was probably the youngest member of
the boat's crew, turned pale with fear, but it was nothing more serious than
that Big Findlay was without a smoke. Big Findlay – or *Fionnlagh Shò-aigh*
as he was called – apparently knew the Gaelic story of the two suitors who
came seeking a certain young lady's hand. Her father resolved to test their
intelligence, and asked the first man what food it was for which there was
room on top of every other food. The dullard answered: 'Porridge!' and was
instantly dismissed. The second suitor, when asked the same question, said
it was tobacco. He got the lady.

I am sorry to say that one islander was persecuted by the boys, who
sometimes pelted him with sods torn from broken sandy ground when they
found him out in the dark. He was a solitary type, unfairly regarded as
hostile to man and beast, and therefore feared to some extent. A ball of
heather rope hanging from a rafter in his house was an object of curiosity.
Many of us believed it was either used in witchcraft, or held a miser's horde.
But even such a man knew English. When he paid one of his rare visits to
the schoolhouse, he never left without hearing the story of the schoolmaster's
watch. 'Mr Duncan', he would say, 'I am sure that must be a very old watch.'
The schoolmaster would then tell the story of the watch – a silver English
lever-watch – when he bought it, where he bought it, what he paid for it,

and so forth, all of which was of great interest to a man who had never possessed either a clock or a watch. On one occasion at least, he displayed his knowledge of English in public. Another islander had been addressing a visitor in Gaelic, using the singular pronoun instead of the more mannerly plural, when our hero intervened, remarking in English: 'Did ye notice? He did not say "ye" but "you"!'

Apropos of this practice, the late Very Rev Dr Norman MacLean, in his book *Set Free*, tells an amusing story of a Skyeman who habitually addressed Captain MacDonald, Laird of Waternish, as 'thou' and 'thee', instead of the less familiar 'you', until at last the young Laird reproved him. But the tenant not only repeated the dose, but rubbed salt into the wound by saying: *Thubhairt mi 'thusa' ri do bhrathair, agus 'thusa' ri t'athair, agus 'thusa' ri do sheanair, agus their mi 'thusa' riutsa cuideachd; oir bha h-uile 'thusa' dhiubh ni's feàrr na 'thusa'* – 'I said *thou* to your *brother*, and *thou* to your *father*, and *thou* to your *grandfather*, and I will say *thou* to *you* also; for every *thou* of them was better than *you*'.

One island worthy has been celebrated in song. A clever bard from Berneray, who was one of the regular ghillies during the shooting season, composed a humorous song, setting forth the islander's characteristics as observed during his first year as a ghillie.

Although Magnus – or *Mànus* as we called him in our language – did not belong to Scarp, he lived so near that he was a frequent visitor. He was a very interesting visitor. His father had come from another part of the parish to live at the head of Loch Tamanavay, where he had some land on condition that he also worked for the superior. Magnus had a wonderful memory for such events as births, marriages and deaths in the neighbourhood, including our island. This led many to believe that he kept a diary or journal, but his knowledge of such things was probably due to his interest in family history, and an unusually retentive memory. He was the type of person who would have had a distinguished scholastic career, had such a course been open to him. But, 'even the worthy Homer sometimes nods', and Magnus had his blind spot. The story ran that he had found a case of galoshes that had drifted ashore. When he next called to see my mother, she asked him why he did not bring her a pair. 'Oh!' said Magnus in his fine musical voice, 'These things were of no use! They were all for the same foot!'

As our island must have been tolerably free from the Celtic gloom attributed to Highlanders generally, we found good entertainment in the visit of an Irish dealer known to us as Barney. He always spoke in Gaelic, the difference between his dialect and our own causing much amusement. Having once crossed over to our island from Brenish, to the north of us, he kept repeating in a way that is still imitated on the island: 'Bad folk, Brenish folk. Brenish folk care not if they kill you!' Either on this occasion or during a later visit, he was offered a bull's hide for sale and amused our islanders by asking, as they at least understood it: *Co is maighstir don t-seice tairbh seo?* – 'Who is master of the hide of this bull?'

Poor Barney! The mere name made us smile, not knowing that it was one of the most popular of Irish names.

Barney always came alone, but I believe he had an Irish wife whom he left in charge of a horse and cart somewhere in the neighbouring parish, and for aught I know she may have been 'charming Kitty Callaghan'.

> Beauty's star,
>   Charming Kitty Callaghan,
> That's what you are,
>   Sighs poor Barney Brallaghan.

CHAPTER TWENTY-FIVE

Giants of those days

After I left home to attend secondary school, and saw tug-of-war at Highland Games, I used to select in imagination an unbeatable tug-of-war team from among our own islanders. We were well-off in the matter of men combining height, weight and strength much above the average, and I had no difficulty in getting my team together, with *Coinneach Mòr* – 'Big Kenneth', or his brother-in-law, *Iain Peigi* – 'Peggy's John', as the anchor.

I have already given an account of one islander's strength, in the story of the wicked Stronach. *Dòmhnall Bàn*, or 'Fair-haired Donald', had a brother John, known as *Iain Donn*, or 'Brown-haired John'. He was apparently equally strong. A very large stone, set up on edge near the road a few miles from Hushinish, was pointed out as one of his feats of strength. Brown-haired John's sons, our island king among them, were men of considerable strength, but it was left to the next generation to produce a man of abnormal strength. I remember this young man visiting his uncle in Scarp in a large fishing-boat owned by his cousins in Tarbert, where his own home was. At certain seasons of the year they fished for lobsters with their big sailing-boat around Gasker, to the west of Scarp. This young man alas, like the strongest of our island's young men, died in his prime.

A hundred years ago the south end of our parish produced a man of abnormal size and strength. He became known as the Cape Breton Giant, his parents having gone to Cape Breton during the first half of the nineteenth century, taking their young son with them. I have seen a photograph of this giant, whose name was Angus MacAskill. So well-proportioned was he that the photograph might be that of any prosperous American as he stands bareheaded, holding a grey felt hat in one hand. It is only when one looks at his hand, holding the hat slightly in front of him, and notes its breadth, that one realises that it is a photograph of a man of abnormal size. MacAskill was born in Berneray, Harris, in 1825, went to Cape Breton with his parents while still young, and died there in 1863. He was seven feet nine inches in height, with a chest measurement of eighty inches, and weighed four hundred and twenty-five pounds, or over thirty stones!

When I first wrote, many years ago, the story of Fair-haired Donald's encounter with the dangerous Stronach, I was told how another islander, whom I am old enough to remember, carried on his back for a distance of five miles to the long ferry, before any road was made, a boll of meal, a smearing stool and a live sheep. In my early youth this man was the oldest man living in Scarp and was noted for his piety. Imagine my surprise, therefore, when I was once sent on some message or other to his house and heard him narrate some extraordinary exploits of his earlier years. While I sat alone on the bench under the window on one side of the fire, the old man's grandson came in and introduced a visitor to the island. The grandson lost no time in drawing the old man, who sat on a low chair beside the fire, so that he might give the visitor some reminiscences. After listening to a number of harmless experiences, the grandson said, 'Tell him how you defeated the champion'. The old man then told how a certain wrestler came day after day challenging the fishermen at one of the East Coast ports during the herring season. At last his companions prevailed upon Murdo to take up the challenge. No sooner had they come to grips than the islander was forced down, with one knee on the ground. This had the effect represented in the old folktales in similar circumstances. Murdo, enraged, quickly raised himself, got on his feet again, caught the champion wrestler round the waist, and swinging him round and round in true Cumberland style, finally flung him into a pool towards which they had gradually moved.

This was good entertainment, but the grandson wanted more. 'Tell him now', he said, 'how you killed the man!' This seemed an impossible demand, but old Murdo, his tongue now thoroughly loosened, told how a man once tried to prevent the crew of an East Coast fishing-boat of which he was a member from going to sea, the man holding on to the boat even after the crew had gone aboard, determined to keep them in port. It was then Murdo acted. One blow laid the culprit low, and the harbour was cleared as quickly as possible. Murdo believed, as he still did after an interval of many years, that the blow had been fatal. It did not occur to him that in such an event he would have been arrested immediately the boat had returned to port. He was sure he had killed his man.

This same grandson, who encouraged the old man in this way, was the tallest and strongest islander of my boyhood; but alas, he died while still a young man, having over-strained himself while doing spectacular feats of strength, such as hoisting, single-handed, the main mast of one of the big fishing-boats used for the East Coast herring season, before the advent of the steam drifter. His brother, the youngest of the family and nearly my own age, was almost as strong, but he too died in his early manhood many years ago.

As a boy, I used to associate with this family a story my old friend Rory used to tell, but which must belong to an earlier generation. Once when the press-gang visited our island, or one of the small settlements near Scarp – I forget which – a certain man warned his sons to make off, while he himself intercepted the raiders. Meeting the boat, he stood on the landing-stone and as each sailor leapt ashore, caught him and laid him on his back on the rocks, saying: 'Well! You were not used to the landing-stone!' This, according to my old friend, was the origin of the common Scarp saying: *Cha robh thu eòlach air an lic*, or, 'You were not used to the landing-stone' – literally flagstone – said to anyone who complained of having been deceived.

The stalwarts of our island were not confined to one or two families, but were found in several families not related, so far as I know, to one another. For example, the oldest ghillie on the estate when I used to visit the proprietor's seat, was one of the islanders evacuated from Scarp to one of the smaller settlements in 1885. By the time I got to know him, he was lank and lean, but a glance at his hands, strong and big-knuckled, confirmed the tales I had heard of his great strength. A brother who lived and died on our island and whom I therefore knew better, was a tall powerfully-built man. The prowess of these two brothers is admirably illustrated in the story of their sea journey from Brenish to Scarp. When they took their seats, ready for rowing, and being alone in the boat, one of them said to the other: 'This side will not yield at any rate!' To which the other replied: 'Neither will this side!' So off they went for an eight-mile spurt of hard rowing, almost twice the length of the Oxford and Cambridge boat-race course, and as our island tradition has it, the boat ran straight, without deviating to left or right, until it at last grounded at the spot from which it had been launched on the island beach when they left home. Having known both men I can well believe they were capable of such a ploy in their younger days.

Great strength was not the prerogative of our giants only. A certain man of average height had such strong hands that he often made us squeal with pain when we were foolish enough to shake hands with him. In this connection, a friend of my own tells how a French pugilist wanted to fight the Cape Breton Giant. MacAskill, a peace-loving man, would have nothing to do with him, but the Frenchman persisted. MacAskill at last agreed, and offering to shake hands, as professional boxers do, before the fight began, he reduced the Frenchman's hand to pulp with a good squeeze. Hugh Miller tells a similar story of his cousin Walter and a strong Dutch sergeant from a transport lying in the Cromarty Firth. 'The strong Dutchman', he writes, 'stretched out his hand, and, on getting hold of Walter's, grasped it very hard. Walter saw his design, and returned the grasp with such overmastering firmness, that the hand became powerless within his. "Ah!" exclaimed the Dutchman, in his broken English, shaking his fingers, and blowing upon them, "me no try squeeze hand with you again; you very *very* strong man."' (*My Schools and Schoolmasters*, Chapter XX.)

Our islanders developed muscular strength in rowing and digging, with the result that men of only medium height and weight showed remarkable strength when the occasion called for it. The baker at Tarbert, the one and only baker of my boyhood, told me of an islander who once called at his shop for a half-boll of flour which the baker had laid out for him. The baker came forward to lift the load of five stones onto the islander's back, but the purchaser did not wait for him. He picked up the sack with one hand and walked out of the shop. The baker was so surprised that he followed the islander into the street and watched him from the end of the road, until he disappeared in the distance on his way to the boat. He had not stopped to rest nor to change hands. The islander in question, who was our island elder for as long as I remember, was only of middle height and few would have expected of him the feat of strength that astonished the worthy baker.

I have been thinking here only of the men, but the race that produced bone and brawn in its male members, did not overlook the other sex. Indeed in some families the women got away with the honours in both strength and stature. And some are still left, I am glad to say, to remind us of the rock from which they were hewn, and of the stalwarts, both men and women, of former days.

CHAPTER TWENTY-SIX

Herding

As the herding of cattle has gone out of fashion in Scarp, I am glad to have known this practice from personal experience.

In my youth herding was necessary. Once the seed was sown in the late spring, that is in the month of May, the cattle were driven daily to the common hill-pasture. As there was no wall or fence protecting the crops, crofting families, in rotation, gave a day to watch the beasts. Those families having no active lads or men, hired young lads for the occasion. Our duty was to keep an eye on the cattle and to prevent them wandering off and ultimately reaching the cultivated fields furthest away from the village.

In the late summer and autumn, when the cattle were left out all the time, they grazed on the western half of the island, far from the village, and did not require herding. This was the case even before our first fence was erected. I remember the erection of this fence. Its chief value was that it kept all the island's sheep at a safe distance while the crops were still in the ground.

A drystone wall built along the top of the crags and across the gullies above the village in my time did away with the necessity of herding, at least on a large scale, but the weather or an animal might knock some part of it down and cause trouble.

When herding, we used a small hut or booth with stone walls and a flat roof of large sods laid on rough wooden spars. As we were given tea and sugar and milk, as well as bannocks of oatcake, we made a fire in the open, preparing wood-shavings for kindling, using a pocket-knife, and selecting good dry peat from one of the peat stacks near us. As soon as the women came for the milking late in the evening, we could go home.

There is evidence that herding on a large scale was the rule on Scarp once upon a time. At several places the foundations of large booths, or shielings, can still be seen, while a few still retain enough of the stone wall to show the recesses or shelves where the milk basins were set out. I am aware of our island tradition that such shelves were used for the wooden milkpails left there with the Sunday milking, no milk being taken home on Sunday, but I am inclined to think they were, at some time or other, real shielings, where the younger women lived for some weeks in summer, milking and churning, and carrying out all the ordinary duties of a milkmaid.

There is also in more than one place the foundation of a turf wall which once enclosed a cattle pen. The word 'fold' is still used when referring by name to these places.

The cattle were driven at night into these folds. The one at the near end of the *Mol Mòr* must have been the last to be used in this way. Indeed I think I remember the time when this fold, still clearly marked, was so used.

Heifers were sent in summer across the Sound, where they roamed at will. The island's bull also spent the summer months there. Ferrying the cattle across the Sound was an exciting affair for both adults and children. The shortest route across the half-mile piece of water was always used. The cattle, securely roped by the horns, were driven into the sea from the long beach facing the centre of the Sound. When the bull's turn came, the excitement was intense, especially as it was usually caught and roped on the beach.

This method of ferrying is quite simple and safe in calm weather and when the tide is slack. The boat is rowed in the usual way, while a few men standing in the stern hold the ropes attached to the animals. At first the three or four animals may swim strongly behind the boat, but they must be closely watched, for at any moment they may decide that they have done enough, upon which they roll over on their sides, with their stomachs bulging above the surface of the water. Those watching the boat's progress from the shore can always tell by this bulge when an animal has stopped swimming. Its head must then be held above water, and as near to the boat as possible, while its inert mass is drawn along. When the other side is reached the ropes are removed and the animals show no reluctance to wade ashore.

Our cattle were of the Highland breed, with an occasional Ayrshire, or a black polled animal. Although not heavy milkers, the Highland cattle stood the conditions better than any other, it being easier, as I have heard it expressed, to feed three Highland milch-cows than one of any other breed.

At first our islanders provided their own bull, but in or about 1912 the Congested Districts Board undertook to send bulls on loan to outlying districts. The description, 'the Congested's bull', with the letter 'g' pronounced hard, as in 'guest', owing to Gaelic influence, was often heard in those days. I may add that the Board of Agriculture for Scotland, later known as the Department of Agriculture, continued this valuable assistance to our crofting communities, sending to the Outer Isles shorthorn bulls, for the sake of their beef, as well as Highland bulls.

For many years now, our island cattle have spent the summer and autumn months beyond the fence erected during my boyhood. This ensures the safety of the crops, but entails a great deal of labour on the part of our women, who are obliged to go long distances twice daily to do the milking. In my time our women carried on these occasions a creelful of fodder, the gathering of which took some time whether it consisted of grass plucked round the cultivated fields, or of weeds gathered in potato fields – chickweed for example – or of potato shaws which might be safely snipped off in late autumn when the crop was ripe. Each Saturday a double supply, involving a double journey, was carried, Sunday's fodder being left in large bags just inside the fence, or on a rock high enough to be out of reach of any animal passing by.

When the milch-cows were not found waiting at the usual rendezvous, the women set out to look for them and to bring them to the pen for milking. Many a late night has a woman's voice sounded among the hills as she called her charge by name. There were really two pens, our island cattle being divided into two herds for milking, the South Hamlet using one milking ground, and the North and Mid Hamlets the other. A curious point is that the two rendezvous changed over regularly, a herd using a pen for only one year and changing to the other pen the next year. It is interesting to learn that this segregation still takes place, even in such a small community, and that the time-honoured changeover, year by year, is still observed.

The improved transport facilities now enjoyed by our islanders have greatly lightened the labour associated with milking-time. As sacks of feedingstuff now arrive regularly on the island, the creelful of fodder and the weekend bag are things of the past. The milkmaid of today, I am told, merely throws a few handfuls of feedingstuff onto the clean grass in front of the cow she is about to milk. The round wooden stoup or milkpail, broad-based and tapering towards the top, with its narrow hoops and sheepskin cover, has given way to the light metal pail which can be carried in one's hand. But I hope that the moggans are still worn. The *mogan* – to give the Gaelic word, which according to its form must be original, while the Scots word is a derivative – is a short soleless stocking made of thick wool closely knitted and held in place by the big toe put through a single loop. It gives protection from the cold, while supplying all the advantages of bare feet on wet, muddy or slippery ground.

I need hardly say that anyone meeting our isleswomen returning from the milking in daylight will find his capacity for rich warm milk tested to the full. Once at least my father was caught in this way, and afterwards suffered for it; and I remember the visiting evangelist, Murdo MacLeod, having gone out early for a long stroll, playfully holding our milkmaids off with his walking-stick, as they pressed stoup after stoup upon him.

As mentioned earlier, there was a time when the whole of the island's livestock was sent to the other side of the Sound for summer pasture. When the milch-cows went, it was necessary for a woman from each croft to spend July and August at a shieling attending to the cattle, with the assistance of a few cowherds, to prepare the summer produce of butter and cheese.

This annual trek must have been a major event. There was to begin with the ferrying of the animals in the way described earlier, but on a larger scale. This was followed by the long journey to the shielings, the men carrying implements and tools, as well as material for repairing the summer booths, and the women looking after bedding, milk churns, cheese vats, and basins, as well as food and cooking utensils. There was more than one shieling site, the nearest being at the head of Loch Cravadale and known to this day as, *A' Bhuaile Dhubh*, or 'The Black Shieling', and another further away, behind the high hill that juts out into Loch Resort. As I have walked all the way from our short ferry to the head of this long loch, and vice versa, I know the rough nature of the moor beyond The Black Shieling, and can imagine the time taken and the fatigue endured in reaching the second shieling. The story is told of how one of our islanders, asked to say grace before the communal meal prepared on their arrival at this distant shieling, began by quoting the proverb: *Ruigidh each mall muileann* – 'A slow horse will reach the mill'. This is our Gaelic equivalent of the English proverb about the lame horse.

In my youth all the villages on the western seaboard of the parish to the north of us sent their cattle to some inland shieling for part of the summer. It so happened that two of these shieling groups were situated at no great distance from Luachair, the small village at the head of Loch Resort, where my aunt lived. Some of the girls crossed the intervening moor to pay an occasional visit and seemed pleased to exchange their turf huts, even for a few hours, for an ordinary dwellinghouse. They were bright and merry, and full of talk, and ready to tease the life out of any young man who came their way.

One day my eldest cousin there, named like myself after The Deacon, received a letter from one of the shielings. As he read it in silence his mother, much amused but slightly apprehensive, made a guess at the correspondent's identity, mentioning a girl whose forebears had once lived in the small village and who was distantly related to us. But my dear cousin, who has passed from the scene long ago, kept his secret as he pored over the shieling-girl's letter. At last he read aloud a passage his shieling friend had copied from her Gaelic Bible, which, I am sure, lay on the turf seat beside her heather couch. It was the famous passage from the Hebrew idyll known to us as The Book of Ruth :

Na h-iarr orm t'fhàgàil, no pilltinn o bhi 'gad leantuinn: oir ge b'e taobh a thèid thusa, thèid mise, agus far an gabh thusa tàmh, gabhaidh mise tàmh: is e do shluagh-sa mo shluagh-sa, agus do Dhia-sa mo Dhia-sa. Far am faigh thusa bàs, gheibh mise bàs, agus an sin adhlaicear mi. Gu'n deanadh an Tighearna mar sin ormsa, agus tuille mar an ceudna, ma chuireas ach am bàs dealachadh eadar mise agus thusa.

The English words, from the King James Bible, are:

Intreat me not to leave thee, or to return from following after thee: for whither thou goest, I will go; and where thou lodgest, I will lodge: thy people shall be my people, and thy God my God: Where thou diest, will I die, and there will I be buried: the

A fine view of thatched houses in Scarp, with Fladday Island and the hills of Lewis in the background. 'North Hamlet' can be seen near the shore, while washing dries beside the MacInnes home in the foreground. (R.M. Adam, July 1937.)

The same house today, showing the roof construction described in Chapter 16: couples meet at a ridge-pole, there are two horizontal purlins, and light laths support the turf and thatch covering. Old anchor-stones lie on the wallhead. A 'tin shed' had replaced the stone peat shed of 1937. (July 1994.)

Extensive cultivation at the north end of the village. A wall and gate, built to keep animals away from the growing crops, is at the bottom right. The gate was on a steep path to one of the milking grounds of Scarp. (R.M. Adam, July 1937.)

Annie Duncan, an Aberdonian cousin of the author, poses in Scarp with a willow creel containing milkpail and fodder for the cow. She wears stockings and shoes rather than 'moggans', and knits a sock as she goes along. (Marjory Duncan, 1930.)

Viewed from the south, *Clach a' Chomharra*—the asbestos rock mentioned in Chapter 1 and described in the note on Geology—with its perched boulder, lies just above the centre of the picture. (May 1994.)

The granite-gneiss boulder left on *Clach a' Chomharra* by retreating glaciers some 20,000 years ago. A hammer and rucksack give it scale. The mottled surface of the fibrous asbestos rock can be seen in the foreground. (May 1994.)

Scarp men busy sheep-shearing on Fladday Island. In those days the sheep's legs were tied to facilitate the work. (R.M. Adam, July 1937.)

A Blackface ram, with fine horns and a very black face, at the fank in Scarp. (August 1994.)

A twelve-week-old lamb stoically awaits its fate—to be dipped then weaned from its mother. (August 1994.)

A strong Scarpman carries a bag of peat to the boat on Fladday Island. The peat are carefully packed to protect the carrier's back. The mouth of Loch Resort lies beyond *Greine Sgeir* towards the left of the picture. (R.M. Adam, July 1937.)

A *turskar* or peat-iron, used in Scarp until 1970. The iron head is old, but the wooden shaft and step had been renewed. The implement needs to be 'conditioned' before use, by soaking in water or standing it in a bog. (May 1994 photo.)

Two millstones, each thirty inches in diameter, lie in *Allt a' Mhuilinn*. The watermill had gone out of use by the mid-1800s. It would have had a horizontal waterwheel driving a vertical spindle to turn an upper stone—the lower one seen here. A third millstone stands in a nearby chamber. (July 1994.)

A rotary quern for grinding meal. Such a quern was still used in Scarp in the author's boyhood. (Two August 1994 photos, courtesy of The Highland Folk Museum, Kingussie.)

A 'knocking-stone' with wood pestle for pounding grain. The unlucky Hushinish stone of Chapter 22 may have been used like this, rather than as a font.

In 1934 a German inventor, Gerhardt Zucker, chose Scarp to demonstrate his Rocket Post, designed to carry mail across the Sound.

The experiment was a failure, for the rocket exploded. The despondent Zucker was comforted with tea in the mission-house.

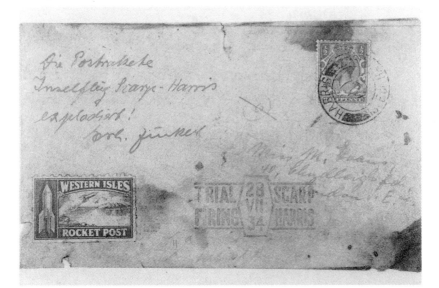

A scorched envelope from the rocket mail, with a halfpenny stamp, and a special stamp for the two shillings and six pence rocket fee. The inventor's German inscription says: 'The postal-rocket island-flight, Scarp—Harris, exploded! Gerh. Zucker'. The back is stamped: 'Damaged by first explosion at Scarp, Harris'.

A fank day in Scarp, when the flock was sorted out and dipped. The ewes were treated first and driven beyond the fence, then the lambs were dealt with. (August 1994.)

A lamb about to experience its first dipping. The Grazings Clerk, partly hidden here, records the details, while the other men lower it into the dip bath and help it on its way. The lambs were later released in the village for weaning. (August 1994.)

The rams are driven towards the jetty. Strong-willed, they are always ready to defy man and dog, so close attention is needed to keep the flock together. (August 1994.)

A boatload of rams prepares to leave for Fladday Island, where they will remain until late November. Winter storms can complicate their return to Scarp. (August 1994.)

Two fine Scarpmen of the past: (left) *Aonghas Ruadh*, Angus MacInnes (1843-1936) , the author's uncle, dressed for the Manish Communion; (right) Norman MacInnes (1839-1920), the island's merchant, known as *An Rìgh*, or 'The King', features in Chapters 6 and 25.

Luachair, at the head of Loch Resort, where two Scarp families settled in 1885. The author spent boyhood holidays there. On Census night 1891 seventeen people shared four rooms in the two thatched houses. (Alasdair Alpin MacGregor photo, circa 1945-49, with permission of The Scottish Ethnological Archive.)

Amhuinnsuidhe Castle, tenanted by J.M. Barrie for several weeks in 1912, was built in 1864-67 for Lord and Lady Dunmore. On Census night 1891 *Fionn Castle*—as it was then called—was occupied by two housemaids, sharing sixty-five rooms! (November 1993.)

One of the knots at the Castle doorway. A Scarp boy was asked if he could untie them! (November 1993.)

In 1912 J.M. Barrie scratched his initials on a window of The Harris Hotel, at that time owned by the North Harris Estate and run by the Cameron family. (November 1993.)

'Our islanders developed muscular strength in rowing and digging...' (Chapter 25). A fine illustration showing the hard physical effort of rowing a heavy boat down the Sound, sometimes against wind and tide. (1930s photograph.)

A unique 'briefcase mail' was introduced when the island Post Office closed in 1969. (Left) The ferryman accepts a locked postal briefcase in Scarp, and (right) the official postman carries the Scarp mailbag ashore at Hushinish. (Copyright: Bill Lucas, Hebridean Press Service, Stornoway.)

Lord do so to me, and more also, if ought but death part thee and me.

And I still remember my aunt's great glee as she cried *A 'sì! 'S i Mairi Iseabail a th'ann!* – 'Ah yes! It is Mairi Iseabail!'

Island Flora

Some of the flowers which grow on the Scarp machair have already been mentioned. The sheep unfortunately nibble the machair bare, as long as they are left free to roam about the village, and it only receives its rich floral mantle after these animals are driven away to the hills and moorland beyond the protective iron fence. The most conspicuous flower growing here is the early purple orchid.

Even in spring the lesser celandine may be seen in large numbers in the kailyards and neighbouring ditches, this small golden flower being the earliest island flower, that is, if we omit the mountain daisy, which I have seen in the month of December. In the spring too, the yellow primrose blooms, first in sheltered corners and crannies of the foothills and later in fragrant clusters on the grassy slopes and ledges of the hills overlooking the village. What a picture those clusters make, the essence and fluorescence of the spring in all its sweetness and freshness! The sweet violet is usually found near the primrose, growing in single blossoms, thinly distributed, and therefore not seen from a distance. The dog-rose or briar has flourished for many years at the foot of a cliff-like rise above North Hamlet, as if guarding the entrance to the small caves and passages formed by the vast boulders that have fallen from this steep rock face. In a similar position beyond South Hamlet, but more difficult to reach, the sweet-scented honeysuckle grows.

The lesser celandine is followed by the marsh marigold, which is larger and stronger and truly golden in its rich colour. Forget-me-nots hide modestly round the base of some large stones, and the scarlet poppy takes possession of any of the potato fields of The Croft left uncultivated for a season. So far as I remember, this flower grows only there. In the same way, the ox-eye daisy grew only in a corner of the schoolhouse garden, where they were plentiful and reached a great height.

The dandelion, with the pretty Gaelic name, *Beàrnan Brìde*, or 'Bride's-notched-one', from its scalloped leaves, and probably taking its name from St. Bride's festival at Candlemas – compare Michaelmas daisy – rather than from the saint herself, had a good grip on most parts of the grassy ground; but having been told in childhood that it was deadly poison, I have never liked this flower. My father sometimes made dandelion tea when he needed medicine, but even this has not reconciled me to it. On cultivated ground behind the mission-house grew both white and red clover, an abundance of which was thought to presage a good harvest.

In the autumn the yellow iris proudly crowned the tall flags that stood erect in many a ditch and drain. Sea-pinks, poised on their green cushion, could be seen on the rocky shores, for example near the school and along our southern coast as far as the *Mol Mòr* islet, where those same cushions were a welcome relief to bare feet pricked and stung by the goat's-beard lichen covering so much of this islet's rocky surface.

On the island's hills and moors grew a large variety of plants and flowers, including butterwort, wood sorrel, wild pansies, ragged robins, carl-doddies or ribwort, bog-asphodel, bladder campion, bluebells (or harebells), and the conspicuous bog-cotton with the lovely Gaelic name, *canach an t-slèibhe*, or 'moor canach'. *Cho geal ri canach an t-slèibhe* – 'As white as moor canach' – was an expression often heard in conversation among our seniors.

Waterlilies, though growing so profusely in other parts of Harris, were absent from our lochs – at least I cannot recall any. Ferns were only found in rare groups, at ground level under overhanging rock, but in spite of their paucity I remember a royal fern being brought proudly home.

Watercress, which the schoolmaster himself had sown soon after he came to the island, grew in slow-running watercourses above Mid Hamlet, but only he himself ever harvested it.

Ours was a treeless island. The nearest approach to a tree was seen in the tall bushes which grew on the islands in the loch that lay between the two ranges of hills. Trees can nevertheless grow on Scarp. Some years ago a native of the island planted several young sycamore trees, both in front of and behind his home. These have grown in a normal healthy way and have now reached an imposing size.

Heather of course abounded, only one sort being so scarce as to have any interest for us. This was white heather, which grew in very small quantities in a few places and was therefore difficult to find. On a fold day, as we often called the day of a sheep-gathering, one of the lads scouring the topmost heights sometimes brought in a few sprigs of white heather, in which all present then showed a keen interest.

In the autumn when we were young, we always had at least two trips to pick blaeberries, the only edible berries growing on the island. I well remember these trips, the first one being to, *A' Chlach Mhòr*, or The Big Stone, as we called a certain rock covered with heather and grass and easily climbed on the nearer side. This site was apparently left unvisited by sheep, with the result that the blaeberry plants escaped the fate of flowers and plants growing in the path of sheep grazing on machair or moor. As a rule we only found a mere handful of berries on this rock, but so long as we could return home with our lips and tongue dyed a purple colour we felt satisfied. The second trip was longer, passing by The Big Stone and climbing the heathery hill-breast above it until we came to The Big Slope, or as we sometimes called it, The Big Slope of Blaeberries. Here the plants and berries were larger than those of The Big Stone, the soil being deeper, and at the right season a fair number of berries were found. We had two or three other patches of blaeberry ground on the island, but I was not so familiar with these. Blaeberries growing among thick heather are easily missed. We had to get down on our hands and knees at the first sign of a blaeberry plant, light green in colour, and push the heather aside to expose the berries, which often grew low on the plant.

It is of some interest that we were always given an oatmeal 'lump' before setting out on those trips. This consisted of raw meal, with a liberal sprinkling of coarse crystal sugar, mixed with a little water. I feel quite sure this was the 'lump' used by native Hebrideans when travelling long distances from their homes, as well as by shepherds and drovers during their long trips to Falkirk and Carlisle. When it was time for a meal, they merely sat down by a burn or a stream, and mixed some oatmeal with water from the burn, kneading it into a lump, or *cnap* as we called it. If they could add a little *aqua-vitae*, the lump would serve the double purpose of a meal and a stimulant. At any rate, we children enjoyed the *cnap* as we nibbled at it, sitting in the heather, and why should strong healthy men not exist on it for several days?

No brambles grew on Scarp, the nearest being on the north side of the long herring-loch, Loch Resort. An alarming boyhood adventure has fixed this place indelibly in my memory. Once when my big cousin and I crossed over by boat to pull brambles, I left him after a while and pulled the anchored boat towards me so that I might board it alone. Having given it a gentle push before jumping, I suddenly remembered that I had my cousin's watch in my vest pocket. I dared not jump in case the watch was smashed against the boat's gunwale, but instead, shouted for help. Extended to full length as I soon was, but still holding on to the boat, I could see my cousin race over the big boulders to my aid. When he reached me he quickly caught the boat's land-rope, not me, and pulled it tight. The sudden jerk had the effect of throwing me off my balance, and plunging one of my feet into the water, but this partial wetting and a good fright was all my escapade cost me.

Island Fauna

Compared with some of the islands of the Inner Hebrides, which are less exposed and have more vegetation, including woods, our island was poor in its birdlife. On the other hand, in summer it was rich in the matter of landbirds compared with St Kilda, where I saw only one small bird during several hours ashore there two years before the island was evacuated. This was the St Kilda wren, found only on that island and resembling our tiny brown wren in its movements. But compared to Scarp, St Kilda had a prolific seabird population, both in numbers and diversity.

When I recall the large number of nests we discovered each spring, most of them found in the foothills, I realise that we had a large variety of small birds, though not in large numbers, the wheatear, with its hard sharp call, being the most conspicuous. The wheatear's markings are like those of the wagtail, which we also had, but the wagtail is larger, and walks instead of hopping like most small birds. Sparrows, mavises, and starlings were plentiful, finches, blackbirds and wrens but rare.

Our seniors, who seemed to have a hereditary love for small birds, discouraged us from harming them. When we went nest-hunting in the evening or on a Saturday, any adult seeing us was sure to caution us and even threaten us with dire penalties if we harried any bird's nest. The greatest deterrent, however, lay in the rhyme we learned when very young; a translation of this childhood rhyme follows the Gaelic version:

> *Big, big, bigean,*
> *Cò chreach mo neadan?*
> *Mas e duine beag e,*
> *Cuiridh mi le creig e,*
> *Mas e duine mòr e,*
> *Bogaidh mi san lòn e,*
> *Mas e duine beag gun chiall gun nàir' e,*
> *Gun gleidheadh Dia d' a mhàthair fhèin e.*

> Chirpie! Chirpie!
> Who robbed my nestie?
> If he be a little man,
> O'er a crag I'll cast him;

If he be a big man,
In a bog I'll thrust him;
But if he be a senseless man,
To his own mother home I'll send him.

I used to wonder, and other boys no doubt did the same, to which of the three categories we belonged, that is to say from the bird's point of view.

The larger landbirds were few, at least in numbers. Hoodie crows were common all the year round, while rooks were sometimes seen in winter. Ravens, with their raucous cry, frequented the heights, keeping a sharp lookout for a carcass on which to feed. A silent eagle, flying high, might sometimes be seen on the same heights, but the broad-winged buzzard, which has noticeably increased in the Outer Isles within recent years, was rare.

While I was still quite young, an owl was caught by some lads, who brought it to our house. It was released in the kitchen and after flying round the room, it perched on a high shelf in a corner of the room, where it sat motionless, solemnly surveying us – it was quite uncanny. In a good summer, the cuckoo could be heard across the Sound, but I am told it has also been heard in Scarp, presumably when the island enjoyed an exceptionally good summer. Pigeons were inconspicuous, those on the island preferring the rocky coastline far from the village, where a creek is known as Pigeons' Creek. There were no game-birds, though once as a boy with my father on one of his Saturday outings, we heard on The Big Blaeberry Slope the crowing of a moorcock, or grousecock, which my father at once recognised. Other parts of our parish, even as near as Hushinish, are familiar with the golden plover, with the short warning call that has given it the Gaelic name, *Feadag*, or 'Whistler'.

Living on an island, we naturally took notice of the seabirds and shorebirds that shared our isolation and our perils. Waders, though not numerous, were sometimes seen feeding quietly on one of the beaches. When home on holiday some years ago, I surprised a flock of small waders on the shore of our main harbour, where the boats were drawn up. They flew off silently as if going out to sea, but soon wheeled round and alighted on another part of the coast.

Spring was the time to observe the birds as they came ashore to nest. The lively Arctic tern or sea-swallow, with its pretence of diving, was a regular visitor. It made no nest, but laid its spotted eggs, about the shape and size of a bantam's egg, on the fine shingle above high-water mark. The oystercatcher with its shrill cry, was a familiar bird. Its eggs were larger, and sharper at one end, than a tern's eggs, but were mottled in the same way. It is so much a shorebird that when an oystercatcher, or a small flock of them, is seen inland, our islanders regard the circumstance as a sure sign of stormy weather. As a matter of fact, the oystercatcher, except in the Outer Isles, frequents rivers and inland lochs, and might therefore be in its natural element sauntering in a field. One of the most delicious meals I have ever had, consisted of trout from an inland loch, and a fresh oystercatcher's egg from a nest by the side of the loch. *Faoileag-an-sgadain*, or the herring gull, and the great black-backed gull, laid their blotched eggs in grassy patches among the shore rocks. They were of course larger than an oystercatcher's eggs, but of the same shape.

As we knew of no deterrent where 'mottled eggs', as we called the whole class, were concerned, we had no hesitation in taking these eggs when they were found to be fresh. There are at least three ways of testing an egg to see whether it is fresh. Our invariable way in testing mottled eggs was to put them into one of the lochans, or small pools, abounding on islets and even on coastal rocks. Those that floated – not those that failed to float, as a certain modern writer says – were returned to the nest.

Three or four varieties of waterbirds might be seen near our shore, the diver spending the best part of a day fishing off shore and frequently submerging for long intervals. When the beautiful eider appeared in the Sound, well out of reach, it was a matter for comment, anyone seeing it drawing the attention of others to it. It is strange that Martin Martin only knew the eider by its Gaelic name, *Colc*, which he wrote phonetically as 'Colk'. Once at least I saw an eiderduck at very close quarters. This was in the late spring, when we had a spell of settled weather, otherwise a crew could scarcely have gone as far as the two small islands immediately behind Scarp, for seaweed. As we approached the landing-place, we saw a duck sitting on her nest near the water's edge. It was at once recognised as an eiderduck. The bird, which was not used to such intrusion, sat on, whereupon the oldest member of the crew – I was only a boy – seized the tiller, and was on the point of striking when the duck rose from the nest and flew off. We lost the fowl, but found three fresh eggs in the down-lined nest. They were larger than those of the domestic duck, and of a much deeper green colour. The mottled eggs and duck eggs found round our shores and across at Fladday, a favourite haunt of the tern, did not taste fishy and were as mild, or almost as mild, as a hen's egg. The main difference was that the white of the wild-bird's egg was of a bluish-white colour, and the yolk red rather than yellow.

Guillemots could often be seen in the water of the Sound when we were crossing to Hushinish. A rock at the back of Scarp is indeed named, *Geò nan langaid*, or Guillemots' Rock. The puffin, with its peculiar beak, deep and brightly coloured, did not nest on the island, but I have seen a captured puffin brought home alive by a fisherman.

Cormorants or shags, 'tumbling their wilkies' as they fished, or flying low over the surface of the Sound with outstretched necks, were common. Their eggs, white as any hen's egg, were not sought. This indeed was as well, for they nested on the inaccessible ledges of steep precipices. The cormorant and shag are surely unique among our seabirds in spreading out their wings to dry when they land, and in remaining in this position for hours on end.

Geese never landed near our village, but often passed over us in their migrations, flying lower than they do near towns and cities. Their flight was a fascinating sight. They could be followed for several miles after they had passed overhead, their formation changing repeatedly as they travelled onward.

But of all large birds, the gannet – the *Sùlaire* or the solan goose – was the most familiar to us. In season and out of season, this big strong-winged bird made our Sound its own and the waters of the Sound its habitual fishing ground. Soaring to a great height, it flew swiftly along, then suddenly checking its flight, swooped down with outspread wings to plunge headlong into the water, apparently closing its wings the moment its beak touched the water. When it emerged, its buoyancy almost shot it clean out of the water. Gannets were busiest in a storm, large numbers of sand-eels then being wrested from their sandy bed and becoming easy prey for the ever-watchful birds. Although it looks all-white with the exception of the wing tips, which are black, a close view reveals that the gannet's neck and head is not white, but ochre.

We had few wild animals on our island, none perhaps except the 'wild cat', or more correctly the feral cat, which was occasionally seen. This cat was a fierce brute which we feared exceedingly, often keeping a lookout for it when we played among the rocks near the shore.

Wild goats, with dark brown coats, browsing on the high hills we passed as we sailed up Loch Resort, added to the interest of such a trip, but we had none on Scarp.

The prolific rabbit, though numerous on the other side of the Sound, has never gained a foothold on Scarp.

Sea mammals were more conspicuous. Porpoises were often seen passing either up or down the Sound, giving the impression that they rolled along with the motion of large slow wheels. An occasional whale went blowing past, keeping well out, but once at least a school of small whales ran aground at our main harbour. I am not likely to forget the excitement and fear of that far-off day. Those of us at home at the time, hearing shouts, went to the door, when we heard someone say what we understood to be: 'So-and-so drowned!' the person named, as we thought, being a cousin of mine. We soon discovered, however, that what was said was: 'Whales on the shore!' a very different thing except in its vowel sounds. We were greatly alarmed, made the door fast, and awaited the outcome of the battle on the North Hamlet beach, as the men of the island attacked the stranded whales with any weapon upon which they could lay their hands. What was said to have driven the whales ashore in this way I do not now remember. It may have been a very low spring tide.

The Atlantic grey seal often appeared near our shores. It was however very watchful and sounded if anyone went near, reappearing after a considerable interval a great distance off. Once a cousin of mine, who lived in the house nearest the main harbour, found an all-white baby seal in the doorway early one morning. There had been an exceptionally high tide during the night.

At one time the men of Scarp carried out seal hunts on Gasker, using for the purpose a heavy wooden club still remembered by the name *slacan*. Martin Martin's account suggests that the seals on Gasker were caught with ropes fastened to the sea-tangle, but this presupposes a larger-scale seal hunt than our islanders would be likely to undertake.

I have left to the end, though not on the principle of, *gach dìleas gu deireadh*, or 'friends last', the common otter, known throughout our parish by the prosaic name, *a' bhiast dhubh*, or 'the black beast'. This provincial name accounts for a mistake I myself made as a boy. I still remember the amused smile playing on the face of the Ladies' teacher up the long herring-loch as I told him, during an expedition to some rabbit-warrens, that 'the black beast' had been shot by one of our islanders, whom I named. This no doubt was true, the mistake being that I thought 'the black beast' was the devil. 'Yes!' I assured him, 'the black beast' had been shot, and there was nothing to fear now!

The otter is commonly of a tawny or dull brown colour, rather than black. That was the colour of the otter celebrated in a humorous song by Neil Morrison, the Pabbay bard, when he found it in his smearing shed: *Am beathach grànda lachdunn 's e cho fada ri slat-iasgaich*, or 'The ugly, tawny beast, as long as a fishing-rod'. Seen at sea with its tail at full stretch as it swims along, it certainly looks a considerable length. This has suggested to some observers that the so-called Loch Ness Monster is really an otter. As it happens, I myself once saw a pair of otters cross the River Ness below Bona Ferry, at the old Bona Ford. As they swam with the one closely behind the other, frequently submerging simultaneously, they gave the impression of something unusual, but they would have been quite inconspicuous out in the loch itself and would have attracted little attention. Those I saw ultimately clambered out of the river, the one still following the other closely, and disappeared through a hedge into the duckpond on the north side of the river at that point.

As is well known, the otter, in spite of its inelegant gait when seen ashore, can cover long stretches of land to reach a stream, and if caught will show fight and give anyone who meddles with it a nasty bite. It is an interesting animal and its movements are well worth watching, whether it be on land or in the water, and whether its colour be tawny or black.

Standing one day with a few of our islanders at *Am Port a Tuath*, or 'The North Port', at Hushinish, I saw an otter swimming towards the shore, and drew attention to it. One of the party at once said that it was bringing ashore something which it could not deal with at sea. This proved to be right. As soon as it scrambled onto the slippery rocks, which it did with little difficulty in spite of a heavy swell, we saw that it had a large flounder in its mouth. After it had taken cover we searched for our friend 'the black beast', but could find no trace of it.

The usual Gaelic name for an otter is *dòbhran*, as used in one of our best known songs, a lullaby. The better name, *dobhar-chù*, or literally 'water-dog', is, however, known on Scarp, the tradition being that our first public schoolmaster sometimes told a pupil that he was, *cho rag ris an dobhar-chù* – 'as perverse as the otter'.

The Mainland of Harris, Part 1

The story of Scarp would be incomplete without some account of the rest of the parish, at least of our end of it.

Just as the largest of the Orkney Islands is known as the Mainland of Orkney, the undivided portion of our parish, from which we were only separated by a narrow sound, was always referred to as *An Tir Mhòr*, or 'The Mainland', the custom showing how conscious we were of our isolation and of the restrictions imposed on those living on an island. I have heard a young boy or girl told, on setting foot for the first time across the Sound, 'You are now on the Mainland!'

While still a young boy, I spent the better part of a day with my brother Arthur at Hushinish, before anyone came to live there. My brother brought his bathing pants, and took me to a sandy cove facing south and known as *Tràigh Shanndagaigh*, or 'Sandy Bay Beach', where I watched him swim. It is a delightful place, with golden sand, and unlike *Tràigh Hùisinis*, or 'Hushinish Big Beach', is sheltered by a rock face on the west side.

A couple of miles further on was Bedersaig, the nearest of the settlements made in 1885, where two crofters' families lived. Boys paying a visit to such a place needed food and I still remember rabbit being fried for our tea while our host entertained us with his lively talk. We afterwards went with a big lad to look for rabbits and wanted to know his dog's name, but he would only say its name was *Bi-gu-math-ris*, or 'Be-good-to-it', which was a fine example of the evasive answer so common in Gaelic folktales and generally known as the retort courteous.

Further on, but much further from the road and out of sight, was the second settlement, Govig, also on a narrow bay, and consisting of three families. The modern houses built there since my boyhood can, however, be seen from the road.

Before I ever crossed the marshy ground to that settlement, I had paid my first visit to the next village, Amhuinnsuidhe, five miles from the long ferry. This village was different from anything I had seen or even conceived, for here the owner of the estate had built a castle, and here the estate workers lived. How old I was I cannot definitely say, but as my father had some business there and the weather was good, he took my sister Rachel and me with him. Here were no thatched houses, but two rows of modern dwellinghouses. A large house for the ghillies employed during the fishing and shooting seasons was above the nearer row, and the massive walls of the castle were visible beyond an arched gate at the far end of the other row, where the stables also were. Here too were real roads.

There was a small school, housed in a long building, apparently of wood, with both roof and walls covered with tarred felt. A Scarp girl who had been a pupil-teacher in our island school, was schoolmistress, and although it was but a side-school, she had about thirty pupils.

As my father's visit was connected with the school, he directed us to a row of buildings and asked us to wait for him at the coachman's house. Instead of keeping to the road we cut across to the end of the nearest house and passed in front of it. I well remember that moment. There was a noise like thunder and in a moment all the children poured out of the house. We stopped and stared at them. The youngest boy, standing with his legs wide apart, was the first to speak, and he asked the questions: Where had we come from? Whose children were we? After answering him and thus breaking the ice, we were bold enough to ask for the coachman's house and were told how to find it.

Subsequent visits, especially during 'the season', which began early in July and lasted until mid-October, showed what a busy hive this place could be. Then the worthy blacksmith could be seen at his forge, with his two eldest sons assisting him. What a fascination it was to watch him hold a piece of red-hot iron on the anvil while his sons hammered it.

Another centre of interest was the stable, with its harness-room, where pony harness was kept and cleaned. There were large grain boxes upon which we could sit. The coachman had three sons who helped him during the season. As no cars were used, the ladies and gentlemen who went fishing or stalking rode along the glens of the deer-forest, to a point as near their destination for the day as possible, with the ghillies in attendance. When the time for returning drew near, a sharp lookout was kept from the archway near the stable, and as soon as a pony with rider appeared on the road beyond the castle, the coachman hurried out in order to meet them at the front door of the castle, and lead the pony back to the stable.

The proprietor's yacht, a large steam yacht with a golden eagle as figurehead, made a fine picture in the middle of the round sea loch. This loch, with its narrow entrance, must have called for watchfulness and skill when bringing the yacht in. A small steamer used for daily trips to the shopping centre, twelve miles away, also anchored there, as well as a small steam launch which looked odd with its short funnel.

The castle was a modern building of considerable height, occupying a small site. The only piece of carving took the form of a thick rope, knotted at both ends, above the main entrance. Boys took a great fancy to this rope. I remember an island boy of my own age being asked by his uncle, who lived at the other side of the loch, if he could untie the knots on the castle rope. After considering for a while, the boy said quite seriously, 'Well, no!'

The solitary house seen on the other side of Loch Leosavay, the name of which means 'Bright Bay', belonged to the family of one of our island 'emigrants' of 1885, and was therefore often visited by us in spite of a difficult walk round the end of the loch, and the crossing of a stream by means of wide stepping-stones. This place had a peculiar name, being called 'The Blind Man's Creek', after a native of an island on the east coast of the parish, who was blind and once lived there. The story goes that a crew from Scarp, having put in here one dark night, were surprised to hear what sounded like hammering on the shore. On investigating the matter, they found the blind man busy fixing a mast-step in his boat, all in the dark.

As children we were always glad of an opportunity of visiting the proprietor's seat, especially during the busy shooting season. We sometimes went with cockerels, for example, getting a shilling each for them at the castle. My mother was in the habit of ordering roast-dripping from the castle cook. Once when it arrived, we found some apples thrust into it by a thoughtful housekeeper or cook, with the result that to this day I associate apples with dripping. I thought they grew in the dripping!

Once or twice during the season the yacht visited the Sound of Scarp, where it remained while a party went ashore opposite the village to shoot rabbits. When the shooting party was a small one, and the weather was favourable, the steam launch came instead of the yacht. On these rare occasions, a pair of rabbits was landed for each family on the island before the yacht or launch departed. The boys meantime longed to get across the Sound to pick up the empty cartridge-cases thrown away by the sportsmen.

When I had reached my teens, my mother and I were shown over the castle by the housekeeper, who startled me by taking a long broom and with one sweep setting all the bells in the castle ringing.

Visits to the homes of the estate workers, who included the head gamekeeper, joiner, and gardener, as well as those already mentioned, made us familiar with the names of those staying at the castle during the shooting season, whether members of the proprietor's family or his guests. An islander who had served as ghillie for many seasons liked to go over the names: Packe, Farquhar, Cadogan, as well as Scott.

When the proprietor did not come for the season, he sometimes let the fishing. In this way he unconsciously put his Highland seat on the literary map, the castle being occupied by James M. Barrie for six weeks or more during the summer of 1912. Three other well-known authors, namely Anthony Hope (Hawkins), E. V. Lucas, and A. E. W. Mason, were among Barrie's first guests there. Barrie was to become a baronet the following year.

It is difficult to say how much of the play *Mary Rose* was inspired by that visit. The theme had apparently been noted by him prior to the visit, but it is certain that when he wrote it after the First World War, the recollection of his visit gave to the theme a form it would not otherwise have had. As the years went by, he himself seems to have associated the play, in its conception as well as its form, with this Hebridean visit, referring to the Outer Hebrides in the Dedication to *Peter Pan*, as 'the place where we caught Mary Rose'. *Peter Pan*, although produced in London as early as 1904, was not published until 1928, and the Dedication belongs to the latter date.

The whole of Act II of *Mary Rose* – first performed in 1920 – takes place on an island in the Outer Hebrides. This island has been identified as the nearest of the islets on the big freshwater loch named Loch Voshimid on the Ordnance Survey map, eight miles from the village and castle of Amhuinnsuidhe, and it is now sometimes referred to as 'Mary Rose's Island'.

I have some doubts about this. For one thing it is too small. Mary Rose's mother described it in Act I as an island of six acres, with quite a number of trees – Scotch firs and rowans – and a pool with a stream flowing out of it. It also had hillocks and a glade, while whins and bracken are added in Act II. It is true that in Act II, only two trees are mentioned, a fir and a rowan, but even in Act II the incidents presented require a larger island. The three other islets in the loch are smaller, and there is no sign of 'the greater island of which this might be but a stone cast into the sea by some giant hand'. It does have a cluster of rowan trees at one end, and this, I believe, is the reason for identifying it with the island from which Mary Rose disappeared so mysteriously on two occasions. Barrie's reference to the sea, in the quotation just given from Act II, suggests, rather, that he may have been thinking of one of the islands in the long sea loch which almost cuts Harris in two, and which he could see from the castle. It would, however, be as easy for him to invent an island for his purpose, as it was to invent a name for it, and the attempt to locate 'Mary Rose's Island' may fail just as surely as if it had disappeared with her. [*Note*: But see comments on this in the Appendix.]

The weird stories told by Cameron, the ghillie, in Act II, creating such an eerie atmosphere, are the fruit of Barrie's fertile imagination and should not be attributed to Hebridean lore, as some of his biographers have done. The play, on the other hand, has invested 'Mary Rose's Island' with an air of mystery; so much so that the appearance of a hiker on the islet, after swimming out to it, gave rise to rumours of some unearthly visitant being seen there! As the head gamekeeper pointed out to me, the name of the ghillie in the play was probably suggested by the name of the Tarbert hotel keeper or his sons. Mr Cameron's hotel – at that time closely associated with the castle – was no doubt the prototype of the Inn mentioned in the play. Mary Rose and her parents during her childhood visit, and she and Simon after their marriage, were represented as staying at an Inn, and not at a castle, or even a shooting lodge.

For trout and salmon fishing only a few ghillies were needed, four local men being, I think, used during Barrie's visit, in addition to Johnnie MacKay, of Scourie, Sutherland, who attended on Michael, one of the Llewelyn Davies lads. The estate factor was responsible for the local ghillies' hire, but Barrie, thoughtful and generous, as well as whimsical and inventive, walked along to the ghillies' house the morning he left and presented to each of them a cheque, as a personal gift.

CHAPTER THIRTY

The Mainland of Harris, Part 2

At the time the bells of Amhuinnsuidhe Castle startled me there was no conveyance to the shopping centre at Tarbert, twelve miles further on, for which my mother and I were making on that occasion. There was, however, a road all the way from Amhuinnsuidhe. It was summer, and we walked leisurely. The private telephone line, connecting the castle to the factor's office at our destination, kept us company.

The first novelty encountered was the deer-park at Cliasmol, with its high fence, where four Scarp families have since then settled. When we reached Meavaig, or 'Narrow Bay' – so called by the Norsemen – we descended to the side of the bay, opposite a gamekeeper's house, and waited for the gamekeeper to ferry us across, which he did. This saved us a long walk round the end of the bay. Today there is a colony of seven or eight crofters where we waited for the boat to come over. They were transferred there from another village in 1919, at the same time as our islanders got the deer-park. The large number of old lazybeds, many of them heather-grown as well as grass-grown, on both sides of the road above this new settlement, shows that intensive cultivation was carried on here at one time.

After a rest in the gamekeeper's house, we climbed up to the road, which is both high and steep at this point, and walked on until we reached a solitary house below the road, where my mother had decided beforehand to spend the night. The owner of the house was one of those evacuated from Scarp in 1885 and settled on Soay Island, in the middle of the long and wide sea loch which lay on our right during the whole of the two days' walk. After spending three years on Soay, the crofter moved to this spot, where he was obliged to reclaim the ground for cultivation on the lazybed system. This was a convenient halfway house, and those of the family still left, and living in a modern house near the site of the old thatched house, remember large numbers of people passing a night with them. Today motorcars and motorbuses pass and re-pass on the road above the house. There is now no need for such hospitality as my mother and I received that far-off night at *Bun-na-Gile*, or 'Gorge Foot', as the place is called; although 'Peat Garth' or 'Shore Garth' – both names being known – would be more precise, the narrow gorge to which the accepted name applies being several hundred yards further west.

The old means of travel, namely on one's own legs, made a journey such as we undertook a real social occasion. Next day my mother and I set out on foot as before, and soon reached the nearest hamlet, Bunavoneadar, if a single house on each side of the road can be described as a hamlet. We called at both houses, receiving a great welcome in each, as we did in the other roadside houses around the bay here – a much wider bay than the one over which we were ferried the previous day.

Two years later, in 1904, this bay became a busy whaling station at which many men from our parish, including a few from our island, found employment. The whalers, three I think in number, and manned by Norwegians, were sometimes seen by us as they returned from the hunting ground around St Kilda with their 'kill' of two or three whales in tow. There was only one objection to this successful industry, namely the smell that made the long walk or drive round the end of the bay unpleasant. J. M. Barrie must have known this smell, for he makes Mr Morland say at the beginning of *Mary Rose*, 'There is a whaling station'. On the face of it this is an unnecessary remark, but one that surely points to the recollection of some unusual personal experience. The whaling station operated for a number of years, both before and after the First World War, eventually closing down in 1925. It reopened for a short period between 1949 and 1951. A whalebone arch was for many years a conspicuous object at the roadside, where the main gate had been.

My first visit to Tarbert, the largest settlement in the parish, was full of interest. Staying at least two nights, my mother, who seemed to know everyone, took me to a number of houses. We must also have visited most of the shops, although I remember only one distinctly. Of that shop I have a vivid recollection, for it belonged to a little old lady who had a parrot as her constant companion in the shop. A display of coloured beads on the counter showed where the beads so much loved by our island girls came from. There was also a heap of spectacles on the counter, reminding me of the story in our school reader of *Moses at the Fair*, from Goldsmith's *Vicar of Wakefield*, and of his foolish investment in a gross of green spectacles. My mother bought a pair of spectacles, for I think a shilling, and afterwards maintained that they would suit anyone.

This then, was the famous shopping centre to which Scarp boats came for provisions. Here were the carding mill which made the long rolls of wool sometimes seen on our island, the factor's house, doctor's house, post office and large hotel. Although many of the houses on the west side of the village were then thatched, those on the east side, where the shops were, were either slated or had roofs of tarred felt. Many large private houses were afterwards built on the west side of the narrow isthmus which gives Tarbert its name, and within recent years high sharp-roofed council houses have been built there. The school was also on the west side, but the church of our own denomination was hidden in a hollow beyond the pier in the East Loch, near the water. The church and manse of another denomination had a commanding site at the eastern end of the village, overlooking the road leading to the pier at which passengers and goods were landed from the mail-boat and the Glasgow cargo-boats.

In my youth, and for many years after, a long boat journey was necessary when supplies were needed for our island. There was a small shop on Scarp, but even when our shopkeeper supplied the islanders with meal and flour, it was necessary to make the sea journey to Tarbert, seventeen miles away, to bring it home. When a dispatch of lobsters was ready for Billingsgate, the boxes were taken by sea to the same place. It was our nearest port. To find a crew preparing for such a trip was an event on our island. As such trips were infrequent, those who made up the crew were overburdened with the odds and ends they were asked to bring back. The return of the boat was eagerly awaited. How often have I sat at the south end of Scarp in the gathering darkness, watching the extreme point of Hushinish for the returning boat. When the boat appeared, the cry went up: *Tha i air tighinn am fianais!* – 'It has come into sight!' – and the news soon spread throughout the village. In winter the returning boat might reach our shores unnoticed, but the crew usually gave a warning shout or whistle as they came abreast of the village.

In my early youth Scarp had no regular postal service and we, therefore, depended on anyone going to the shopping centre, whether on foot or by boat, to post letters for us, and bring back any that might be kept for us at the Tarbert post office. However, in 1899 a weekly postal service began. A man who lived in Tarbert brought our mail on horseback to Amhuinnsuidhe, where the road ended. He walked the rest of the way to our short ferry. A large wooden letterbox with a zinc roof was set up in a sheltered hollow behind the banks of bent-grass, so that our mail, both incoming and outgoing, could be left there safely.

After four years our postman unfortunately lost his horse, which fell on the road under him, and as he could not continue the service, a man who had returned to the parish from Canada was appointed. The new postman soon got a pony and trap, but for five years he was obliged to make the difficult five mile journey from Amhuinnsuidhe to our Scarp letterbox on foot. In good weather he was usually met at the ferry, and I well remember his perspiring figure as he sat in his shirt-sleeves on the grass, transacting business with our island postmaster.

In 1908 a supernumerary was appointed to meet the postman at Amhuinnsuidhe, to bring our growing volume of mail on his back to the short ferry, returning to Amhuinnsuidhe with any outward mail before the postman left for Tarbert the next day. Anyone acquainted with our climate will readily believe that the foot postman, living at Hushinish and making four journeys in two days, got many a drenching. I once heard his wife complain that he brought home to her every drop of rain that fell from the skies.

I often travelled in the postman's gig. A most genial man, with a strong sense of responsibility, he was good company on the long winding road. Although he often urged his horse on, he was careful not to overdrive it. Both he and his passengers got out at the steepest parts of the road and walked. The greatest nuisance was the number of gates, every one of which had to be opened and carefully closed again. A wide grid fixed in the road over a deep cavity now serves the purpose, holding up sheep as effectively as any gate, and allowing cars to proceed without stopping.

When a road was at last made in 1925 along the five-mile track to Hushinish, and the regular postman was succeeded in 1926 by his supernumerary, the latter was able to use a motor-van for the whole distance. This speeded up the island's mail considerably, and gave travellers a faster conveyance than anything known before then.

This road and the increase in motorbuses and lorries solved Scarp's greatest transport problem. Our islanders were however not satisfied until, in 1937, an extension of the road was built across the Hushinish machair to the long ferry.

For many years now – since the summer of 1930 – there has been a post office on the island, and in September 1947 a new link was established with the island, when a submarine cable was laid down and a telephone service provided. There is also a mail service three times a week.

Our islanders had for long been pressing for a jetty at the Hushinish end of the long ferry, a concrete jetty having been constructed at the Scarp end in the late 1930s. The Member of Parliament for the Western Isles loyally kept the matter before the Secretary of State for Scotland. At last in 1962 work began on the construction of the long-awaited Hushinish jetty. It was ready for use in the autumn of the same year. It has been built in the small bay, with a road leading down to it from the wooden shed used as a store by our islanders.

The isolated nature of Scarp has sometimes drawn public attention to it. This was the case in the summer of 1934, when a young mother gave birth to a baby girl on the island, but had to be removed by road to Stornoway hospital, a distance of nearly fifty miles, before she safely gave birth to the first baby's twin sister. The children, though twins, were thus born in different counties.

It is not surprising then, that when in 1934 a young German technician, Herr Zucker, supported by a London stamp-dealer, Herr Dombrowski, received permission to experiment with a Rocket Post, he should choose Scarp for the experiment. A postal dispatch of letters was used for the purpose, each letter having a special stamp in addition to the ordinary postage stamp. The special stamp, oblong in shape, had the words 'Western Isles Rocket Post' on it. On the left was the picture of a rocket standing upright, while the centre of the stamp had a design showing a rocket in flight over water. Each envelope was stamped 'Trial Firing, 28.VII.34, Scarp-Harris'. Although no value was shown on the special stamp, a 'rocket fee' of half-a-crown was charged for each letter. The experiment was a failure. When fired, the rocket exploded, scattering the letters over the beach from which it was to be launched.

EDITOR'S NOTE

The author concluded his manuscript here, by expressing a hope that his *Memories of Scarp* would bridge the Sound more effectively than Herr Zucker's rocket had done!

The last Scarp missionary died in September 1966. The remaining islanders and the author lobbied strongly for a successor to be appointed, but that was not to be. The population had by then fallen to no more than thirty souls.

Scarp school closed in June 1967. The author travelled from Edinburgh to take part in that – for him – poignant occasion.

The last of the settled population left the island in December 1971. This was the end of an era for Scarp, but not the end of Scarp's story.

Scarp is still treasured by the families who retain crofting rights there, and by the people who are privileged to own holiday homes on the island. But it is also treasured by all whose forebears and relatives lie at rest in the graveyard on Scarp. The author died in Edinburgh in September 1971. He was buried, by his own wish, 'in the fine sandy soil' of the graveyard at Kingskettle, Fife, where he had himself conducted many burial services. It had always reminded him of the soil at *An Teampall* in Scarp.

Appendix

CHAPTER ONE: SCARP GEOLOGY

In Chapter 1 the author refers to that Scarp curiosity, 'the asbestos rock'. Dr J. D. Peacock, BSc, PhD, FRSE, author of the British Geological Survey report, *Quaternary geology of the Outer Hebrides*, has provided the following note on the geology of Scarp. He writes:

The gneissic bedrock of Scarp, the Lewisian Gneiss, is a continuation of that which forms much of the Outer Hebrides. These highly metamorphosed, often granite-like rocks, are some of the oldest in the British Isles, having been formed as long as 2700 million years ago. In more detail, the ice-moulded landscape is underlain by steeply north or north-east dipping beds of grey gneiss in which there are small enclaves of schist. Much of the gneiss is veined by much younger granite – only about 1700 million years old! – and locally by very coarse-grained quartz-feldspar rock – pegmatite. Towards the north-west part of the island the veins and layers of granite greatly predominate over gneiss and schist. Shallow gullies have been eroded along prominent north-south joints. Except for the area of blown sand along the east coast – where the village lies – the bedrock is at or near the surface, being overlain merely by thin peat, or peaty soil.

The unusual asbestos rock which crops out about seven hundred yards north of Manish, is composed chiefly of a felted mass of star-shaped clusters of finely fibrous amphibole in which are embedded blades of green actinolite (Jehu and Craig, 1934). The lenticular outcrop, which is some thirty-five yards long by fifteen yards broad, is aligned in a north-westerly direction in conformity with the layering of the surrounding gneiss. From a photograph in Jehu and Craig (1934) the rock mass is an ice-moulded whaleback on which there rests an erratic boulder. That this soft asbestos rock still forms an upstanding feature in an area that has been intensely eroded by glacier ice is probably due to the strength afforded by the randomly interlocking crystals and the lack of close-set joints, in contrast to the surrounding gneiss. The erratic boulder would have been carried there by ice and dumped randomly on top of the whaleback as the ice melted away.

The Outer Hebrides were extensively glaciated during the last part of the Ice Age, about 20,000 years ago, only a small area in the extreme north of Lewis remaining free of ice. Though the great Scottish geologist James Geikie, writing in the late nineteenth century, thought that the Outer Hebrides were crossed by ice flowing from the Scottish mainland at this time, more recent work has suggested that the glaciers on the Long Island were local, with centres of ice dispersal in the mountains of South Lewis and North Harris, and on the west coast of Barra and the Uists. Hushinish, and probably Scarp, were crossed by glacier ice moving in a westerly direction from the South Lewis-North Harris icecap, though no confirmatory observations have yet been made on the island itself.

It is of particular interest to read in Douglas Peacock's note above that the asbestos formation is part of the solid geology of Scarp and is not, as has sometimes been suggested, a foreign mass carried to that location by glacial action. However, as mentioned here, it is surmounted by a granite-gneiss boulder – a glacial erratic – deposited there by melting ice as the last of the Hebridean glaciers retreated.

It can be rather difficult to locate the asbestos rock – known as *Clach a' Chomharra*, or 'the marker stone' – for many of the glacially-moulded rocks in the west of the island carry perched boulders. After following the directions given in Chapter 1, and the location 'about seven hundred yards north of Manish', the next point to look out for is colour. In good light conditions, even from some distance, the rough mottled surface of the asbestos rock appears a shade darker – or in sunshine sometimes of a pale fawn colour – compared to the cold light-greyness of the surrounding rocks. A scan through binoculars can help if approaching from the lower ground to the south. Colour, and the general shape – see photographs – along with the surmounting one-cubic-yard boulder, should help a keen visitor to find *Clach a' Chomharra*, although this involves a good five miles round trip from the village.

The tradition of the author's boyhood, that it was a woman carrying a sickle, who had been turned to stone on the spot, has been amplified by a younger islander: the erring lady had been gathering limpets on the Sabbath, and the boulder was her creel! So there was a strong Sabbatarian message behind the story. The author – perhaps as a matter of clerical propriety – missed out that aspect of the tale.

Dark-banded pink/brown rocks, exposed on the foreshore beside the Scarp sheep-wash or fank, are also of geological interest. A 1977 Nature Conservancy Council report, *Outer Hebrides: Localities of Geological and Geomorphological Importance*, summarises their interest as: 'Outcrops invaluable in appreciating relationships established during Scourian times in the Lewisian basement'. In other words, these outcrops, including the dark 'Scourie dykes' which cut across the pink/brown gneiss, help geologists to examine the sequence of events which formed the rocks of the Western Isles.

Near to the same location, 'The Red Stone', mentioned in Chapter 14, can be seen near the fank. Whether – as tradition suggested – the shore was at one time further out and the stone a hazard for the plough, is another matter.

CHAPTERS FOUR & FIVE: THE BOATBUILDER

The two chapters dealing with fishing mention three types of boat as being used in Scarp: firstly, the open eighteen foot fishing-boats; secondly, the larger boats used for ferrying seaweed, bringing home peat, or going for supplies to Tarbert; and lastly, the still larger boats once used for long-line fishing well out to sea. The first two types were familiar in the author's boyhood, but the big long-line boats were just a memory by then.

Some of these boats were built in Scarp, and issue No.1 of the magazine *Alba*, published in 1948, contains a splendid Gaelic article entitled *Fear-baile*, in which the building of such a boat is described. Its author, Allan MacLean, a former schoolmaster and himself a native of Scarp, was a skilled boatbuilder and boat-restorer. With his agreement, an English version of that article follows. Sadly, since helping with the wording, Allan died in April 1994 at his home on the Beauly Firth. It is to his great credit that the sentiments expressed here were in many ways 'before their time'.

I am indebted to Peggy MacClements for providing the literal translation from which this note has been prepared, and to Allan MacLean for having explained the more unusual technical terms. His original title, *Fear-baile*, could be translated as 'A Man of Parts'. Readers might keep in mind that the original article was written some forty-seven years ago, or twenty-three years before the last of the islanders left Scarp. Much has changed since then, but thankfully the Gaelic language is – to continue his own metaphor – still sailing steadily along.

The Boatbuilder, by Allan MacLean

My first memory, from about thirty years ago, is that there was no householder in the neighbourhood who was not a tradesman in one way or another, and I am sure that this was true of all island peoples. The man who was a fisherman would make his own tackle by hand, and a man of the land would, to some degree, make every tool he needed. Not only would these men build their own houses, but they would furnish them inside with elegance and neatness.

Even so, a visiting tourist thought – and it is still sometimes their attitude today – that those men and women were backward, with little intelligence. But the truth is that an unintelligent man had no place in the islands in those days. When such a man appeared, he was looked down upon as a useless man, as happened to the St Kildan man who could not get a wife, *bho nach robh ball aige* – 'because he had no rope'.

Things are different today. If a lady has a little money, she will get goods and materials from the Lowlands. A man no longer needs to cut seaweed with a sickle, he will get artificial fertiliser from the merchant; a coir rope is used instead of a hand-made heather rope; and a Kelvin engine is used instead of oars. They had a saying in Scarp, where I was brought up, *Ma tha luga agad, tha h-uile rud agad* – 'If you have a sandworm, you have everything'. Today it is, *Ma tha an t-airgiod agad, tha h-uile rud agad* – 'If you have money, you have everything'. And they do have money – I know of no one without it. But even so, they lack something else – Youthfulness! – and in no time many corners of the islands will belong only to the birds, unless some things change.

Indeed, we have already seen old ways set aside. That is good in many respects if continuity remains; but it is inevitable, when old skills and practices are abandoned, that the language that was their heritage is also in danger. I believe that we should try to hold on to words, customs and knowledge which are going out of use, before they too are lost or forgotten. If we retain the language, these other things will be preserved. Though the wind is so much against us just now, who knows but that it may change again before the boat sinks altogether? There are many on board who wish to let it run, but *An Iùbhrach Ghàidhealach* – 'The Highland Cutter' – has not gone so far on its side that it will not recover if there were a good man at the helm.

I shall give a short account of how I saw them building boats, and the kind of boats they used to build, in the hope that others will, *cuir clach air a' chàrn* -'put a stone on the cairn'.

There is no wood at all in the Long Island, save small stunted bushes. Even so, not much wood came from the mainland to build boats. The waves of the Atlantic in those days sent enough wood of every kind, to every beach and creek between the Butt of Lewis and Toe Head – wood which the sailing-ships lost on the way home from Sweden and Canada. *Tha am muir ag iarraidh a bhith 'ga thadhal* – 'The sea wants to be visited'. This material would often be claimed before daybreak, and the islander would retrieve with a clear conscience the wood he found along the tidemark on the shore. It was not stealing, nor even 'taking' it, but his own rightful share, if it was he who saw it first and brought it up. None but the Custom House could give them a formal right to it, but what use had the Custom House for material like this, taken from the sea!

A man who hoped to build a boat would throughout the winter gather on the shore every kind of wood he required – but wood which drifted slowly ashore in the heat of summer would be of little use, because of barnacles and timber-worms. Then he would take a pit-saw and cut the good timber into the planks he thought might be of most use. There was hardly a village which did not have a pit-saw. If they did not use it to build boats, they used it for coffin-making. The making of both started in the same way – with the pit-saw. It was said that the pit-saw worked by itself at night, and there were many who would never give it lodgings within their homes.

The pit-saw they used for boats was about eight feet long, with a cross-handle at each end. Before the sawing began, a line was put on the log by a string blackened from the bottom of a pot. This would make a straight black line by one man holding it taut at each end and another raising the middle of it from the wood and letting it go with a snap. Then the log would be put over the sawpit and two men would come to grips with the pit-saw, one standing above and one below. Only a skilled man could produce a half-inch plank from an eighteen inch log, but *Coinneach Mòr* could handle the wood as well as any sawmill. I can see him yet – his eye on the black line, and the great saw pouring sawdust onto his face and beard, and making eerie music.

Usually it was an experienced carpenter who built the boat – a carpenter who had learnt the trade from his father. But there were men who built boats without any formal training at all. The two that *Dòmhnall Mhurchaidh* built were good, and he made no claims to being a carpenter. A carpenter would take only about twenty days to build an eighteen foot boat. As was customary for tradesmen of old, the carpenter would come to stay with the man who wanted the job done, and remain there until the boat was finished. The crew for the boat would give him plenty of help with the rough work. When the boat was ready, his pay would be three or four pounds.

He had few tools except an adze, a hand saw, a band saw, and a plane. I never saw *Calum Geal* put a scarf on a boat but with the adze. He said that you would never do that with an adze unless you kept it tight to your hip. The outside of the plank would get a scrape of the plane, but the inside was left rough as it came off the saw.

Both galvanised and non-galvanised iron nails were used, but I never saw copper used. They required four kinds of nails: for the ribs, for the end wood, for riveting the planks, and for the gunwale. If he had his choice of wood, the carpenter would put oak in the stem and the stern, red fir in the keel, grey elm in the gunwale, and he would use larch for the ribs and the planks.

I never saw two boats on the Harris or Lewis shore that you could not distinguish one from the other. Even so, they were of a common pattern, and you would recognise a stranger in their midst very quickly. The fishermen would say, *Cumadh an eisg cumadh an eathair* – 'The shape of a boat was the shape of a fish'. That is still the first rule today among people who design boats and spaceships – to make them 'streamlined'. It does not matter much what shape a boat is above the sea, it is what is below the waterline that makes a boat, and if it is not fine at the stern it will not sail well.

A Lowland carpenter places the ribs as soon as he lays the keel, shaping them first according to a full-scale template. After that he has only to drop the planks onto it, as if he was putting sarking onto the rafters of a house; but the carpenters I saw working on boats, shaped them with no ribs at all, as they proceeded with the work. He was no beardless boy who could do that. From the time he started on it until he finished, the critics would – as they say – be under his feet. There would be plenty men to discuss how he was getting on. Even before a plank was laid there would be no lack of advice. But notwithstanding, the carpenter would cut and shape and bend and rivet, and let the critics talk.

Usually nine planks would be put on each side. On the first two from the keel, the sandstrake and the garboard, depended what grip the boat would have on the water. The sandstrake planks stood very much on edge – the heel of your boot would hardly go between the two of them. The next three, the floor or bottom planks, gave the boat breadth, and made it curved or straight, as you wished. The next two, the rising planks, lifted the sides, and the last two, the top planks, gave the freeboard. The Brenish carpenter liked the third floor-plank to be nearly flat. This may seem too flat, but he would make such a sweet curve with it that the eye would not be offended, and he would give it a long sweep towards the ends, until it was trim and right.

The preparation of the wood was a key step. They had no steam-box, so they steeped the planks all night in a pool of water, and then steamed them over a fire of shavings, which crackled and sparked. Then they took the prepared wood in hand and twisted and tortured it until you took pity on it! But despite that they would not break or split it by overdoing it. If there was difficulty in getting it right they would again soak and steam it. They had a heavy stick called the *madadh*, or 'the hound', to help bend and twist the planks. There was a slot at the end of the madadh, to hold the edge of the plank, and the weight of the stick itself would shape the plank. The call, *Cum cuideam air a' mhadadh* – 'Lean on the madadh', was often heard. If the carpenter wished to make a tight curve the men would, if need be, put weight on the madadh till after nightfall.

Space does not allow me to go into more detail about the carpenter's boat. I would like to tar every seam and rivet every nail, and go to sea in her with the brave, skilful, good-humoured men who knew how to make full use of her. One day *Alasdair Bhèidearsaig* said to *Fionnlagh Chaluim*, when they had the boat under sail, *Saoilidh mi, Fhionnlaigh, nan cuireadh tu an darna cas a nuas air an tobhtaidh gu seòladh an t-eathar na b'fheàrr* – 'I think, Findlay, if you put one foot aft of the thwart, the boat would sail better'.

'An ignorant villager', said the tourist. 'A senseless tourist', say I!

THE NINE PLANKS OF A SKIFF

GAELIC	ENGLISH
Druim	Keel
1. Fliuch Bhòrd	Sandstrake
	(or Keel Board)
2. Meanbh	Garboard
3. Urlar (1)	Floor (1)
4. Urlar (2)	Floor (2)
5. Urlar (3)	Floor (3)
6. Bòrd Togalach (1)	Rising Plank (1)
7. Bòrd Togalach (2)	Rising Plank (2)
8. Timcheall Iseal	Lower Top Strake
9. Timcheall Ard	Top Strake
Beul Mòr	Gunwale

The challenge for the carpenter was to get a sweet-flowing line from the keel to the gunwale. [See sketch overleaf.]

CHAPTER SIX: SHEEP GATHERING

In Chapter 6 the author explains that a sheep-gathering was an exciting event in a child's life, and that the whole of the able-bodied community was involved when a 'fank' took place at Islaca on the south of the island, beyond the *Mol Mòr*. Some things have changed since those days, but other aspects of island sheep-raising are much the same.

The winter task of smearing the sheep with a tar and butter compound to protect them from parasites and damp, has long since given way to dipping, with the sheep being immersed in a bath containing a chemical dip. Not only was smearing an expensive and laborious task, for it is said that a man could smear little more than a score of sheep in a day, but it also depressed the value of the wool of the treated animals. The practice of smearing Blackface sheep on hill farms had been common throughout Scotland up to the 1850s, but by 1880 it had largely been replaced by dipping. The practice survived longer in the north and west Highlands.

It is unclear when smearing ended in Scarp, but it was still current when the author was a young boy, for on 5 December 1890 the schoolmaster reported that the smearing of sheep had interfered with school attendance for several days that week. A later schoolmaster noted a day in November 1915 as being 'sheep-dipping day', and therefore a school holiday. So smearing had been replaced by dipping sometime between 1890 and 1915. A gap in the school records prevents a closer identification of the date.

The fank at Islaca is now used only in May, when the lambs in the west of

CROSS-SECTION ILLUSTRATING
THE NINE PLANKS OF A SKIFF

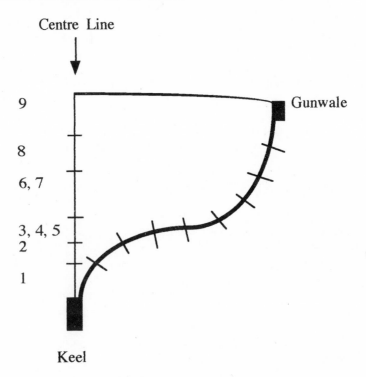

(Diagrammatic only, not to scale.)

BASED ON HAND-SKETCH BY ALLAN MACLEAN

the island are marked. Today the main fank is at the north end of the village, not far from the concrete jetty.

The lambs are no longer ferried to Fladday for weaning. Now that no crops are grown around the village, the lambs are weaned on the fine machair there, while their mothers are driven beyond the fence, to the north and west. Fladday is still used for grazing the rams, while the island of Kearstay, just off the northern shore of Scarp, is used for wintering some of the hoggs.

Although direct evidence is sparse, it seems likely that Scarp once had the small native Hebridean sheep, sometimes described as 'having been goat-like in appearance', before the larger Blackface and Cheviot sheep began to displace them throughout the Western Isles. This happened between 1780 and the mid 1800s. For example, Rev J. L. Buchanan's *Travels in the Western Hebrides from 1782 to 1790*, refers to the sheep as being, 'Of various colours, such as black, grey, dun, and party-coloured, many of them with four horns', adding that the tacksman of Bernera, Norman MacLeod, had introduced improvements including, 'English sheep, and large horses and bulls to mend the breed of cattle; as also jack-asses to breed mules'. And Robert Heron, writing in 1794, reported that Harris may then have had eleven thousand sheep, which were, 'of a diminutive breed . . . sixteen of their fleeces make up a stone of wool . . . a ewe and her lamb are sold for 3s 4d . . . the mutton of those small animals is uncommonly delicate and well-flavoured'.

W.Anderson Smith, in his book, *Lewsiana: or Life in the Outer Hebrides*, published in 1875, wrote:

> The ordinary native sheep of the cotters are rags of creatures, manufacturing sweet mutton out of the memory of sweet summer feeding on the moors, and their share of the seaware. Superior sheep have been introduced by some of the farmers; but the best suited for the country generally is, no doubt, the hardy black-face, which is, at the same time, a decided advance upon the original small native breed.

All these 'small native sheep' are believed to have been the descendants of sheep introduced to the islands during Viking times. Although they eventually died out as commercial stock in the Western Isles, a few survived in mainland parks – perhaps from the times of long overland droves to southern markets – and their descendants now flourish, with their own association, 'The Hebridean Sheep Society'. There are now some two hundred registered flocks in Britain, including at least three groups in the Western Isles. As selectively bred they are by now a most attractive animal, light-boned, dark brown or black in colour, with two or four flowing horns – although there is a suggestion that the two-horned are now preferred. They are hardy and can tolerate difficult grazing conditions. Sometimes misnamed 'St Kilda Sheep', the Hebrideans are quite distinct from the Soay sheep of St Kilda.

Chapter 15 refers to, 'the tacksman's Blackface sheep and the proprietor's

Cheviots', as using the fank at Hushinish, and *The New Statistical Account* of 1841 mentions that Cheviot sheep had by that date been introduced into Harris. The Blackface breed proved more suitable for the harsh conditions of North Harris and the use of Cheviots there declined. But Scarp must have had at least a small flock of the native sheep – of one sort or another – at the time the tacksman introduced the Blackface to his Hushinish farm. His tenants would soon have followed his example, and switched to the more marketable Blackface.

Scarp normally carries some six hundred and fifty Blackface ewes, and four hundred lambs are raised each year. The larger male lambs are sold in early September, and the other lambs are wintered on their owners' crofts, or sent to mainland farms on the east coast. It is interesting that the Napier Commission of 1883 was told that Scarp then had five hundred and seven sheep and seventy-three cattle. In addition there were then extensive crops on all the arable ground. Scarp now has no cattle and there are no growing crops to restrict the grazing land available for sheep. With the exception of the wintering lambs, the Blackface sheep can happily survive on the island without the need for imported feedingstuff.

The following table of main activities shows that the cycle of shepherding involves careful attention throughout the year:

Introducing the rams	last week of November
Lambing	mid April to end of May
Shearing & dosing	end of June and end of July
Dipping	late August
Weaning the lambs	August to September/October
Lamb sales	first week of September
Wintering	October to April

The families who keep sheep on Scarp, and who retain inherited crofting rights there, have to work hard, in all weather conditions, in attending their flocks. Manning the boats for ferrying sheep is not always easy. As with many aspects of crofting life, close collaboration is needed between neighbours. This has always been an accepted tradition of life in the islands, and it remains so today. One change from the days of which the author wrote, is that in deciding when to hold a sheep-gathering, the telephone has, to a large extent, replaced the traditional Scarp 'parliament'.

I am indebted to Murdo John MacInnes, Govig, a member of the last family to leave the island, and Clerk to the Scarp Common Grazings Committee, for providing the information on today's Scarp sheep and shepherding.

CHAPTERS TEN & TWENTY-TWO: MEDICAL CONDITIONS AND BELIEFS

In Chapter 10 the author refers to 'the great pain', a mysterious illness which was invariably fatal. In Chapter 22 a Scarp charm for 'the rose' is given in full, and mention is made of 'the king's evil', 'the evil eye', and death portents. Dr Una MacLean, MD, PhD, FRCP, a distinguished 'grand-daughter of Scarp', has provided the following notes on these Medical Conditions and Beliefs. She writes:

Chapter Ten

The 'great pain': It is difficult to be sure what could have caused such a condition, since severe abdominal pain requiring surgery to avoid a fatal outcome could have had a number of possible sources. If folklore is to be believed and the pain did lead to death, it must have been due to a rupture of some organ, giving rise to peritonitis. The appendix seems the most likely culprit, and it was apparently associated in the minds of Scarp people with this organ, about which they had heard in the early years of the century, when King Edward VII was saved by an emergency operation. But such agonising and dangerous pain could be caused by a strangulated hernia or by the rupture of a peptic ulcer. Very severe pain in the abdomen can also arise from the gall bladder, from a kidney stone or from pancreatitis, although these conditions would not necessarily be fatal. The real problem we face, in such a small population of islanders, has to do with probabilities and the rarity of particular diseases or symptoms over the period of one generation's memory. In the absence of more detailed and written records, the matter can never finally be resolved.

Chapter Twenty-two

Charm for 'the rose': The disease called 'rose' here refers to mastitis, that is to say, an inflammation or incipient deep abscess in the breast. It is extremely painful and, should it spread to the blood-stream, can be fatal. In the Hebrides the condition, as it affects both women and cows who were producing milk, was recognised as essentially the same. In the absence of specific, anti-biotic treatment, recourse was had to an incantation in which the sickness was strongly urged, in the name of the Virgin Mary, to quit the breast or udder and go into the ground.

'The King's Evil': This was the name used widely throughout Scotland for tuberculosis of the glands. Within living memory, older people could frequently be observed bearing ugly scars in their neck, where the glands had broken down and discharged on the surface when the victim was young. The seventh son of a seventh son was believed to have the greatest healing power in such cases, but even a seventh son – as the author reports of Scarp – would possibly be considered more effective than an ordinary mortal.

Witchcraft: The author refers to a man on Scarp who was believed to possess 'the evil eye'. The writer recalls her great-uncle speaking of his childhood in Scarp, in the 1870s or 1880s, and how he had been warned not to take the cows near a certain *woman* for fear of her evil influence.

Portents. With regard to the author's report of his mother's belief that a 'tinkling in the ears' foretold a death, the belief has also been recorded in Quebec. Dr Margaret Bennett, of the School of Scottish Studies in Edinburgh, met Christie Mackenzie (nee Murray) in 1976. At that time the lady was 76, and she was a fluent Gaelic speaker. Her grandparents emigrated from Lewis in 1852 and settled in the Eastern Townships. The verbatim quotation went as follows:

'I'll tell you my own experience. I get a whistling in my ears, and as true as I do, I hear of a death soon after! . . . They told me I was awful foolish to believe in that, but just as true as I hear it, I hear of a death somewhere.'

  (*Reference*: Bennett, Margaret (1980). *Folkways and Religion of the Hebridean Scots in the Eastern Townships,* in, *Cultural Retention and Demographic Change: Studies of the Hebridean Scots in the Eastern Townships of Quebec,* Edited by Laurel Doucette, National Museum of Man, Mercury Series, No.34, Ottawa, pp. 45-144.)

CHAPTERS ELEVEN, TWELVE & THIRTEEN: FOLKTALES

It is not entirely clear which of the folktales came directly from the island's oral tradition and which from the author's own later scholarship, but the internal evidence suggests that most of the tales were first heard during his boyhood in Scarp. Chapter 11 gives the Scarp version of the tale, 'Big Birken and her Son', in which little Birken came to an unfortunate end, and from which the island saying, 'I am not obliged to do that, said the cat', was derived. The story of 'Niggardly Mary', given in Chapter 12, must also have been well-known in Scarp, for the tag, 'William-be-seated', was sometimes quoted in fun to the author's younger brother, William James.

  Chapter 13 details the local origins of 'Big John, The King's Son'. A tinker woman had brought it to Scarp, and a gifted storyteller had added it to his repertoire. The author later noted it down during visits to the narrator's home, and in 1946 he broadcast a Gaelic version on the BBC Scottish Home Service, as part of the series, *Sgeul na h-aon oidhche* – 'Tale for one night'. The relationship to the J.F.Campbell tale, 'The Brown Bear of the Green Glen', led him to speculate as to whether John MacDonald, the wandering tinker who had in 1859 told the 'Brown Bear' tale to Campbell's collector Hector Urquhart, might have been the husband of the tinker widow who brought it to Scarp. Unluckily her family name does not seem to have been remembered. One motif, deliberately left out in the broadcast version, and the Chapter 13 English version, contrasts with the Campbell tale, and perhaps with the Scarp oral version: 'the fairest creature ever seen' – 'the prettiest little jewel' of Campbell's version – was delivered of a baby son before she, guided by a mystical bird, came to claim the hand of Big John!

The great collector, John Francis Campbell, or *Iain Og Ile*, was born in Edinburgh in 1821. He was brought up in close contact with the Celtic culture of his father's tenants in Islay, before receiving a formal education at Eton and Edinburgh University. He was the first scholar fully to recognise and make a systematic collection of West Highland traditional tales. Campbell made wide use of collectors and contributors, and although he was himself an accomplished linguist, and prepared the English translations, he relied upon Hector MacLean, the erudite schoolmaster of Ballygrant, Kilmeny Parish, Islay, to prepare and see the Gaelic text through to publication. The author sometimes felt that MacLean had received less than due recognition for his part in the *Popular Tales*, and for his wider scholarship, suggesting that the schoolmaster should be described as, 'Campbell's collaborator'. A commemorative article on Hector MacLean, by the author, can be found in *An Gaidheal* of January 1964.

The first three volumes of Campbell's *Popular Tales of the West Highlands* were dated 1860. The School of Scottish Studies in Edinburgh possesses two original volumes of the Tales, with the first one inscribed, 'To Hector MacLean from his friend J. F. Campbell'. These particular books, once part of MacLean's own library, were donated to the School by an Islay lady who remembered Hector MacLean well. She passed them on via the author, who had been parish minister of Kilmeny between 1929 and 1936.

Hector MacLean died in 1893. A Celtic cross stands near the former school at Ballygrant. It carries the following Gaelic and English inscriptions:

> *Chuir an Comunn Ileach suas a' chrois so*
> *A ghleidheadh air chuimhne cliù*
> *Eachainn Mhic 'Illeathain*
> *A rugadh 's a chaith a bheatha anns*
> *an Sgìreachd so.*
> *Ileach ceanalta agus sàr sgoilear.*

> In Memory of Hector MacLean, M.A.I.,
> A native of Islay
> And a distinguished scholar.
> Specially eminent in Celtic Literature
> and Anthropology.
> Born, 1818. Died, 1893.

J. F. Campbell died at Cannes in the South of France in 1885. A Celtic cross was erected there in his memory. A commemorative monument also stands on a hill at Bridgend, not far from Islay House, where he had spent much of his youth.

Scarp must at one time have had a vigorous tradition of oral history and folktale – these three chapters are testimony to that. Much would have come there during times of population movement in the eighteenth and nineteenth centuries. It had never been an introverted community, for the active men engaged in fishing and agriculture travelled widely, and would have brought in regular infusions of contemporary lore, as would visitors and itinerant tradesmen. But with the passing of each generation much of this traditional knowledge has been lost. What has been recorded – here and elsewhere – must be but a small fraction of the island's folk history.

CHAPTER TWELVE: A SEER AND AN OUTLAW

Chapter 12 tells of the prophesies of *Coinneach Odhar*, 'The Brahan Seer', and how his prediction of the building of 'three white houses' at Hushinish was fulfilled in 1900.

The Seer also predicted that a dark-haired man, 'would cross and re-cross', the Sound of Scarp on foot, and that this would happen only once. It is said that this was done, before witnesses, one day in 1784 when the tide was unusually low. In Chapter 2 the author tells of watching an adventurous Scarp youth crossing the Sound on foot, as the same boy's father had done years before. Whether anyone has actually 'crossed and re-crossed' on foot since the 1784 pioneer reportedly did, is not recorded. As already mentioned in a footnote to Chapter 2, this would be a hazardous enterprise due to fast currents and possible quicksands – it is *not* recommended.

It has proved difficult down the years for scholars to establish the historical facts about the Brahan Seer. Not unexpectedly, there were contradictory versions of his place of birth, his life and his death. Indeed it has been suggested that the traditions associated with his name encompass parts of the lives of a number of people with such predictive gifts. Whether such powers were based on unusually good deductive observation, or on more mysterious, or even sinister, influences, is a matter for personal judgment. Most people today would suggest that the former was the case.

The facts surrounding *Mac an t-Srònaich*, or 'Stronach', are also uncertain. That such an outlaw did roam the moors and hills of Lewis and Harris seems clear, but whether all the crimes attributed to him actually occurred is less so. At a time when news depended wholly on oral dissemination, it would be quite understandable should fact and fiction become entangled, with unexplained events being fitted into the context of what was already known or believed.

Many of the Stronach 'incidents' occurred during moorland journeys by his victims. Lonely moorland treks were an everyday occurrence at the time. A private manuscript, written over one hundred years ago by Murdo MacLeod, the evangelist mentioned in Chapters 2 and 26, describes life in Lewis two hundred years ago. No roads connected the parishes or settlements, and the population was thinly spread. The transit of goods, when not by sea, was wholly on foot, sometimes with the help of, 'small but spirited horses with two small creels slung across their backs'. Just as often transport was on the backs of the people: 'Men would be seen with their uncomfortable burdens – which might include wood for house roofing, or agricultural implements – wading through the fords of rivers, the stepping-stones of rapid burns, the mossy bogs of moorlands, and going over steep heathery hills and deep glens, all of which made their short-legged horses quite useless for carrying purposes in these emigrations.' It is not difficult to imagine the hardships of those times, nor how an accident or a fright might be attributed – whether seriously or in fun – to the outlaw Stronach.

In February 1914, at a time of unusually bad weather, a twenty-one year old cousin of the author was found dead on the moor near Loch Voshimid. He had been bringing goods from Tarbert to one of the settlements on Loch Resort, when he was overcome by the elements. A police report gave the cause of death as, 'supposed exhaustion and exposure'. While the word 'supposed' hints at an element of doubt, the atrocious weather that winter – well covered in newspaper reports of the day – must have played a central part in the tragedy. In earlier times Stronach's name might have arisen, for the Ulladale Cave, which the outlaw was said to have used, was not far off.

CHAPTERS FOURTEEN & TWENTY-ONE: HISTORICAL REFERENCES

1.   In Chapter 21 the author refers to a small church having been built in Scarp by Alasdair Crotach, the 8th Chief of the MacLeods, who died at Rodel in 1547. This church is referred to in a document, known as 'The Bannatyne Manuscript', held at Dunvegan Castle. This deals with the early history and genealogy of the MacLeods. Dating from around 1829, it appears to have been based on much older papers and on the oral traditions of the day. It explains how Alasdair Crotach, one of the great chiefs of the Clan, built the 'Fairy Tower' at Dunvegan – the muniment room, holding early MacLeod records, is in this tower – and how he retired to the monastery at Rodel in South Harris several years before his death. There he repaired and completed the Church of St Clement, and prepared the fine tomb in which he was later laid to rest. In the words of the manuscript:

Allister Crottach [sic] built two other Beautiful Small Churches dependent on this Monastery – one at Nic Capevale and one in Scarpa – both now in ruins.

So Scarp can claim to have had a place of worship over four hundred years ago.

Although no 'ruins' are to be seen there now, the name, *An Teampall,* used for
the graveyard, and the presence on the nearby shore of *Sgeir an Teampaill* –
'The Temple Rock' – suggest where it was. Exactly who inhabited the island at
that time remains uncertain, but Dean Monro's observations – which follow –
indirectly confirm the presence of an active population in Scarp during Alasdair
Crotach's days, for the Dean's travels took place just two years after the 8th
Chief's death. The other 'beautiful small church' at 'Nic Capevale' – spelt 'Nic
Caperrall' by an early transcriber – was probably that at *Rubh' an Teampaill,* at
the south side of Chaipaval, near Northton.

2.   Donald Monro, or Dean Monro, the High Dean of the Isles, prepared his
Description of the Western Isles of Scotland, called Hybrides, following travels in
1549. He described 251 islands, not all of which were visited. His entry for
Scarp reads:

> Besides this out in the sea above Usiemes in Heray lyis ane Ile callit the *Scarp,*
> manurit, fertile and frutfull, gude for corn, store and fishing, perteining to Mccloyd
> of Haray.

> [Beside this, out in the sea above Hushinish in Harris, lies an island called
> Scarp, cultivated, fertile and fruitful, good for corn, cattle and fishing, owned
> by MacLeod of Harris.]

As the author points out, this is not unlike his description of many islands of the
Hebrides, but it does indicate that Scarp was populated and under cultivation
at the time of Dean Monro's travels, over four centuries ago.

3.   Martin Martin, writing around 1695, mentions Scarp in, *A Description of
the Western Islands of Scotland,* saying simply:

> ABOUT two Leagues farther North [than Gasker] lies the Island *Scarp,* two miles
> in Circumference, and is a high Land covered with Heath and Grass.

In fact Scarp exceeds two miles in diameter, the longest chord being just over
three miles. Martin, a man of culture who used the style 'Gentleman', took a
Master's degree at Edinburgh University in 1681. His *Description* is a most useful
book, although it is disappointing on Scarp. The above extract is taken from the
actual 1703 volume carried by James Boswell and Dr Samuel Johnson during
their tour of the Hebrides. Boswell's own inscription on the flyleaf reads:

> This very Book accompanied Mr Samuel Johnson and me in our Tour of the
> Hebrides in Autumn 1773. Mr Johnson told me that he had read Martin when
> he was very young. Martin was a native of the Isle of Sky where a number of

his relations still remain. His Book is a very imperfect performance; & he is erroneous as to many particulars, even some concerning his own Island. Yet as it is the only Book upon the subject, it is very generally known. I have seen a second edition of it. I cannot but have a kindness for him notwithstanding his defects. 16 April 1774, James Boswell.

This historic volume is in the possession of the National Library of Scotland. Boswell and Johnson's own tour, which must at least partly have been inspired by Martin's descriptions, took them no nearer to the Outer Hebrides than Skye and the island of Coll. While staying at Dunvegan, Dr Johnson's room was in the 'Fairy Tower'. He later wrote: 'At Dunvegan I had tasted lotus, and was in danger of forgetting that I was ever to depart, till Mr Boswell sagely reproached me with my sluggishness and softness.' Boswell confirmed that both had 'slept well, and lain long', at Dunvegan.

Gasker – probably stocked from Taransay rather than from Scarp – received slightly better treatment from Martin:

> [Gasker] ... excels any other Plot of its extent, for Fruitfulness in Grass and Product of Milk; it maintains 8 or 10 Cows. The Natives kill Seals here, which are very big.

4.   Harris estate records as early as 1698 list 'the twopenny land of Hushinish' and 'the twopenny land of Scarp' (ref. Alick Morrison's *Harris Estate Papers, 1724-1754*, in *Transactions of the Gaelic Society of Inverness, vol. XLV*). The penny was an archaic measure of land value. Harris had about 90 pennylands in MacLeod ownership, but information on the population and forms of tenure on Scarp at that time is limited. Among the 'Dunvegan papers' is a schedule of the land of Harris belonging to Norman MacLeod of MacLeod, dated 1772. It shows Scarp as having 2,328 acres of pasture and 72 acres of arable land.

5.   John Knox of London, on behalf of the British Society for Extending the Fisheries etc, travelled in the Highlands and Islands of Scotland in 1786. He did not visit the west coast of Harris, but after sailing from Rodel, he visited Scalpay and Tarbert, before proceeding up the east coast of Lewis to Stornoway. After referring in his narrative to the main islands of the Sound of Harris, he added: 'These, with Scalpay, Taransay, and Scarp, compose the inhabited islands on the coast of Harris. Some of them produce good crops of grain, and all of them good pasture.' So Knox, who was at that stage of his journey accompanied by the Harris proprietor, Captain Alexander MacLeod, heard of successful pastoral activity in Scarp at that time.

6.   Robert Heron's *General View of the Natural Circumstances (of the) Hebrides*, was published in 1794. He gives a useful general description of agriculture

and the ways of life in Harris. He grades the classes of rank as: the Proprietor, MacLeod of Harris; the tacksmen; the small tenant-farmers; the tacksmen's tenants; the tacksmen's servants; and 'the begging poor'. He suggests that the main hardships of the 'scallags', or servants, arise from their being tied to a particular master and having no freedom to choose where to work. Of Scarp he says:

> Scarp, another insular division of the parish of Harris, lies from that isle [Harris], about half a mile N.W. consists of one lofty rock, the diameter of which, at its base, may be 3 miles; and is inhabited by fifty souls.

It is interesting that Heron at the same time reports Taransay as being, 'inhabited by about 140 souls', and Scalpay as being, 'inhabited by two or three families – from fifteen to twenty souls'. Today, by contrast, Scarp and Taransay have no settled populations, while Scalpay thrives, a population of around 380 having been recorded there in the 1991 census.

7.   John MacCulloch M.D. published, *A Description of the Western Islands of Scotland*, in 1819. He says a good deal about the geology and the minerals of Harris in general, but little about Scarp. His wording suggests that he did visit the island, although he could not have examined it very closely:

> [Scarp consists] . . . of one rocky mountain of gneiss about 1000 feet in height . . .
> I discovered nothing in Scarpa worthy of particular regard.

His mind was on the geology here, suggesting that Scarp was, in his view, geologically dull compared to Taransay and Scalpay, both of which had excited his interest. He tells us nothing about the island's human settlement at that time.

8.   The first full account of conditions on Scarp is seen in the written and oral evidence given on behalf of the people of Scarp to the Napier Commission, sitting in Tarbert on 13 June 1883. This is contained in the minutes of evidence of the 1884 *Report of Her Majesty's Commissioners of Inquiry into the condition of The Crofters and Cottars in the Highlands and Islands of Scotland.* Norman MacDonald, crofter and fisherman, Scarp, reported that there were about forty families, or two hundred people, living on the island, although only sixteen names were on the rent roll. Beyond that, the land was split up informally among families and friends, to the extent that it had reduced them all to poverty. The island was overcrowded, partly as a result of the clearing of thirteen small villages between Loch Resort and Bunavoneadar, and partly through the loss of summer grazings across the Sound. In earlier days the islanders had sent their horses – this confirms the early use of horses – and cattle to these grazings while the crops were growing on Scarp. That right was withdrawn in favour of the sheep flock of the tacksman,

Alexander MacRae, around 1820. Mr MacDonald confessed that most of the Scarp tenants were in arrears of rent, some by more than a year. He was clear that the island could not support its current population.

MacDonald also gave useful evidence on fishing. Every man who could be was also a fisherman. They had small boats for long-lines and lobsters, but no herring boats. A man on the island bought the cod, ling and lobsters, at prices set at the start of each season. Payment was usually by way of meal supplies. The Scarp coast, without a harbour, was not suitable for the larger boats which would enable them to fish further out, for in winter they had to haul their boats out of the water every night.

The evidence of Kenneth MacDonald, the factor for North Harris, confirmed this picture. He said: 'There are sixteen tenants in Scarp on the rent roll, but without leave asked or obtained, the father gives his son a bit of the croft, and the brother gives his brother a bit of the croft, entirely against the rules of the estate'. His view was that emigration was the only solution to this chronic overcrowding. He meant emigration from the Hebrides, rather than from the island of Scarp alone, for the possibility of resettlement in parts of the deer-forest or sheep-walks had not yet been conceded by the proprietors. Emigration was, in the words of the factor: 'the only remedy to drive away from Harris the chronic distress that every year occurs in our congested country'.

The findings of the Napier Commission led directly to the *Crofters Holdings (Scotland) Act, 1886* – once described as being the crofters' Magna Carta. This Act introduced the principles of security of tenure, rent regulation, compensation at the end of a tenancy for any improvement carried out, and the right to bequeath the tenancy of a croft to a member of the same family. The Commission's enquiries must also, directly or indirectly, have opened the way for the resettlement of Scarp families in some of the small hamlets originally cleared to make way for sheep or deer.

9.   Good information on the population of Scarp is available from the Decennial Censuses from 1841 to 1891. Later censuses will not be open to public scrutiny until 100 years after the event. Figures after 1891 are given here, based on census data, with the assistance of the General Register Office for Scotland:

POPULATION OF SCARP 1794-1971		
Year	Inhabited houses	Person
1794	-	50 (Robert Heron)
1841	23	129 Census
1851	25	145 do.
1861	27	151 do.
1871	33	156 do.
1881	41	213 do.
1891	29	143 (normally 157)
1901	30	160 GRO Scot.
1911	31	154 do.
1921	32	141 do.
1931	25	95 do.
1951	20	74 do.
1961	-	46 do.
1971	-	12 do.
post 1971	-	last family left in Dec. '71

The drop between 1881 and 1891 reflects the 1885 resettlement of families in seven nearby locations. This migration may have spilled over into 1886, but not later, for the H.M.Inspector's Scarp school report for 1886 noted that about one-third of the previous year's pupils had been lost due to the migration of families.

The author's father, W. S. Duncan, was enumerator for Scarp, Cravadale and Bedersaig, for the 1891 Census. He noted that on census night there was one visitor on the island, but that fifteen residents were absent at the Uig Communion in Lewis. This means that the normal population of Scarp was then one hundred and fifty-seven people. Among those missing was the author's uncle Angus MacInnes. He could be found on census night 1891 staying as a visitor in a house at Crowlista, Uig, no doubt playing his full part at the Communion. This was for many years a traditional event on the Scarp calendar, for Uig was in those days just as accessible as their own church at Tarbert.

Once, probably in the year 1930, when the author was home on holiday, he found the men preparing to leave for the Uig Communion. He joined them, sailing first to Brenish, where they spent the Thursday night. The Scarp company was invited to conduct the evening meeting, the author sharing the pulpit with the Brenish missionary. He later recalled how impressed the Lewis congregation had been by the Scarp men's power of public prayer.

10.   The Statistical Accounts add a little to this picture. *The (First) Statistical Account of Scotland*, published in 1794, refers to the Hushinish farm as having some extent of arable land, including it with other lands worked with the

Scotch plough drawn by four horses. Reference is also made to some patches of cultivation along the Harris shore of Loch Resort. Scarp is listed as an inhabited island, but few other details are offered.

The New Statistical Account of Scotland, dated 1841, mentions Scarp as being 'peopled' but nothing else is directly said about it. A general comment on the parish no doubt includes the natives of Scarp: 'The people are generally sober and industrious. Some of their articles of dress are of the most primitive description, and of the coarsest materials, all manufactured by themselves.' Rev John MacIvor, who compiled the Harris report, would have himself enjoyed fine black clerical garb, rather than the functional home-produced tweeds worn by his parishioners!

Much better detail is to be found in *The Third Statistical Account of Scotland.* The County of Inverness volume, in which this appears, was not published until 1985, although the Harris section had been prepared in 1953, and was updated – by Rev D.A.MacRae – in 1966. The report gives a fine historical perspective of the Parish of Harris, and good information on Scarp was provided by Mrs Joan MacLennan, the last teacher on the island. The following summarised points relate to Scarp:

> The crofts were all on the machair on the east side of the island; their size ranged from three and three-quarters, to five and a quarter, acres; grazings were common and shared by the crofters and the other inhabitants; an average of sixty sheep and two cows were kept by each of the crofts; oats, barley and potatoes were the main crops; and some crofts had small walled gardens in which vegetables were grown.

> There were four or five small boats, used for lobster fishing, on the island.
> The inhabitants no longer made tweeds, but the women knitted socks and pullovers. Scarp had one shop, supplied with provisions by boat from Hushinish.

> The island had a Church of Scotland mission, the services being in Gaelic, but with an occasional summer service in English for the benefit of visitors.

> Paraffin lamps were in use, and peat was burned, but most houses by then used Calor Gas for cooking. There was no general water supply.

> By September 1963 the one-teacher Primary School had only four pupils.

11.   Chapter 14 describes how Hushinish was resettled in 1900, by three families who, in 1885, had moved from Scarp to Dirascal, a small bay on the southern shore of Loch Resort. Contemporary legal papers confirm that the move to Hushinish was a voluntary one, which benefited the Proprietor by freeing part of the North Harris deer-forest, and benefited the crofters by

giving them better and more accessible land. The annual rent paid for each croft at Dirascal in 1890 was two pounds. The fair rents fixed in 1900 for the new Hushinish crofts were also two pounds each per year, and the Proprietor provided a grant of fifty pounds to each tenant to help build a dwellinghouse of stone, lime, wood and felt. The extent of the promontory, including arable and grazing land, was stated to be 'about 300 acres', out of which a small enclosure of three acres was used by cottars from Scarp for growing potatoes. Hushinish was said to have good green pasture and machair land, and: 'The situation is very favourable for lobster fishing, is at the terminus of a good footpath [from Amhuinnsuidhe] and within a reasonable distance from a school.' The souming – the number of livestock supportable by a given unit of land – for each croft, was given as: 'three cows with their followers, and twenty-five sheep'. Ninety-five years later Hushinish is still occupied, with a healthy stock of sheep and a cow or two still being seen; the 'good footpath' is now a well surfaced, if single-track, road; and lobsters can still be caught around the coastline. Hushinish remains the terminus for visitors crossing to Scarp, and it still has a crofting community of its own.

CHAPTER SIXTEEN: THE PROVISION OF BYRES

Chapter 16 describes how in the author's early youth the cattle occupied one end of a typical thatched house, and the family the other end. Reports by the County Sanitary Inspector for Inverness show just how seriously the authorities viewed this practice. His report for the year 1892, for the District of Harris, contains the following graphic description. It relates to the whole of Harris, but must have applied to some dwellings in Scarp. These reports were examined through the courtesy of the Regional Archivist in Inverness:

LABOURER'S HOUSES: The crofters' houses are as a rule the most active insanitary agents in the district, and are fitly described by the term 'black hut': low, roughly-constructed enclosures without gables, chimneys or windows; the interiors dark and grimy with smoke, the walls streaming with moisture, and the atmosphere heavy with the exhalations from the dung, which is only removed from the houses once a year. This is a marked peculiarity of the district and is evidently adopted not so much from necessity, but in preference to any other method of disposal. The question of providing separate accommodation for cattle and other bestial, apart from dwellinghouses, is one which requires immediate attention. This and other kindred matters have recently been under consideration by the Local Authority, and definite instructions have been issued by hand-bill throughout the district.

The same official's report for 1897, shows that a marked improvement had been seen:

A very considerable reduction has taken place in the number of dwellinghouses in which cattle are kept. Thirteen houses now contain twenty-three cattle. The progress made each year since the Committee resolved to stamp out this class of offence, is shown by the following figures:

31 December 1894:	167 dwellinghouses contained	431 cattle
31 December 1895:	87 dwellinghouses contained	171 cattle
31 December 1896:	25 dwellinghouses contained	71 cattle
31 December 1897:	13 dwellinghouses contained	23 cattle

Separate byres have been provided for 408 cattle removed from 154 dwellinghouses, within three years.

By 1913 the County Sanitary Inspector reported that, despite repeated warnings to discontinue the system of harbouring cattle in dwellinghouses, two cases still existed in the District of Harris. An earlier report had suggested that some defaulters were: 'helpless old men, widows, or paupers, who were quite unable to provide byres unaided'. These last two cases no doubt fell into some such category. The Public Health Acts, and the Inspectors, had done their work well over a comparatively short period.

CHAPTER NINETEEN: HARRIS TWEED

James Shaw Grant, CBE, writing as a former Chairman of the Harris Tweed Association, has provided the following note on Chapter 19:

The 'still newer loom' at Hushinish was, presumably, a Hattersley automatic loom. These looms were introduced by the first Viscount Leverhulme when he was attempting to develop industry in Lewis and Harris in the 1920's. They were smaller and simpler to work than either of the old types of loom described, but heavy, and weaving became almost entirely a male occupation, except insofar as efforts were made by a few individuals to keep the old methods of production alive. A loom, using modern materials and technology, much lighter to operate than the Hattersley, capable of weaving a wider cloth, as the market now demands, and likely to attract women back into the weaving side of the industry, is now – in 1993 – being introduced. Harris Tweed is protected by Act of Parliament. The Harris Tweed Act 1993 set up a Harris Tweed Authority to 'promote and maintain the authenticity, standard and reputation of Harris Tweed' and to take over the functions of the Harris Tweed Association – a voluntary body – which for over eighty years successfully protected the name Harris Tweed, and prevented it from becoming a purely generic term. The 1993 Act defines Harris Tweed as 'a tweed which has been handwoven by the islanders at their homes in the Outer Hebrides, finished in the Outer Hebrides, and made from pure virgin wool dyed and spun in the Outer Hebrides'. The new Statutory Authority also has power to make regulations to ensure that the traditional quality and characteristics of the cloth are maintained. As the author explains, the sale of *clò mòr*, the marketable version of the indigenous island tweed, was first promoted for philanthropic reasons by people who had no commercial stake in the industry but were deeply concerned by the poverty in the Western Isles in the middle of the last century. The element of voluntary service to the industry for social reasons was maintained throughout the life of the Harris Tweed Association, and is enshrined in the 1993 Act. The members of the Authority, appointed by the Sheriff Principal, and the Western Isles Islands Council – *Comhairle nan Eilean* – must be people who are not involved in the Harris Tweed industry and have no interest in it, financial or otherwise, which might prejudice their performance. The protection of the geographical origin of the cloth, and the element of social control in the interests of the community, make Harris Tweed unique among British manufacturing industries.

CHAPTER TWENTY: THE SCHOOL

The author's father, W. S. Duncan, became schoolmaster in Scarp in October 1883. In mid 1886 he transferred to Obbe Public School, South Harris. In August 1889 he was reappointed to Scarp, where he served until his retirement in February 1901. The following extracts are selected from his weekly entries in the Scarp school log-book. Editorial comments are shown in italics. These extracts are reproduced with the kind permission of the Director of Education of The Western Isles Islands Council, Neil Galbraith.

12 October 1883: Commenced work here yesterday – Thursday 11 October. Weather fair then and today. W. S. Duncan, teacher.

10 November 1883: Must get a bell or a whistle to intimate the approach of the school hour.

28 March 1884: Miss Marion MacInnes commenced duty as Sewing Mistress on Monday.
Family tradition has it that Marion MacInnes stuck sewing-pins into W.S.Duncan in class, to tease him. It clearly worked, for on 8 January 1885 the schoolmaster married his sewing mistress at Amhuinnsuidhe!

4 April 1884: Some of the older boys were absent assisting in bringing seaweed from Loch Resort to be used as manure for the land. Weather a little fairer.

22 August 1884: Had a holiday on Thursday because the children were required to assist in driving sheep on that day as they were collected to have the lambs separated. Many were absent on Friday too, being engaged about the lambs.

21 November 1884: The attendance a good deal affected this week by many of the boys being employed cutting bent-grass across the Sound and bringing home boatloads of it.

5 December 1884: Many boys were often absent this week employed in catching and bringing home sheep to be smeared.

Extract from H.M.Inspector's Report for 1884: The managers must be congratulated on the appointment of the present Teacher, who seems thoroughly qualified by conscientiousness and professional ability, for the charge of this remote school.

4 September 1885: Lady Scott called at the school on Monday afternoon and expressed her kindly interest in the children.
The Scotts had purchased North Harris – including Scarp – from the Dunmores in 1871. This Lady Scott, formerly Emilie Packe, was the widow of Sir Edward Henry Scott, who had died in 1883. His heir, Samuel Edward Scott, was then just ten years old, so Trustees, including Lady Scott, dealt with his affairs until he came of age.

2 October 1885: The men are now home from the N.E. coast fishing.

11 December 1885: A severe snowstorm prevented the youngsters from attending, and also some others who had no shoes.
The 'youngsters' were presumably the very youngest children.

Extract from H.M.Inspector's Report for 1885: Fifty-four scholars ... Great intelligence and very commendable proficiency are shown in the various oral and written Examinations. The tone of the school is superior and the children are under kindly and effective control. The disinclination on the part of the parents to give Girls a full Elementary Education should be resolutely opposed by the Managers.

1 June 1886: Announced three weeks as part of Summer holidays. *Followed by a note –* 'W. S. Duncan went to Obbe Public School'.

The succeeding teacher seemed to have had a very difficult time in Scarp, especially in coping with absenteeism. He died in July 1889. The registered cause of death was 'narcotic poisoning'.

9 August 1889: *Once again in W. S. Duncan's hand –* Entered on the duties

of this school on Wednesday 7 August 1889. It may be seen that this is not the first time I have made a commencement in Scarp. Arthur (my son and pupil-teacher) commenced today. A great number of the children stayed away on Thursday afternoon owing to the arrival of a boat with my family at 2 p.m., and I dismissed those who did put in an appearance, without holding a class, being averse to spoiling the averaging in my very first week. I have warned the children, however, not to stay away in this way again without receiving permission.

The 'boat with my family' doubtless contained his wife Marion, his eighteen year old twin daughters Helen and Christian – by an earlier marriage, for he had been a widower on coming to Scarp – his thirty month old daughter Alexandrina, and the author, then aged ten months. It was characteristic that the schoolmaster had not made the day an official holiday, as well he might have. Getting the school back into good order was clearly his priority.

19 August 1889: Compulsory Officer called after visiting the houses. He informed me that the elder children were required today to assist at gathering the lambs, and that many of the younger were staying away to see the fun.

17 January 1890: The attendance was unfortunately affected this week by the celebration of the Old New Year's eve by the young generation male, which consists of watching together all night, drinking tea etc. Many pupils in consequence had to busy themselves next day in sleeping off the bad effects, and had thus no time to spare for school attendance on that day. One boy at least is still on the sick list since then.

As explained in Chapter 23, Old New Year's Eve, or Hogmanay, was celebrated on 12 January.

28 March 1890: Only seven meetings held this week, the children having taken Wednesday and part of Thursday to pay up arrears of sleep incurred in connection with the festivities of a wedding. Influenza is still very prevalent and many pupils are absent from that cause.

6 June 1890: Some mornings the youngest set of infants could not get out of bed in time to attend in the forenoon, but I cured that evil to a great extent by giving a sweetie to those who came in time.

29 August 1890: Attendance affected on Monday by many assisting to take the lambs to the weaning island, and on Friday by many assisting at the peats.

The lambs were taken to Fladday island, lying towards the northern end of the Sound, in late August or in September, and returned to Scarp in October.

5 December 1890: The smearing of the sheep interfered with the attendance for several days.

This treatment, with a tar and butter compound, protected sheep from parasites and damp. It had given way to 'dipping' by 1915.

The year 1891 appeared to find Scarp troubled by extensive illness, with influenza, 'sickness', and whooping-cough, causing more than one school closure.

19 February 1892: No meeting held on Friday because only two pupils made an appearance. There is a serious sickness on the island. The peats are done on Scarp and the weather is fearfully cold and snowy, so that it was impossible to keep the schoolroom warm during the week. I have asked the school managers for coal.

15 April 1894: Very stormy with so much snow that many who had no shoes could not come to school.

28 December 1894: Only nine meetings this week, as Mrs Duncan was dangerously sick on Friday (today) afternoon. It was very stormy on the forenoon of that day.
The schoolmaster's youngest daughter, Christina Ann, was born in the schoolhouse early that afternoon. The 'dangerously sick' condition of his wife, Marion, must imply that a difficult birth was under way or had just taken place. Happily, both mother and baby survived and flourished, each eventually attaining the age of eighty-four years.

Extract from H.M. Inspector's Report, 1894: Painstaking devotion to duty on the part of the headmaster continues to characterise this remote island school.

24 December 1895: Attendance very poor today – 19 in the forenoon and 13 in the afternoon. A marriage of a Scarp couple was being celebrated at Amhuinnsuidhe and the children stayed away in great numbers – especially the girls – to look at the preparations being made in the island for the marriage feast.

14 August 1896: *Mention of Saturday 1 August, then –* On the same day I received a letter informing me that my daughter was alarmingly sick in Glasgow, and desired to see me before she died. I therefore left the school in charge of my son, Arthur, who is an ex pupil-teacher of 1890. He along with the P.T. appear to have conducted the school work with much diligence during my absence for the last fortnight.
This low-key entry relates to his daughter Helen, married in Glasgow, who died on 5 September 1896, one day before her twenty-sixth birthday. The schoolmaster's short visit must have been of some comfort to her, though tragic for him as he returned home to Scarp, knowing of her imminent death. Her twin sister Christian had died in Renfrew in 1892, aged twenty-one. Both daughters had been struck down by pulmonary tuberculosis.

25 June 1897: Tuesday was observed as a holiday for the Queen's Diamond
Jubilee, and the children were after the sheep on Friday.
Queen Victoria (1819-1901) had been crowned in 1837. Family tradition has it
that W. S. Duncan – a keen royalist – once bowed to Queen Victoria as she passed
in her carriage on the way to Haddo House, Aberdeenshire. This may have been in
1880, for the Queen visited Haddo that year, and W. S. Duncan was teaching in
Oldmeldrum at that time.

Unfortunately the next school log-book, covering September 1897 to July 1915,
is missing from the official records. This would have taken us to W.S.Duncan's
retirement in 1901 and beyond his death in 1912.

These extracts contain a wealth of detail of a now forgotten way of life.
All the early Scarp teachers seem to have been troubled by absenteeism; but
the older children played an essential part in many of the activities of the
island. Fank days were – at least in later years – an official school holiday,
but it is understandable that other activities should sometimes – for example,
when the weather suddenly opened to permit work on the land or across the
Sound – take priority over classes. The schoolmaster needed to be pragmatic
on such occasions. W. S. Duncan seemed to be so, despite his reputation as a
disciplinarian.

Scarp has had many able and dedicated teachers since those days. A few
extracts from later log-books are of particular interest here – the reporting
teachers' identities were not always made clear in the log-book:

22 October 1915: Before school on Monday a pedlar appeared in the place from
Brenish and only a handful of pupils turned up, as North Scarp was as if a Fair
was being held.
This might have been another visit by Barney, the Irish dealer who features in
Chapter 24!

4 August 1916: On Monday last all Scarp – old and young – were at Fladday
lifting peat, so no school was kept.

The winter of 1917-18 seems to have been exceptionally bad. A series of entries show
that the island had run out of meal and that a Scarp boat, returning from Tarbert,
was stormstayed in Loch Leosavay. The men carried meal the five miles to Hushinish,
but there was great difficulty in getting it across the Sound to Scarp. The following
extracts illustrate the hardships of the time.

24 November 1917: Tuesday was promising and a boat went to Tarbert. Boat
put to Amhuinnsuidhe Wednesday and is still there, the men coming overland
yesterday with what they could carry on their backs. No meal in Scarp past
few weeks.

1 December 1917: Boat still at Amhuinnsuidhe and women cannot get across the Sound to go for meal . . .

21 December 1917: Boat got home safely this week, to the great relief of many families, including our own . . .

25 January 1918: No Tarbert yet. Week very stormy. Food problem on island very serious. Quite apparent that School children are suffering much from subsisting almost solely on potatoes.

5 February 1918: Five men crossed today for Tarbert to endeavour to get food relief somehow.
They carried a 'wire' to the Rear Admiral, Stornoway, written out the week before by the schoolmaster, but only then ferried across the Sound. The next entry records the outcome.

8 February 1918: Two patrols appeared in Sound yesterday afternoon. One had our meal etc. and the five men who went to Tarbert on Tuesday. Day very stormy and pouring rain. Boats had great difficulty in reaching the patrols against a strong southerly gale. We would have been in dire distress had we not been relieved now, and we are very grateful to the Rear Admiral for responding to the SOS sent by Dr Ross and me.
The drama of that afternoon can well be imagined. A large proportion of the island's population – then about 150 – must have turned out to see the naval patrol boats, with their own Scarpmen braving the gale to bring the 'relief' ashore.

8 May 1945: The Second World War has ended. Today and tomorrow given as Holidays to celebrate. The children marched in procession to the top of the hill, where a bonfire was lit at night.

30 June 1967: *By the last schoolmistress, Mrs Joan MacLennan* – This school is being closed today. The remaining pupils are to attend Sir Edward Scott Junior Secondary School, Tarbert, next session.

The author travelled from Edinburgh to be present at the closing of the school. The following particulars were taken from his own notes of the occasion: Angus MacInnes, the island's elder, presided; Donald MacLean, the missionary of Maaruig, opened with prayer; the last schoolmistress, Joan MacLennan, was thanked by Murdo MacInnes on behalf of the islanders; and she in turn praised the hospitality she and her husband had received during their years in Scarp. Norman MacLean, postmaster, presented prizes to the last two pupils, Salvia MacDonald and Donald John MacDonald; and Salvia, on behalf of all the islanders, made a presentation to the schoolmistress. The author gave a short address on the history of the school and later closed the proceedings with the Benediction. The entire proceedings were conducted in Gaelic. A *Stornoway Gazette* contributor reported that most of the company then took part in a game of football with the children's ball.

CHAPTER TWENTY-ONE: THE MISSION

The Rev Donald A. MacRae, Minister of Tarbert Church of Scotland from 1956 to 1988, and now living in active retirement at Maaruig, has provided the following evocative note on the Mission in Scarp. The loss of the last resident missionary in 1966 greatly troubled the islanders, and the author, among others, made strong efforts to help the Home Board of the Church of Scotland to find a replacement. Sadly that was not successful. Seen from today's perspective it had an inevitability, even if its timing might have been different. Scarp by then had no more than eight families and less than thirty people, but they felt the loss of their resident missionary none the less keenly. Mr MacRae writes:

> There is a tinge of sadness in reflecting on the demise of a lively community. This is especially true when one thinks of bygone village clearances in the Highlands and Islands, where people were constrained to leave homes, relatives and modes of life, unwillingly, to face a future of unknown hazards.
>
> This however was not the case with the Scarp people. Force of circumstances brought about their exodus from the island of their nativity, which they loved so dearly, where so many blessings and joys were shared by them.
>
> When the last resident lay missionary of the Church of Scotland vacated the island on his retirement he was not going to be replaced. The dwindling population acknowledged that the end of an era was commencing in the history of the village. Across the Sound, however, on the mainland of Harris, they had friends and relatives who shared their language and culture and worship.
>
> Thus they were fortunate in being able to establish good homes in more accessible locations, where it was easy for them to integrate into the community.
>
> The younger ones could avail themselves of new opportunities of employment, and those who desired to retain their crofts in Scarp did so, and continue still to graze their sheep stock there.
>
> Only the narrow Sound separates them from their ancestral birthplace. Though nostalgic longings and memories are naturally aroused, they know that hardships and anxieties which followed the lot of dwindling populations in small isolated islands do not now overwhelm them.
>
> But even after the missionary gave his farewell blessings to the island people, they knew that the Mission Church would always be open on the Lord's Day

for worship, as long as anyone remained who could read the Bible. The Kirk Session of Tarbert Church were able to send a saintly elder over regularly for weekend pulpit supply, and if the weather should be so atrocious as to prevent a sea crossing, it was fortunate that one of the last families to leave the island was the household of the godly Scarp elder, who was capable of conducting worship himself.

A stranger coming to Scarp for Sabbath worship always made reference to a custom peculiar to the island. At the conclusion of the evening service after the benediction, the missionary called the worshippers together to kneel in prayer in the pews, and after prayer they all rose quietly from their knees and departed homewards. This was probably a recurring symbol of the Christian family kneeling for night-time prayers before bedtime.

Another custom which was uncommon in Lewis and Harris, was the singing of a Gaelic Psalm by the menfolk gathered round the open grave in the burial place. The funeral service was held, as in the other islands, usually in the home of the bereavement. Thereafter the cortège arrived at the graveside, and when the coffin was laid reverently to rest in the sandy soil before the committal prayer, the officiating missionary, or minister if he was able to be present, read verses in Gaelic from Psalm 16, including the last two verses, or from Psalm 107, including verse 30, and the precentor led the singing. On a balmy summer's afternoon that was a very moving and wonderful service – the choir of melodious skylarks singing overhead, the cadences of the singing surf beside the cemetery, the solemn dark-garbed menfolk encircling the grave bidding farewell to the mortal remains of their fellow islesperson, earnestly singing the ancient psalmist's song of resurrection, hope and joy.

The island today is lovely, as it always was, but sadly so. The visitor reminisces among the ruins of a deserted hamlet, but still has the mystic sense of being 'surrounded by so great a cloud of witnesses' and the wonderful knowledge that there were godly men and women converted here, who became Christian witnesses and ambassadors, not only to our own kith and kin in the islands, but to many many others further afield.

Salm CVII, rann 30:

An sin tha iad ro-ait, air son
   gu bheil iad sàmhach beò:
'S gu'n d'thug e iad do'n chaladh sin,
   's do'n phort bu mhiannach leo.

Psalm 107, verse 30:

> Then are they glad, because at rest
> and quiet now they be:
> So to the haven he them brings,
> which they desir'd to see.

CHAPTER TWENTY-THREE: A RÈITEACH AND A WEDDING

In Chapter 23 the author refers to the enjoyment children and adults alike derived from a wedding. Dugald Campbell, schoolmaster in Scarp from 1949 to 1953, has described a wedding which was celebrated there in the traditional style. On that occasion the betrothal and marriage ceremonies took place on successive days, rather than a fortnight apart, as in older times. The groom – John MacDonald – came from one of the notable families of Scarp, and the bride – Janet MacDonald – was from Manish, in South Harris. The schoolmaster himself was the piper who features in the narrative. Sadly, Mr Campbell died in Inverness in July 1995. He had already cleared the printed text of this splendid composition.

A Rèiteach and a Wedding,
by Dugald Campbell

During the early days of summer 1952, word spread through the community that an islander from the north end of Scarp was about to marry a young lady from furth of the island. The news greatly excited the population. Other marriages there had been, but it was many years since a bride had come from outwith the island to settle in their midst. An event like this had to be celebrated in true traditional manner. A *Rèiteach* must be held. Such was the unanimous decision of the islanders.

But what is a *Rèiteach*? It is a word which does not translate easily – it is a type of Betrothal or Espousal Ceremony, for which there is no single comparable English word.

Once the date of the wedding became official, preparations began in earnest. These were not just confined to the family concerned, but seemed to be the responsibility of all the islanders and particularly the womenfolk, as the preparation of a wedding feast fell mainly on their shoulders. Food rationing was still in operation, but the word was never mentioned.

There was no calling of committee meetings. A few of the women would get together in one of the houses just to ensure that the necessary arrangements were moving along smoothly. Yet there was a lot to be organised – the food, the cooking, the baking, the collection of dishes and cutlery, and the acquisition of tables and chairs. The list seemed endless, but all had to be attended to and, most important of all, the accommodation had to be secured.

There was only one building on the island capable of accommodating such a gathering – the school. The bridegroom, whom we all regarded as a close personal friend, and whom we often referred to as *Ar Bàilidh*, or 'Our Factor', because of his unfailing helpfulness, had made a practice of visiting us at the schoolhouse every Wednesday evening after the prayer meeting in the mission-hall. On his first visit after news of his impending marriage had become widespread, we discussed the event at some length. I quickly mentioned that the school would be made available and that I would contact the Education Authority for formal confirmation of the closing of the school for the three days required – a Wednesday, Thursday and Friday. All this was readily agreed.

At last the day of departure for the wedding arrived, and during the afternoon all those travelling to attend the *Rèiteach* at the bride's home gathered at the boat at the north end of the village, the bridegroom being piped aboard to the strains of 'Leaving Port Askaig'. When all were safely aboard, we were ferried to Hushinish. There we boarded a bus and proceeded to Tarbert, where a stop was made for necessary supplies. Leaving Tarbert, we proceeded on our journey to Manish, where we arrived at the bride's home at about six in the evening.

Here it was evident that the ladies of the community had been just as industrious as their counterparts in our own island. After the usual welcoming hospitality, we relaxed for the next hour or so, until at eight o'clock the guests filed into the dining area. This was the largest room in the house, from which all surplus furniture had been removed and replaced by a number of tables in the shape of a large 'T', and more or less filling the whole room.

There was a definite order of seating. At the top table sat the bridegroom and on his right sat the chief speaker from our island, who would act on his behalf. The chair on the bridegroom's left was kept vacant while the next one was occupied by the best man. The chair on his left also was kept vacant. Seated on either side at the top of the other table were the chief speaker and his assistant from Manish. From there towards the foot of the table sat the remainder of the guests, but it was noticed that there was a kind of descending order of superiority. Those who seemed to be considered more important, perhaps because of age, being placed nearer to the top two speakers.

The tables were draped with snow white tablecloths on which mountains of food had been placed – no sign of rationing here either! On all being seated, Grace was said in the native tongue, after which the ladies served the tables. This was done with a great deal of banter as all those dining were male. The banter and the conversation were entirely in Gaelic.

At last the meal ended and everyone relaxed over a welcome cup of tea, while one or two of the older generation lit their pipes. At this point the chief local speaker seated at the head of the main table leaned across and spoke to his friend, in a voice audible to all. 'We have a lot of visitors with us tonight', he said. 'Yes,' replied his friend, 'we have indeed. I wonder what has brought them? I wonder if they are looking for something?' 'Perhaps they are,' said the spokesman, 'would they be looking for a horse?' 'No,' replied his friend, 'they don't have horses in Scarp, but they might be looking for a cow.' 'No,' said the spokesman, 'they have plenty of cattle on the island.'

This type of conversation continued for some time until at last the speaker said: 'If we only knew what they are anxious to find, then I am sure we would do all in our power to help them', and raising his voice slightly he continued, 'Our two communities have had excellent relations with one another over very many years, and if they would only let us know the reason for their mission, I'm sure we would be able to supply their needs'.

This was the signal for the chief speaker from the island to get to his feet. He thanked the villagers for their welcome and for their generous hospitality. He went on to say that we had come on a mission that would further enhance the bonds of friendship which had existed between the two communities for so many generations. He explained that his friend beside him – the bridegroom – was a close neighbour, and proceeded to extol his virtues to the utmost. He told of his friend's reliability. He it was who was responsible for conveying the lobster boxes to Tarbert on their way to Billingsgate. This task he performed extremely efficiently. However, over the past few months it was noticed that his journeys to Tarbert were taking longer than usual and, after some discreet enquiries, it had transpired that he was making the return journey to the island via Manish, hence the reason for their visit. They had come to seek the assistance of the community in procuring a wife for his friend.

The speaker for the Manish group now replied, assuring the visitors that they would be delighted to assist in such a venture. He spoke in glowing terms of the qualities of the local girls and he was sure that this young man need not return to his island as a despairing bachelor.

Now came the most important part of the proceedings – the choosing of a bride. Suddenly there was the sound of hilarity and scuffling in the kitchen area. Then all at once two young men appeared in the doorway, dragging in a supposedly reluctant candidate for approval. They held her just inside the doorway, so that she could be seen by all. The local speaker asked if she could be regarded as a suitable bride. The visiting speaker looked at the girl and shook his head. He agreed that she had many fine qualities, but she hadn't the type of legs required for climbing the hills to attend the shieling! The young men bundled her back into the kitchen, where there were further scuffles and hilarity before they again appeared with a struggling victim. Her virtues were also extolled, but again they didn't match the requirements of the visiting speaker. She had eye-shadow, painted nails and dyed hair – all this was out of keeping with local tradition. A third young girl was brought in but again rejected. The speaker could always think up some amusing reasons for his decisions, much to the enjoyment of the company. When the fourth candidate was hauled in, the speaker seemed quite impressed. She was not quite what they were looking for, but in case they might not get anything better, they would hold onto her in the meantime. She was led to the vacant chair beside the best man. This in reality was the bridesmaid.

Thereafter several girls were brought in, one by one, but each was rejected in the usual hilarious manner. But when the next member of the fair sex was brought in, the bridegroom looked up at the speaker and nodded, whereupon the speaker started to proclaim her virtues. But looks of concern appeared on the faces of the local people, and their chief speaker whispered that this was not 'the chosen one'! All was taken in good part and she too was dismissed with various hilarious excuses. Finally the real bride was brought in and this time there was no mistake. All possible praises were bestowed upon her and she was led to and placed in the vacant chair beside the bridegroom.

Peace returned to the kitchen regions, while the entire party toasted the health of the young couple, and listened to speeches from both sides of the table. Once these were completed and the bride safely chosen, those of the company already served, moved to a neighbour's house where a room had been prepared for singing and dancing. An accordionist and a piper provided music for the dancers, while at intervals singers entertained the company with Gaelic songs.

At five the next morning the company sat down to another meal, after which it was decided we should have some sleep in preparation for the day ahead. Each person from Scarp was just told: 'You are going to stay with such and such a household', and everyone was accommodated without any fuss or difficulty.

By nine o'clock that day everyone seemed to be afoot and in remarkably good fettle. At one o'clock we gathered together and proceeded to Leverburgh, where the young couple were duly married with the utmost solemnity, and all in the Gaelic tongue, by the local Free Church Minister assisted by the Church of Scotland Minister from Tarbert. Once the necessary clerical business had been attended to and photographs taken, the young couple were piped from the church to the strains of 'The Highland Wedding'. The entire company retraced their steps to Manish where an excellent lunch awaited us. This interval gave the bride the opportunity of changing out of bridal raiment and into travelling clothes more suitable for the long journey to the Sound and the sea-crossing to Scarp.Eventually we boarded the bus and set out for Hushinish, arriving there at about eight in the evening, to be met by a large contingent of friends and relatives, who had gathered to congratulate the young couple. Among those present were my good friends the doctor and the Tarbert headmaster complete with his cine-camera. The weather was perfect, and as bride and bridegroom were piped towards the waiting boat the camera began to roll. I remember thinking that this part at least would be preserved for posterity. Arriving at Scarp another welcoming party awaited us, and the young couple were piped to the open door of their home to the strains of *Mo Dhachaidh*, or 'My Home'.

Having delivered the young couple safely, the entire company were distributed amongst the island homes to relax for a short time, while the bride once more donned her wedding outfit for the reception about to take place in the school.

I made my way to the schoolhouse where we found that the kitchen area had taken on the appearance of a top class hotel carvery. The ladies had worked wonders to have everything organised to perfection.

On looking into the school itself, I found it devoid of school furniture. The few men who had been left on the island and the school children had cleared the room, enabling the ladies to set the tables in the traditional manner of a 'T' shape. The white-draped tables were laden with a wonderful variety of the good things of life – evidence of the quality of the cooks and bakers within our midst. In the fireplace I noticed an article which had not been placed there by the ladies – a stoutly built gantry on which rested a fifty gallon barrel of ale. Truly nothing had been omitted.

As the cameraman was anxious about the fading light, I made my way to the newly-weds' house, for they had to be piped to the school. I was joined by others anxious to take part in the procession, but as we approached the door we found to our dismay that the occupants were securely locked inside.

When the young couple had entered the house, the bridesmaid had locked the door so that there would be no opportunity for the young lads to play pranks on the newly-weds. Alas! The key had broken in the lock and now they were prisoners in their own home. There was only one way out of the dilemma – the bride must be taken out through the window. Tools were quickly procured and the bride and retinue were extricated via the window space.

The newly-weds were now piped from their home to the school, where over two hundred guests had gathered to welcome them. They took their allotted seats at the top table, flanked on either side by the bridesmaid and best man. The young couple would remain in their seats throughout the entire night, while successive relays of guests were fed. Speeches of congratulation and welcome, full of wit and humour, were delivered, after which Grace was said, and the ladies proceeded to serve a sumptuous meal. Once the first contingent had finished, the tables were set for the next group of diners. An interesting feature in all this was that as each male took his seat, he placed a bottle of whisky on the centre of the table in front of him. During the meal he would go round topping up the glasses of the diners and then replace the bottle. It remained there until it was empty. The relays of diners continued until all had been served.

While this was going on, all those who had been served engaged in dancing in the clear area of the room. Here again the accordion and the pipes provided the music. However, as the night was beautifully clear and calm, and the space inside rather confined, the dancers moved outside, where the doctor organised dancing and community singing. The dancers continued to dance on the green sward of the children's playground, leaving the schoolroom for the singing of songs and the telling of traditional tales, while the dispensing of tea or ale went

on throughout the night. It was a night to be remembered by all who had the
privilege of being present.

As the rays of morning sunshine told of the passage of time, at about eight
o'clock a.m. it was decided that the celebrations should be concluded. One last
cup of tea, and the singing of 'Auld Land Syne', brought the event to an end.

Eventually I turned the key in the school door and watched the last of the
boats ferry the departing guests over to Hushinish. As I turned away I realised
that a group of children were on the sands just below the school. I made my
way down to where they were, to find, as they put it: 'We are just playing here
until it is time for the school to open'. I was completely astonished. They had
sang and danced the whole night through, yet here they were waiting for the
school to open. I suggested, as gently as possible, that they should go home and
have a few hours sleep, as the school would not be ready for classes until Monday
morning.

I went to bed pondering over the inexhaustible energy of youth.

CHAPTER TWENTY-SEVEN: FLORA

This chapter gives the author's memories of the flowers of his boyhood. Unlike
his schoolmaster father, William Smith Duncan, the author was not himself a
naturalist. His descriptions should nevertheless be of interest to the reader, giving
a feeling of the diversity of plantlife found on Scarp.

Andrew Currie, the Broadford naturalist, was good enough to read Chapter
27, and that part of Chapter 9 dealing with the use of flowers in children's
games. It was decided to leave the manuscript, including the flower names,
as written, covering things as recollected by the author, rather than to give
a botanical commentary on the plants mentioned. But in editing the chapter,
account has been taken of some suggested adjustments.

Referring to Arthur Bennett's writings, Mr Currie pointed out that W. S.
Duncan had enumerated two hundred and forty seven plant species found on
Scarp, and that he had noted the orchids of Harris in particular detail, recording
their habitats more fully than was at that time usual. He writes:

> I, as a botanist, conclude that W. S. Duncan made a major contribution to the
> flora of the Outer Hebrides, and in particular Harris, over a period approaching
> twenty years. Specimens were sent as well as letters, and this was at a time when
> the flora was little known. His contribution was therefore a very valuable one.

W. S. Duncan's life is covered in an introductory Biographical Note and he
features in Chapter 20, *The School.* A number of plants, new to the outer islands'

records, are attributed to him in issues of *The Scottish Naturalist* between 1889 and 1891; and his botanical work is recognised in Arthur Bennett's *Contributions towards a Flora of the Outer Hebrides*, published in the quarterly magazine, *Annals of Scottish Natural History*, during 1892, 1895, 1905 and 1910. The following extracts from Bennett's writings are of interest here:

> *January 1892*: A wish to see the western isles of Scotland thoroughly explored for their botanical productions has induced me these five years past to endeavour to interest anyone who I knew was likely to help on the work; and by the kindness of Messrs Duncan, King, Somerville, and Cotton I have been enabled to see a good series of plants from the Outer Hebrides.

> *October 1895*: Since my first notes on the flora of these islands, various additions have been made, more especially by Mr W. S. Duncan and Dr W. A. Shoolbred.

> *July 1905*: It would seem by Mr W. S. Duncan's researches that the alpine element (noted as so poor by Babington in 1844) is richer than had been supposed.

> *July 1910*: I regret to say that my correspondent Mr W. S. Duncan has (since the last report) been seriously ill, and able to do scarcely any collecting and observing; but the following pages will show that while he could he has done good work.

The majority of plants attributed to him were from Scarp itself, but his collecting extended to the North Harris hills and to South Harris. The latter arose from his time as schoolmaster at Obbe.

In 1888 he collected, from a loch near Obbe, a stonewort plant new to the British flora, but already known from the Continent. This was a delicate green alga with the current botanical name, *Nitella confervacea* – in his day known as *Nitella batrachosperma*. The *Scottish Naturalist* for 1889-91 said of the discovery: 'Here is another inducement to our botanists to search every piece of water accessible to them on the chance of finding something new.'

Flora of the Outer Hebrides (Natural History Museum Publications, 1991), mentions W. S. Duncan some thirty times, mainly as the collector of British Museum specimens dated 1889 to 1896. Of special interest is a microspecies of Hawkweed – Gaelic name: *Lus na Seabhaig*, or 'The falcon's plant' – with the botanical name *Hieracium scarpicum*. This Latin name acknowledges Scarp where he first collected it, in the 'North Bay' of the island, in 1890. Several specimens, dated 1890, 1891 and 1894, were contributed to Arthur Bennett's herbarium, now held by the British Museum. In 1941 H. W. Pugsley described it in detail and gave it this botanical name. The entry on page 122 of *Flora of the Outer Hebrides* reads:

H. scarpicum Pugsley: Endemic in the Outer Hebrides, and only known from Scarp (hence the name), Lewis and North Harris. The type specimens were collected by W. S. Duncan, 1894, (BM)

The *Flora* notes that Hawkweed – of which over two hundred microspecies are known from the British Isles – is found on 'Rocky banks, cliffs and crags, ravines and walls', and that 'It can only survive when it is out of reach of grazing animals'. It may therefore not have been particularly common in Scarp, where grazing was and still is widespread.

Annals of Scottish Natural History for July 1910 lists the orchids recorded in Scarp by W. S. Duncan. The table below shows those which have familiar English names. The names here are derived from *Wild Orchids of Scotland*, HMSO, Edinburgh, 1993. Only botanical names – some of them now obsolete – were given in the *Annals*. The modern equivalents are used below:

ENGLISH NAME	GAELIC NAME	BOTANICAL NAME
Bog Orchid	Mogairlean Bogaich	*Hammarbya paludosa*
Common Twayblade	Dà-dhuilleach	*Listera ovata*
Lesser Twayblade	Dà-dhuilleach Monaidh	*Listera cordata*
Early Purple Orchid	Moth-ùrach	*Orchis mascula*
Early Marsh-orchid	Mogairlean Lèana	*Dactylorhiza incarnata*
Heath Spotted-orchid	Mogairlean Mòintich	*Dactylorhiza maculata* var. *ericetorum*
Frog Orchid	Mogairlean Losgainn	*Coeloglossum viride*
*Lesser Butterfly-orchid	Mogairlean an Dealain-dè Beag	*Platanthera bifolia*

*Note: The Lesser Butterfly-orchid – with its 'white, slightly tinged yellowish green flowers' – was described as being 'frequent from Amhuinnsuidhe to Bedersaig', a footpath route which the Scarp people were very familiar with in his day. It is unclear whether this orchid had been found on Scarp itself. In addition, the Greater Butterfly-orchid *Platanthera chlorantha* – not listed for Scarp – was in 1891 recorded by W.S.Duncan at Obbe.

Visits to the island during 1994 and 1995 confirmed a point made at the beginning of Chapter 27: the rich carpet of spring flowers, usually seen on the machair around the school and mission buildings, is lost when heavy grazing by the island's sheep occurs. The flowers recover quickly once sheep and lambs are driven beyond the fence to the north and west of the village. Andrew Currie has pointed out that some degree of grazing is normally beneficial in such locations, for it keeps down the rampant grassy vegetation which would otherwise choke many of the more interesting plants. The ending of arable cultivation, once the last families had left the island in 1971, must also have had an impact on the diversity of wild flowers to be found on Scarp.

Most of the Forest of Harris lying west of a line starting just inland from Bunavoneadar and curving northwards to the head of Loch Resort, became a 'site of special scientific interest' – an SSSI – in 1984. The Hushinish peninsula falls within this area, but the island of Scarp does not. A few small coastal pockets – e.g. at Bedersaig, Govig, Amhuinnsuidhe, and Cliasmol – also fall outside the North Harris SSSI. The notification summarises the area as being: 'A fine example of an ecosystem which is the result of strongly oceanic conditions acting on some of the rockiest British hills'. In contrast, Gasker and Gasker Beg are part of a group of 'small seal islands' which form another SSSI. They are: 'notable for the grey seal colonies which they support'. The notification adds that over one thousand seal pups are born on Gasker annually.

Once an SSSI notification is served, the owner or occupier of land is required to inform Scottish Natural Heritage before doing anything which might damage the features of special interest. When necessary, a consultation process then takes place, and there are circumstances under which monetary compensation could be claimed. The conservation aspects of a declaration need not prevent the occupiers from following traditional practices and ways of life, but they can help to prevent damaging operations should these become a threat in the future.

CHAPTER TWENTY-EIGHT: FAUNA

Peter Cunningham, the Stornoway naturalist, has offered some interesting observations on Chapter 28. On the strength of these, a few names within the original text have been adjusted. His comments are given below:

> Not much has changed since this chapter was written, except perhaps the havoc wrought among ground nesting birds by American mink which, released or escaped from captivity in Lewis in the 1950s, have multiplied and spread throughout Lewis and Harris and offshore islands. Nevertheless this fifty year old account is well worth having, if the author's occasional imprecision in respect of birds' names is borne in mind. For example his Stonechat, a literal translation from the Gaelic *Clacharan*, refers to the Wheatear [Changed to Wheatear in the text] according to his careful description.

His reference to Rooks being seen in winter is interesting, for it is known that there is a regular passage in winter of Continental Rooks up the west of Britain, and the present unique Hebridean rookery in the Stornoway Woods is supposed to have been set up by the survivors of a great flock of Rooks wrecked on the west coast of Lewis in the late nineteenth century.

The captive owl was most likely a Short-eared Owl which is native to the Uists and Benbecula and wanders now and again into Harris, but the Pigeons were without doubt Rock Doves which still breed in coastal caves in all the islands and are regarded as important pure relics of their hybrid metropolitan brethren.

The author had the keen eye for seabirds natural to an islesman but lacked through no fault of his own the finer points of nomenclature. His reference to Sandpipers [Changed from 'sandpipers' to 'small waders' in the text] I should think more properly applies to common waders such as Dunlin and Ringed Plovers, to both of which the behaviour he describes could be attributed. Common Sandpipers are solitary birds of inland lochs and streams, and others of the sandpiper family are rare vagrants.

Great Northern Divers are fairly common winter visitors from Iceland, but local Black-throated and Red-throated Divers could have frequented the Sound of Scarp, as they still do today, together with many Shags which the author refers to, wrongly I think, as the rarer Cormorant.

The wild cat has never been found in the Outer Hebrides, but unfortunately many feral domestic cats have thrived in the wild.

Mr Stewart Angus writes in his paper, *Terrestrial Mammals of the Outer Hebrides*, (in *The Natural Environment of the Outer Hebrides*, Nature Conservancy Council, Stornoway, 1979) that, 'Feral Goats were found in Harris and Uig (Lewis) in the last century and possibly as late as 1930, but they are long extinct'. The author's reference to them in the Loch Resort area is therefore of great interest.

Peter Cunningham refers to the havoc caused by mink. The crofters and house owners on Scarp confirm their unwelcome presence. A few years ago one of the last ladies to leave Scarp went into her hen-house at Bedersaig, near Hushinish, and disturbed a raiding mink which had just killed her hens. She bravely caught and caged it, but not before it had badly bitten her hand. As she crossed to her house she left a trail of blood on the road. An alert vet who chanced to pass soon after, noticed the blood and stopped at the house. He dressed the wound, and Annie duly recovered from her encounter with the mink.

The taking of wild-birds' eggs seems to have been freely practised – at least by the children – during the author's boyhood. Unlike St Kilda, it is doubtful if such eggs, or the flesh of the birds themselves, had ever formed a serious part of the islanders' diet. For one thing, they had access to comparatively few breeding seabirds, and the nesting landbirds and shorebirds, although common, were not present in large numbers. With limited exceptions, it is now an offence under the Wildlife and Countryside Act, 1981, to kill, injure or take, any wild bird, or to take or destroy its eggs.

The author's interest in the otter might have been inherited. Once when his grandfather, Angus MacInnes – The Deacon – was alone at the back of Scarp, he confronted an otter and 'killed' it. He slung the animal over his shoulder, holding it by the tail, and made for home. Along the way the otter revived and took a firm grip of the seat of his trousers. On reaching home he called to his wife: *Na cumhainn ise, ach thoir an aire ormsa!* – 'Don't spare her, but mind me!' – whereupon she grabbed a weapon and struck a blow. She missed the otter and landed a thump on her husband's elbow. The Deacon let go of the tail and the otter made off through the open door and down to the sea below the house: a happy ending – from today's point of view.

Otters were undoubtedly persecuted in Harris – as elsewhere – at one time. Harvie-Brown and Buckley, writing in 1888, quote the 'vermin returns' for 1870-1880, submitted by Murdoch MacAulay, 'head forester' at Amhuinnsuidhe, as: 'Martens 10; Otters 6; Rats 2000; Ravens 100; Crows 200; Peregrines 3; Hawks 15'. This suggests that the otter was not very numerous in North Harris, or that it did not have the highest priority among the estate's 'vermin'. Perhaps the taking of otters was under-recorded, for these writers also say: 'skins of fine [otter] fur often bring as high a price as 15s. each' – a considerable sum in those days.

The otter is now given wide protection under the Wildlife and Countryside Act, 1981, and The Conservation (Natural Habitats, &c.) Regulations, 1994. Under the latter – which implement a European Council Directive – the otter, along with certain other Scheduled species, including the true wild cat, is 'a European protected species'. It is an offence, 'deliberately to capture or kill', or, 'deliberately to disturb', such an animal, or, 'to damage or destroy a breeding site or resting place'. One of the limited exceptions is that it may be disturbed if discovered within a dwellinghouse.

It may be no surprise to learn that the lady who caught the mink is a great-granddaughter of The Deacon, who caught the otter!

CHAPTER TWENTY-NINE: MARY ROSE'S ISLAND

Chapter 29 refers to J. M. Barrie's connection with Amhuinnsuidhe – how the 1912 holiday there with his wards, the Llewelyn Davies boys, helped set the scene for the play *Mary Rose*. The association of Loch Voshimid with the play is rather stronger than the author, when he wrote that chapter, had thought. Nicholas Davies, the youngest of the five boys, was interested in the author's observations. In a letter written to him in 1966, he contributed the following personal note on the subject:

I might just add this about Mary Rose Island in Loch Voshimid. When I first re-saw it in 1962 I more or less ridiculed the whole idea – much the same as I have ridiculed the number of people who claim to have been the first Peter Pan; but on a wild and windy, though beautiful day two years ago, when the boat could not be launched on the loch, I walked round the lochside and chanced to sit down a dozen or so yards from the lochside just opposite the island, and strange as it may seem, I had a most vivid recollection. Which was of a certain day in 1912 when JMB took me and the family nurse (I presume in some form of trap) up the wonderful winding road past Scourst (where my elder brother, George, was fishing) and on to have lunch with Michael, who was on Voshimid with his beloved Johnnie MacKay. JMB and I sat on this very spot waiting for Michael to finish his fishing and have lunch with us. I have not the slightest doubt now that this was the moment when JMB looked across to the island and recalled the old legend, which I think first sprang from Scandinavia, and had been told him previously. It was certainly the only day I went to Voshimid that year and I am pretty sure the only time that JMB himself got there. And yet, as you correctly say, it wasn't until after the war seven or eight years later that he started seriously to write his wonderful play.

Nicholas Davies went on to mention a visit to the whaling station at Bunavoneadar, when he, aged eight, and J.M.Barrie, aged fifty-two, 'were both overwhelmed by the smell'. Barrie later had Mr Morland, in Act 1 of *Mary Rose*, tell of a family visit to the Outer Hebrides, adding, 'there is a whaling station'. This remark – for Barrie enjoyed embedding private allusions within his works – no doubt commemorated the playwright's Bunavoneadar visit with young Nicholas.

Mr Davies added a footnote on Barrie's parting gifts to the Amhuinnsuidhe ghillies. Barrie knew that Nicholas was devoted to his own, 'dear old bearded lame ghillie called Donald', and suggested that he should give the ghillie his own pocketmoney, instead of the gifts being delivered by Barrie to all the others. He ends: 'So – unless JMB slipped him something out of my sight – poor Donald only got three shillings and sixpence for his pains!'

CHAPTER THIRTY: THE FINAL YEARS

Chapter 30 tells of a walk to Tarbert in the early years of this century, and of the postal and other links between Scarp and the mainland of Harris. The laying of a submarine cable across the Sound enabled a telephone service to be established in 1947. Even though this was a boon, the population steadily declined over the next two decades. The death of the last missionary in 1966, and the closure of the school in 1967, were milestone events, but so too was the closing of the island Post Office, when the postmaster and his family left in 1969. When that happened, each of the four remaining households was provided with a lockable official briefcase to use for outgoing and incoming mail. These were put into a regulation mailbag and ferried to Hushinish, where the official postman then conveyed the Scarp mail to Tarbert Post Office.

In the 1960s Scarp was host to a number of enthusiastic visitors, for in June 1965 a visitors' hostel was established, with the help of the Gatliff Trust, in one of the thatched houses in Scarp. The relative inaccessibility of the island limited the number of young people using it, but those who did seemed to thoroughly enjoy the experience. Approximately one hundred and fifty hostellers used it between 1965 and 1970. The depopulation of the island, with the consequent loss of the scheduled ferry service subsidised by the Post Office, meant that the Trust had to close the hostel in 1970. A visitors' housebook from the Scarp hostel, examined by courtesy of Frank Martin, Chairman of the Gatliff Trustees, contains glowing reports by both British and foreign visitors. The kindness and helpfulness of all the Scarp people, including the Warden, is repeatedly acknowledged, and the island's rugged beauty is warmly mentioned. The only 'hardship' occasionally recorded is the hauling of driftwood fuel from *Eilean na Moil Mòire* to the hostel. The weather, from 'uninterrupted sunshine' to 'a thunderstorm', inevitably features in some of the comments. Many of the hostellers expressed a strong desire to return to Scarp.

By late 1971 only two crofting families remained on the island. They then reluctantly decided that it was time to settle on the Harris mainland. The following extract from a contemporary press agency report covers that historic occasion. It is quoted here with the permission of Bill Lucas, of Hebridean Press Service, Stornoway:

> The Hebridean isle of Scarp in Harris was evacuated this afternoon [2 December 1971] by the last of the native inhabitants. Mr and Mrs Angus MacInnes and their two sons came ashore at Hushinish on the Harris mainland with their furniture, personal effects and livestock, to set up a new home at Govig. Their goods were ferried across the half-mile channel which separates the picturesque little island from the Harris mainland, while their two cows swam behind the boat. A few weeks ago Mr and Mrs Murdo MacInnes and their son also left their native isle and moved to Tarbert in Harris.

It is good to know that both these families – and others – retain their crofting rights on Scarp, and that the men are back and forth, across the Sound, during the busier times of the sheep-raising year. The family who went to Tarbert soon moved to a new house at Bedersaig, within sight of their native island.

Scarp has not been entirely deserted since then. One or two people, with an instinct for independent living, have made their homes there from time to time, and a number of houses are now retained as holiday homes by families who appreciate the quiet natural beauty of the land and the surrounding sea.

Access for day-visitors who lack a boat of their own is difficult. There is no ferry, and the crofters who have sheep on the island must govern their crossings according to the needs of husbandry and the vagaries of the weather. Their working boats, used for conveying stock, need a strong crew to launch and to handle, so the casual visitor may have to admire Scarp from across the Sound. This in itself is well worth doing, and it avoids the risk, should the weather suddenly deteriorate, of being stranded on the island, among the memories and ghosts of over four hundred years of human settlement.

THE OWNERSHIP OF SCARP

Chapter 14 explains how Scarp, as part of the lands of Harris, was at one time within the territory of the MacLeods of Dunvegan, before the parish was sold in 1779 to Captain Alexander MacLeod. In 1834 Harris was bought by the Dunmore family, who in the mid 1860s built the Castle at Amhuinnsuidhe. In 1871 the land was divided and North Harris sold to the Scotts, who were the proprietors during the author's boyhood. Ownership later passed through other hands: the names Leverhulme, Venables, Brocket, Sopwith, Lowndes & Miller Mundy, and Hereward Wake are all well remembered. In late 1994 the North Harris Estate was purchased from Mrs Helene Panchaud – the Swiss-based owner whose late husband had bought it in 1977 – by the present proprietor, Mr Jonathan Bulmer.

But in 1978 Scarp had been separated from the North Harris Estate, when it was purchased by Tewera, a company with Swiss majority owners, Mr and Mrs Daniel Fiaux. The following year they purchased the school buildings from the Western Isles Islands Council, and converted them into a single dwellinghouse. In 1983 the island was sold to Orbitglen, a company owned by Mr Nazmudin Virani, a London based Asian businessman. In mid-1995, following the insolvency of the owner, Scarp – including the by now derelict school building – came onto the market once more at 'offers of over £75,000'.

Newspaper reports in August 1995 suggest that Scarp now has a new owner, but public particulars of the purchaser – and his intentions for the island – have not, at the time of writing, been released.

The sale opens a fresh chapter in Scarp's story. Sixteen crofting tenancies remain in force, with all the rights which the Crofting Acts provide. So long as some of these families remain interested in keeping a sheep stock on the island, and enough people are available to work it, that part, at least, of the traditional way of life should remain.

What the future holds depends on the wishes of the new owner, along with the crofting tenants and the other island feuars. It would be good to think that a degree of restoration and conservation would feature among their priorities. Scarp still has a great deal to offer – its story will continue.

Bibliography

Note: The publications listed here are either referred to within the text, or have proved useful while researching the book.

Adams, Ann & Norman Adams. *Island Chapters,* Littlewood, Todmorden, Lancs. 1991.

Allan, Brian, P.Woods & S.Clarke. *Wild Orchids of Scotland,* HMSO, Edinburgh, 1993.

An Gaidheal or *The Gael.* The magazine of *An Comunn Gaidhealach,* 1951–1964 issues.

Angus, Stewart (Editor). *Hebridean Naturalist,* the magazine of Curracag, the Western Isles Natural History Society, Stornoway.

Barber, John & D. A. Magee. *Innsegall: The Western Isles,* John Donald, Edinburgh, 1986.

Barrie, J. M. *Mary Rose,* Hodder & Stoughton, London, 1924.

Bennett, Arthur. *Contributions to a Flora of the Outer Hebrides,* in, *Annals of Scottish Natural History,* 1892, 1895, 1905, 1910.

Bennett, Margaret. *Scottish Customs: from the Cradle to the Grave,* Polygon, Edinburgh, 1992.

Bennett, Margaret. *Folkways & Religion of the Hebridean Scots in the Eastern Townships,* in, *Cultural Retention & Demographic Change: Studies of the Hebridean Scots in the Eastern Townships of Quebec,* National Museum of Man, Mercury Series, No 34, Ottawa, 1980.

Birkin, Andrew. *J. M. Barrie and the Lost Boys,* Constable, London, 1979.

Boswell, James. *The Journal of a Tour to the Hebrides,* with Samuel Johnson's, *A Journey to the Western Islands of Scotland,* Oxford University Press, Oxford & London, 1970.

Boyd, J. M. (Editor). *Natural Environment of the Outer Hebrides,* The Royal Society of Edinburgh, 1979.

Bray, Elizabeth. *The Discovery of the Hebrides: Voyages to the Western Isles, 1745–1883,* Collins, Glasgow & London, 1986.

British Geological Survey. *Geology of the Outer Hebrides,* HMSO, 1992.

Brown, Rev Thomas. *Annals of the Disruption,* Macniven & Wallace, Edinburgh, 1884.

Buchanan, Rev J. L. *Travels in the Western Hebrides from 1782 to 1790,* London, 1793.

Burleigh, J. H. S. *A Church History of Scotland,* Edinburgh Hope Trust, 1988.

Campbell, J. F. *Popular Tales of the West Highlands,* Vols. I–IV, 1890–1893.

Carmichael, Alexander. *Carmina Gadelica, Volume 2, Hymns & Incantations*, Oliver & Boyd, Edinburgh, 1928.

Celtic Monthly (The), Vol. XVII, March 1909.

Cervantes, Miguel de. *Don Quixote*, Wordsworth Classics Edition, Ware, 1993.

Cheape, Hugh. *Kirtomy Mill & Kiln*, Scottish Vernacular Buildings Working Group. (Not dated – but post 1982.)

Clyne, Douglas. *Gaelic Names for Plants and Flowers*, Crùisgean, Furnace, Argyll, 1989.

Crofters Holdings (Scotland) Act, 1886.

Cunningham, Peter. *Birds of the Outer Hebrides*, The Mercat Press, Edinburgh, 1990.

Cunningham, Peter. *A Hebridean Naturalist*, Acair, Stornoway, 1979.

Darling, F. Fraser & J. M. Boyd. *The Highlands & Islands*, Collins, London, 1964.

Duncan, Angus & Jane Mary Duncan (A. D. & J. M. D.) *Bardachd Mhurchaidh A' Cheisdeir: The Songs & Hymns of Murdo MacLeod*, Darien Press, Edinburgh, 1962 & 1965.

Dwelly, Edward. *The Illustrated Gaelic–English Dictionary, 1901–1911*, 9th. Edition, Gairm Publications, Glasgow, 1977.

Fenton, Alexander. *Scottish Country Life*, John Donald, Edinburgh, 1976.

Fenton, Alexander. *Country Life in Scotland: Our Rural Past*, John Donald, Edinburgh, 1987.

Geddes, Arthur. *The Isle of Lewis & Harris – A Study in British Community*, Edinburgh University Press, 1955.

Gifford, John. *The Buildings of Scotland: Highlands & Islands*, Penguin, London, 1992.

Goldsmith, Oliver. *The Deserted Village*, from, *The Oxford Book of 18th Century Verse*, Oxford University Press, 1926.

Goldsmith, Oliver. *The Vicar of Wakefield*, Oxford University Press edition, 1974.

Gordon, Seton. *Afoot in the Hebrides*, Country Life, London, 1950.

Gordon, Seton. *Highland Days*, Cassell, London, 1963.

Grant, Isabel F. *The MacLeods: The History of a Clan: 1200–1956*, Faber & Faber, London, 1959.

Grant, Isabel F. *Highland Folk Ways*, Routledge & Kegan Paul, London, 1961.

Grant, James Shaw. *The Gaelic Vikings*, James Thin, Edinburgh, 1984.

Grant, James Shaw. *Discovering Lewis & Harris*, John Donald, Edinburgh, 1987.

Harris Tweed Act, 1993, HMSO.

Harvie–Brown, J. A. & T. E. Buckley. *A Vertebrate Fauna of the Outer Hebrides*, Edinburgh, 1888.

Henderson, Dr George. *Leabhar nan Gleann: The Book of the Glens*, Edinburgh, 1898.

Henderson, Hamish. *Alias MacAlias*, Polygon, Edinburgh, 1992.

Henson, Elizabeth. *British Sheep Breeds*, Shire Publications, Princes Risborough, 1994.

Heron, Robert. *General View of the Natural Circumstances (of) Hebrides*, Edinburgh, 1794.

Hogg, James. *The Works of The Ettrick Shepherd: Poems & Ballads*. Blackie, 1876.

Hogg, James. *A Tour of the Highlands in 1803*, James Thin edition, Edinburgh, 1986.

Jehu, T. J. & R. M. Craig. *Geology of the Outer Hebrides, Part 5, North Harris & Lewis*, in, *Transactions of the Royal Society of Edinburgh, 1932–33*. Robert Grant & Son, Edinburgh, 1934.

Johnson, Samuel. *A Journey to the Western Islands of Scotland*, with James Boswell's, *The Journal of a Tour to the Hebrides*, Oxford University Press, Oxford & London, 1970.

Keay, John & Julia. *Collins Encyclopaedia of Scotland*, Harper Collins, London, 1994.

Knox, John. *A Tour through the Highlands of Scotland and the Hebride Isles, in 1786*, James Thin edition, Edinburgh, 1975.

Lawson, Bill. *St. Clement's Church at Rodel*, Bill Lawson, Northton, Harris, 1991.

Lawson, Bill. *The Teampull at Northton & the Church at Scarista*, Bill Lawson, Northton, Harris, 1993.

Leigh, Margaret. *Highland Homespun*, G. Bell & Son, London, 1936.

MacCulloch, John, M. D. *A Description of The Western Islands of Scotland, including The Isle of Man*, Archibald Constable & Co., Edinburgh, 1819.

MacGregor, Alasdair Alpin. *The Western Isles*, Robert Hale, London, 1949.

MacDonald, Alexander. *The Blackfaced Breed of Sheep*, in, *Transactions of the Highland and Agricultural Society of Scotland, Fourth Series, Vol. XVI*, William Blackwood, 1884.

MacDonald, Donald. *Lewis, A History of the Island*, Gordon Wright, Edinburgh, 1978.

MacDonald, Rachel, as told to her daughter Morag MacKinnon. *When I Think of Scarp*, in, The Scots Magazine, April 1965.

MacIver, D. *Place-names of Lewis & Harris*, Private publication, Printed by Stornoway Gazette, 1934.

MacKenzie, Alexander. *The Prophecies of the Brahan Seer*, edition edited by Elizabeth Sutherland, Constable, London, 1977.

MacKenzie, John. *The Beauties of Gaelic Poetry*, Edinburgh, 1904.

MacLean, Dr. Norman. *Set Free*, Hodder & Stoughton, London, 1949.

MacLennan, Malcolm. *A Pronouncing & Etymological Dictionary of the Gaelic Language (Gaelic–English & English–Gaelic)*, Acair & Aberdeen University Press, 1979.

MacLeod, Neil. *Clarsach an Doire*, (First published 1883) Gairm edition, Glasgow, 1975.

MacLeod, Rev Canon R. C. *The Book of Dunvegan*, Volumes 1 & 2, Aberdeen, 1938–1939.

MacLeod, Rev Canon R.C. *The MacLeods of Dunvegan*, Clan MacLeod Society, 1927.

Magnus, Philip. *King Edward the Seventh*, John Murray, London, 1964.

Martin, Martin. *A Description of the Western Islands of Scotland (1716 Edition)*, facsimile edition by James Thin, Edinburgh, 1976.

Mack, Douglas S. *James Hogg, Memoir of the Author's Life & Familiar Anecdotes of Sir Walter Scott*, Scottish Academic Press, Edinburgh, 1972.

Monro, R. W. (Editor). *Monro's Western Isles of Scotland and Genealogies of the Clans, 1549*. From the manuscripts of Donald Monro, Dean of the Isles, Oliver & Boyd, Edinburgh, 1961.

Morrison, Alick. *Harris Estate Papers 1724–1754*, from, *Transactions of the Gaelic Society of Inverness, Volume XLV, 1967–1968*.

Morrison, Alick. *The Chiefs of Clan MacLeod*, Associated Clan MacLeod Societies, 1986.

Murray, W.H. *The Hebrides*, Heinemann, London, 1966.

National Sheep Association. *British Sheep*, Seventh Edition, NSA, Tring, Herts., 1987

Nature Conservancy Council & Comhairle Nan Eilean. *The Natural Environment of the Outer Hebrides*, in, *Proceedings of a Symposium held in Stornoway, 16 October 1979*.

Nature Conservancy Council. *Outer Hebrides: Localities of Geological & Geomorphological Importance*, Nature Conservancy Council, 1977.

Napier Commission. *Report of Her Majesty's Commissioners of Inquiry into the condition of The Crofters and Cottars in the Highlands and Islands of Scotland*, Edinburgh, 1884.

Nicolson, Alexander (Editor). *Gaelic Proverbs and Familiar Phrases: based on MacIntosh's collection*, MacLachlan & Stewart, Edinburgh, 1882.

Nicolson, Nigel. *Lord of the Isles: Lord Leverhulme in the Hebrides*, Weidenfeld & Nicolson, 1960.

Pankhurst, R. J. & Mullin J. M. *Flora of the Outer Hebrides*, Natural History Museum, London, 1991, 1994 reprint.

Peacock, J. D. *Quaternary geology of the Outer Hebrides: B.G.S. Reports Vol. 16, No. 2.* HMSO, 1984.

Rare Breeds Survival Trust. *Rare Breeds: Facts & Figures*, RBST, Kenilworth, 1994.

Ross, William. *Gaelic Songs by William Ross*, collected by John MacKenzie, edition revised by George Calder, Oliver & Boyd, Edinburgh, 1937.

Scott, Sir Walter. *Guy Mannering*, J. M. Dent edition, 1906.

Scott, Sir Walter. *The Poetic Works of Sir Walter Scott*, Oxford University Press, 1904.

Scottish Council for Research in Education. *Aithris is Oideas* (Traditional Gaelic Rhymes & Games), University of London Press, 1964.

Scottish Natural Heritage. *Sites of Special Scientific Interest* (SSSI booklet), SNH Publications, Redgorton, Perth, 1994.

Simpson, Dr W.Douglas. *A Chronicle History of Dunvegan Castle*, in, *Transactions of the Gaelic Society of Inverness, Volume XXXVII, 1934–36*.

Sinclair, Colin. *The Thatched Houses of the Old Highlands*, Oliver & Boyd, Edinburgh, 1953.

Smith, W. Anderson. *Lewsiana: or Life in the Outer Hebrides*, Daldy, Isbister, London, 1875.

Smout, T. C. *A Century of the Scottish People, 1830–1950*, Fontana, London, 1987.

Stewart, Rev Alexander. *Elements of Gaelic Grammar*, 1801 & 1812.

The Conservation (Natural Habitats &c.) Regulations 1994. HMSO.

The Statistical Account of Scotland, Volume 10, Edinburgh, 1794.

The New Statistical Account of Scotland, Volume 14, Wm. Blackwood, Edinburgh, 1845.

The Third Statistical Account of Scotland, Volume 16, Scottish Academic Press, Edinburgh, 1985.

Thomson, Derick S. *The Companion to Gaelic Scotland,* Blackwell Reference, Oxford, 1983.

Thomson, Francis. *Islands: Harris & Lewis: Outer Hebrides,* David & Charles, Newton Abbot, 1968.

Thomson, Francis. *Harris Tweed: the Story of a Hebridean Industry,* David & Charles, Newton Abbot, 1969.

Watson, W. J. *Place-names of Ross & Cromarty,* The Northern Counties Printing & Publishing Co., Inverness, 1904.

Watson, W. J. *History of the Celtic Place–names of Scotland,* William Blackwood, Edinburgh & London, 1926.

Welsh, Mary. *Walks in the Western Isles,* Westmorland Gazette, Kendal, 1993.

Wildlife and Countryside Act 1981. HMSO.

Williamson, Kenneth & J. M. Boyd. *A Mosaic of Islands,* Oliver & Boyd, Edinburgh, 1963.

Index